REVIVAL OF THE GNOSTIC HERESY

REVIVAL OF THE GNOSTIC HERESY

FUNDAMENTALISM

Joe E. Morris

First published in 2008 by PALGRAVE MACMILLAN® in the United States—a division of St. Martin's Press LLC, 175 Fifth Avenue, New York, NY 10010.

Where this book is distributed in the UK, Europe and the rest of the world, this is by Palgrave Macmillan, a division of Macmillan Publishers Limited, registered in England, company number 785998, of Houndmills, Basingstoke, Hampshire RG21 6XS.

Palgrave Macmillan is the global academic imprint of the above companies and has companies and representatives throughout the world.

Palgrave® and Macmillan® are registered trademarks in the United States, the United Kingdom, Europe and other countries.

ISBN-13: 978-0-230-61153-5
ISBN-10: 0-230-61153-2

Library of Congress Cataloging-in-Publication Data is available from the Library of Congress.

A catalogue record of the book is available from the British Library.

Design by Scribe Inc.

First edition: December 2008

10 9 8 7 6 5 4 3 2 1

Printed in the United States of America.

Dedicated to Ted Runyon

In Memory of the late Hendrikus W. Boers, Emeritus Professor of New Testament, Candler School of Theology, Emory University

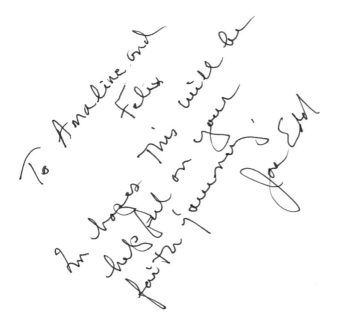

CONTENTS

FOREWORD

In this time of religious pluralism, when we are advised to be open to other religions and tolerant toward points of view different from our own, Joe E. Morris seems curiously out of step, for he asks us to look critically at a movement that, through radio and TV, is attracting millions of followers to Fundamentalist megachurches and conservative causes. Is Morris out of sync with the generous American spirit, which prefers "to think and let think?" Yet he points out that Fundamentalism cultivates a mindset that is anything but generous with those who disagree with its interpretation of Christianity. From a fundamentalist standpoint, rigidity is indeed a necessity, because its attraction is lodged in its certainty that it has the right way, the true knowledge, the only option that is supernaturally guaranteed and endorsed. And the human yearning for such certainty is precisely what makes it alluring.

But Morris goes beyond this psychological appeal, which, in a time of confusion, uncertainty, and unrest, is provided by any brand of fundamentalism, whether Christian, Jewish, or Islamic, to the remarkable parallels between modern-day Christian Fundamentalism and the ancient heresies with which early church councils struggled. Because they were convinced that these heresies distorted the truth of the Christian message. It is these parallels that Morris is persuaded justify, calling Fundamentalism a Gnostic heresy. And from his standpoint truth is what is at stake. While he does not deny that Christianity can be interpreted in many ways, as reflected in the various denominations today, there are nevertheless guidelines hammered out by the debates of the early centuries, which succeeded in defining the boundaries of what could be considered authentically Christian. It is these boundaries which Morris is convinced Fundamentalism has overstepped, and he demonstrates this by comparing it with the early gnostic heresies.

To be sure, Gnosticism came in many forms. Some were legalists, others were licentious, some were literalists, while others made extensive use of allegory. It is not surprising, therefore, that Morris finds he is dealing with a slippery phenomenon when he seeks to draw parallels between Gnosticism and present-day Fundamentalism. In Gnosticism of whatever variety, however, one thing seems to be constant and that is its *dualism*, its sharp contrasts between good and evil, light and darkness, the spirit and the material world, the enlightened and the ignorant, the saved and the unsaved. This dualism is written into the nature of reality, because the creator of the world is not God but a demiurge, a half god or fallen angel responsible for evil and the ambiguity of the human situation. The *gnosis* or knowledge that is necessary for salvation is having the right words, the secret formulas, the names of the gods and demonic powers that one must know in order to pass through the darkness and the various levels of the heavens to where the high God dwells in inexpressible Light.

While Fundamentalism does not posit a duality in God or in the created world, it is dualistic in most other respects, beginning with a clear line between the saved and the unsaved. The saved are those "in the know," those who are certain and believe all the "fundamentals" and defend them against the evil forces and skepticism of the present age. Hence literalism and "creationism" must be championed against those who would favor an allegorical interpretation of the Genesis stories that would place evolution within a more comprehensive view of the Creator's relationship to the world. The unsaved are those who refuse to believe that a rigid dualism is the answer to the world's problems, that all truth lies on one side, and that the other side is bereft of any legitimacy. Yet this is the kind of dualism that characterizes fundamentalist forces, whether they are found in Israel or Arab lands, in India or the United States.

But Fundamentalism, whether of the Christian, Jewish, Muslim, or Hindu variety, will be part of our world for the foreseeable future. This means that the larger question that this book raises is, how are we to live in a world of competing fundamentalisms? The first task, it seems to me, is to understand our own religion in a deeper way than has previously been necessary, to understand how all religions seek to answer basic and universal human needs and questions. Getting rid of religion is not the solution and secularism is not the answer. The human needs still remain, and secularism breeds pseudo-religions like nationalism and ethnic fundamentalism that move in to fill the vacuum. The way lies rather in discovering how the religious answers are complementary and not necessarily in competition, and therefore can cooperate to bring peace and stability. If Allah is, as Muslims constantly remind us, the *all-merciful*, and the Jewish and the Christian God is equally all-merciful, what are the dimensions of divine mercy that have the potential to reduce human strife without the necessity to deny any of our traditions? What is called for is a new *gnosis*, an approach to knowledge and knowing that is healing, a knowledge that penetrates through the barriers that we have used to establish our identity by dividing between "us" and "them," a knowing that penetrates through to the God of the Abrahamic faiths. This is the God who calls us to leave the territories that are familiar and safe with comfortable identities and venture forth out of Ur of the Chaldees (Gen. 15:7) and into a new land where we discover the God who is merciful to humans by making the dualisms and the barriers that Fundamentalism sets up unnecessary.

Theodore Runyon, PhD, Professor Emeritus
Candler School of Theology
Emory University

PREFACE

This book is the culmination of a long spiritual struggle that began over fifty years ago. When I was seven years old, my parents gave me an *Egermeier's Bible Story Book: A Complete Narration from Genesis to Revelation for Young and Old.* In her Preface the writer states that she endeavored to "familiarize herself with the viewpoint of children and to adapt her language accordingly."[1] She succeeded with this young reader. The book launched a personal journey to the heart of Christian scripture, a near obsessional drive back to first principles, to the reasons we believe what we believe and the fundamentals of religious faith.

What was so captivating about this book? First of all, it had pictures. I only had to open the book to the first one, a black and white (lithograph) of Adam and Eve, the first humans, dressed in fur clothing covering them to their thighs. They were standing close together, beneath a palm tree, their hands folded in prayer, their faces glum with guilt. In a distant tree I could see a snake that appeared to be crawling away. Two pages later was the Ark Noah built, a huge boxlike ship in a storm. In the distance was a faint rainbow. From that point, all I did was flip pages and look at pictures: Abraham and Lot; Joseph finding his brothers; Moses and Aaron with the magicians; the Red Sea parting for the Israelites; David slaying Goliath, followed by more popular Bible stories. The pictures in the New Testament were not as exciting, not as heroic. They were too quiet. I quickly flipped back to the beginning and began again, this time lingering, absorbing the Old Testament pictures.

This early introduction to the Bible set the framework for my earliest understanding of scripture. For me, these were true stories. The characters were real. Once past the pictures I settled into reading, one story after another. After dinner each evening, I would go straight to bed, turn on my bedside lamp and read. By my ninth birthday I had read *Egermeier's Bible Story Book* over ten times, though I must confess, the New Testament stories got left behind. I did read them, but only once; the resurrection story twice. But not the ten or more times I read about creation and Noah and the Ark, Joseph and his coat of many colors, Samson, Gideon, and so on. I was too impressed with a different type of power, one that colored my theology and my view of scripture for years to come. I believed these stories and all else I read, were literally true. No other interpretation was available to me. This was God's word and God did not lie. Though I did not realize it until a half century later, a dualism was dominating my thinking. One Testament was becoming more important than the other. I did not *become* a Fundamentalist, as if there existed in that milieu other options to challenge my thinking. I *was* a Fundamentalist. I was born into that religious mindset.

At age twelve, after an eight-week confirmation class, I joined the church and the pastor gave me a handsome, leather-bound King James Version of The Holy Bible. It had pictures. They were slick and colorful. There were maps in the back. When Jesus spoke, the letters were in red. This was all new and fascinating, but it was not *the* Bible. I put down the *King James Bible* and returned to my *Egermeier* storybook.

As I grew older, I was forced to read the King James, the Bible everyone was reading. After all, it was the Bible Jesus used, or so one Sunday school teacher declaimed. Admittedly, it had some advantages. It had chapters and verses, which made it easier to find scripture and follow along, flip back and forth for references. The red letters helped distinguish the word of God through Jesus, versus the word of God through all the other words. The fact that one carried more weight than the others raised an early question. In my *Egermeier* they were all the same. God's word was God's word. Though I did not realize it, in my theologically immature groping mind, this was probably the beginning of my earliest glimpse of dualism. Later it would manifest itself in myriad ways and I would learn the name that went with it: Gnosticism.

I eventually left my revered *Egermeier* at home but took its theological frame of reference with me. Everything I read in the King James Version became as real as the stories of earlier years. Nothing really changed. Same Bible, same theological framework; different book. Everything happened as the first book had said it happened and was now repeated and confirmed, though with different words. *King James* took over, but the power and influence of *Egermeier* never diminished, never lost its magic. At age seventeen, following a terrific struggle, and with young Samuel clearly in mind, I knelt at the altar of my Methodist Church and dedicated my life to the ministry. The preacher that first January Student Sunday had been an influence. Only many years later did he emerge from the closet and announce he was gay, news that did not affect me adversely. He had played a role in my theological development and for that I was grateful. He had tried to get me to look at the scriptures differently, look at the New Testament and its different power, but I was too riveted on the Old Testament, on *that* God. The Old Testament was much easier to understand. The New Testament was too confusing. It lacked energy and excitement. Except for the resurrection of Jesus. Now, there was a touch of the Old Testament power and miracle, God's hand reaching down and touching the Earth. But the parables and the Sermon on the Mount were dry reading. I wanted more excitement and I learned I was in good company. When asked once if he read the Bible, William Faulkner remarked he enjoyed the Old Testament; it was a book about people, the New Testament was one about ideas.[2]

After graduation from Millsaps College in Jackson, Mississippi, with a degree in Philosophy under my belt, I entered New College Divinity School at the University of Edinburg, one of the most noted theology schools in the world. T. F.

Torrance, James S. Stewart, and other great theologians from around the world were there. Other great theologians from around the world came and spoke there. God was there—but only for a short while.

A pivotal moment occurred in James Stewart's New Testament class. Someone had asked a question about a certain scripture and Stewart directed them to a Greek text. From studies at Millsaps I knew the New Testament had been written in Greek, not classical Greek but a form called *koine*. When he remarked, however, about lack of spacing and punctuation in the earliest texts, I became alarmed. A space here, period there, could change the entire meaning of a text, possibly a creed or entire theology. That was just the beginning of the end of my comfortable theology. My hand shot up. I rigorously protested. Dr. Stewart suggested, in gentle professorial tones, "Laddie, you might wish to visit the British Museum in London and the Vatican Museum in Rome and see for yourself."

During spring break that year (1966) I did just that, via buses, trains, boats, hitchhiking, one conveyance or another, I made the pilgrimage to see the ancient texts. Beneath their protected beveled glass casements, there they were. Ancient papyrus, block letters running together . . . no punctuation . . . no indication of when one sentence ended and another began. Stewart was nauseatingly, disgustingly right. My theological framework, developed from a literal and unerring Bible, collapsed.

Thus began my scholarly journey (I would like to think scholarly) to prove Professor Stewart wrong, to prove the Bible was without error and could be literally, word for word, believed. *Egermeier*, the storybook for young and old, was holding on, refusing to let go. Because there could be no either–or. One position was right and the other wrong. I was locked into dualism. The journey has taken over fifty years of preaching and pastoring, study and research, for me to understand that both perspectives share validity, that both voices have something to say.

The purpose of this book is to expand on a dialogue already opened and advanced by others. The worlds of religion and theology are particularly indebted to Bruce Metzger, Bart Ehrman, Martin Marty, Scott Appleby, Philip J. Lee, Harold Bloom, Fisher Humphreys, Philip Wise, and many others whose works and contributions will be cited along the way. In particular, Philip Wise in his scholarly presentation, *Against the Protestant Gnosticism*, issues a clear challenge: "to clarify the distinctions between Gnosticism and the faith of the Church . . . to make plain the differences between infinite claims and earthly gratitude, between *gnosis* and faith, between pilgrimage and escape, between self and community, between the exclusive and the inclusive, between the nebulous and the concrete."[3]

The attempt of this book is not to proselyte. The only agenda is to broaden and deepen the readers' understanding of current theological issues with respect to the history behind those positions. Nor is it my purpose to negatively, or destructively, critique any particular theological approach. There are advantages and disadvantages in any posture of faith. As they surface they will be identified and evaluated. I began this study and research with a single primary hypothesis. But, as is typical of any research, before the experience was concluded not only had the hypothesis been altered but others also surfaced. We learn and grow. Hopefully, the readers of this book will gain greater understanding of their own religious faith and that of others.

Today my *Egermeier Bible Story Book* remains within easy reach. Spineless and tattered, held together by large rubber bands, it rests prominently between a copy of *Young's Analytical Concordance of the Bible* and a *Nestle-Aland Novum Testamentum Graece*, on a bookshelf with *H KAINH ΔIAΘHKH* (The British and Foreign Bible Society's text of the Greek New Testament with revised critical apparatus), a sixteenth-century copy of a *Geneva Bible*, a *Revised Standard Version, New International Revised Version, King James Version*, J. B. Phillips *New Testament* translation, *Cambridge New Testament* (1847), *New English Bible*, and *Harper Collins Bible Dictionary*. On that same shelf are my old Greek, Latin, and Hebrew language study guides, a shelf strategically positioned among others that hold volume upon volume of church history, doctrine, and dogma, church organization, discipline, and ethics, a wall as sacred and dear to me as one for others on the Temple Mount. A single book, though, the lynchpin, where it all began: *The Egermeier Bible Story Book . . . For Young and Old*. And today, as though time had not skipped a beat, I still get in bed each evening and read about God and his Creation, the Christ and his works of compassion, the Holy Spirit and its eternal presence. And sometimes it is the *Egermeier Bible Story Book* I read.

ACKNOWLEDGMENTS

In listing acknowledgements, it has seemed customary over the years for authors to save their wives until last, an indication of special attention by that final placement. In this case, however, my wife Sandi deserves a higher ranking. In addition to her constant emotional support and encouragement, she edited—line by line, word for word—reams of pages. To be successful, Stephen King states in *On Writing*, writers should stay healthy and married. I would add one more criterion: they should marry an English teacher. Nor does it hurt to have children who bring home theological books from college. Thanks to our son, Jason, who sparked this project with one he brought home from medical school. *The Spirit of Early Christian Thought* by Robert Louis Wilkin triggered a year of torrid reading and a pilgrimage back to my earliest religious origins, through seminary and doctoral studies, resulting in *Revival of the Gnostic Heresy: Fundamentalism.*

Ted Runyon, my professor of Systematic Theology at Candler School of Theology, Emory University, also deserves special recognition. Had it not been for him, my interest in theology might well have vanished in the tumultuous '60s of cynicism, "death of God," and nihilism. His lectures were clear, earnest, poignant, and always quietly uplifting. For this reason, and the many hours he, too, used critiquing and editing, this book is dedicated to him.

Roy H. Ryan, former editor of The United Methodist Publishing House, brought a depth that would have been missing without his touch. Several comments regarding inerrancy and literalism, the Apostle's Creed, and right belief versus grace come straight from his marginal editorial comments: "One could make the case that 'knowing Christ' and 'knowing' and 'believing' the Fundamentals are signs of comprehension." He further commented, "This Word is the absolute Truth, letter of the law, binding for all time . . . completely closed to any further additions. . . . Literal interpretation is the hermeneutic. We not only have no further additions, but also no further interpretations." He also receives credit for the statement that exegesis is a hermeneutic not needed by those who take the scripture literally.

A special thanks to Dr. Julian Prince, writer and former Academic Dean of Students at Samford University, who served in the role of affiliate reader. At the request of Palgrave MacMillan, he read an early draft and offered constructive critique that led to the final acceptance of the manuscript for publication.

Others along the way were helpful. To determine the book's readability for laity, members of the book club at St. Luke United Methodist Church—pastor

Mike Hicks, Dr. John Vaughn, John and Mary Lee Reed, and Marvin Hurdle—all read early drafts and provided useful insights. Comments and critique by Drs. Gerald and Julie Waldon, retired professors from the University of Mississippi were invaluable. Linda Sands, fellow fiction writer, reviewed early chapters and put her effective literary scalpel to work. Paul Sudduth, Lay Leader of St. Paul Antiochian Orthodox Christian Mission Station, was helpful in advancing my understanding of Orthodox doctrine and dogma.

Often, publishers receive acknowledgment from a sense of expected obligation. But Farideh Koohl-Kamali and Brigitte Shull of Palgrave MacMillan *were* true shepherds. Not once did I feel neglected, excluded, or abandoned in the intricate and tedious process of publication. I am honored to be a part of their team and proud this book came to light under their guidance.

INTRODUCTION

The heresy of one age becomes the orthodoxy of the next.

—Helen Keller

THEIR NAME COMES FROM A GREEK WORD THAT MEANS "KNOW." THEY BECAME the first Christian *heresy*, a Greek word that means "choice." They were deemed by their opponents to have made the wrong choice, chosen the wrong way, the wrong Christ, even the wrong God. Their "bad" theology was assailed in a scribal battle of pen and parchment, a fierce war of words and books the world may never see again. Their beliefs were scorned and maligned; their faithful excommunicated and run out of town; their books and writings banned and burned.

Because of the successful suppression and purge of their correspondence and writings, we know very little about them. What we do know is filtered mostly from the writings of their opponents—highly intelligent and rigorous Christian heresy hunters or heresiologists—later to become more familiarly known as the "early church fathers." We do know at one time, under the leadership of a man named Marcion, they were a strong presence in the Mediterranean world. They were a highly organized church complete with a hierarchy of bishops, elders, and deacons. This highly stratified *ecclesia* met regularly in sanctioned synods. They had their own bible and creed, their own liturgy and sacraments. Most of them called themselves Christian.

Then, during the third and fourth centuries CE, out-numbered and out-organized, attacked on one side by the populist orthodox bishops and on the other by pagan[1] Greek and Egyptian Platonists, they vanished, faded eastward from the scene across the Syrian Desert toward Persia. So aggressive and thorough was the campaign against them that they were thought to have been permanently extinguished. Centuries later they were well outside the Byzantine Empire but without their identity. Fragmented and spread over a large area (today's Iraq and Iran), they had merged with the Mandaeans, a religion with shared beliefs.[2] Yet, over the centuries, under varying religious cloaks and guises, they have surfaced. They are the *Gnostics*. And they are back.

They are back full force, congregations of them, with their own churches, cathedrals, priests, liturgies, creeds, catechisms, lectionaries, Web sites, and structure. Marcion would be proud. Their churches, much like those of mainstream Christianity, have their own names—The Gnostic Church of St. Mary Magdalene, Ecclesiastica Gnostica, Queen of Heaven Gnostic Church, The Apostolic Johannite. Their beliefs vary, but mostly follow those laid down by their forebears two millennia ago.

Some say Gnosticism is back because of the recent flurry over *The Da Vinci Code* and *The Passion of the Christ*, that the accompanying media hype has created a renewed interest in Christianity, more specifically the history of the early church and its Gnostic challenge. Certainly, Dan Brown and Mel Gibson have contributed, but they scarcely get all the credit. Other less dramatic influences include the 1979 publication of Elaine Pagels' best-selling *The Gnostic Gospels*,[3] a book, some have argued, that paved the way for Brown's astronomical success.[4] But all of these knowledgeable and talented individuals are indebted to something that happened decades earlier. *The Gnostic Gospels* may never have seen the light of day without the 1945 discovery of thirteen leather-bound books in the Egyptian desert: the real Gnostic gospels.[5] A century earlier was another startling discovery. At St. Catherine's Monastery on Mount Sinai, a thirty-year-old forerunner of Indiana Jones, Dr. Constantin von Tischendorf, came upon the now-revered Codex Sinaiticus. This fourth-century volume, found in a wastebasket full of papers used to light the monastery oven, brings us closer than ever to the original New Testament. Biblical scholar Bruce Metzger has called it "the only known complete copy of the Greek New Testament in uncial script."[6] Then there are the Dead Sea Scrolls, by now a story known to all of us, of the Bedouin shepherd boy who, while searching for a lost sheep, cast a stone into a desert cave. Upon hearing something shatter, he explored further and stumbled over tall, slender jars containing scrolls of ancient manuscripts.

No single cause explains the Gnostics rapid and visible return. The mix of history, archaeology, and fiction has always been a good combination for resurrecting old movements and spawning new ones. But it does not fully explain this sudden reemergence. Why *this* rapid visible rise? Why does it seem we are hearing about Gnosticism as though it were some new religious kid on an already crowded ecclesiastical block?

There are some who say that Gnosticism simply never left and that the relatively recent discoveries of old books and publications of new ones had little to do with "jump starting" a movement that never died. Those confident of this belief are members of Ecclesia Gnostica and other Gnostic congregations like them scattered around America and throughout the world. They were here first, before James Robinson translated the ancient Nag Hammadi texts for the world to read and before Elaine Pagels' *The Gnostic Gospels* was published. These latter-day Gnostics will direct your attention to history and point out that the Cathars, Rosicrucians, Knights Templar, Esoteric Freemasons, and Theosophists had roots in Gnosticism.[7] They will remind you that the study of Gnosticism was thriving in the nineteenth century, championed by well-known scholars and writers—such as William Blake (1757–1827), Arthur Schopenhauer (1788–1860), Herman Melville (1819–91), and William Butler Yeats (1865–1939)[8]—and influenced in the twentieth century by the likes of Carl Jung, Eric Voegelin, Harold Bloom, Wallace Stevens, Yeats, and Hermann Hesse. With pride, they will tell you a Gnostic church was reestablished in France in 1890 and is still active today. A well-informed member of the Ecclesia Gnostica will relate how a man named Stephen

Hoeller came from England in the 1950s and in the '70s started the Ecclesia Gnostica Church and the Gnostic Society.[9] And there are others. In 1985, the American Gnostic Church in Texas began reflecting the second century teachings of Basilides.[10] In January, 1962, Tau Rosamonde Miller was contacted and offered ordination by emissaries of the bishop of the Mary Magdalene Order (Holy Order of Miriam of Magdala) in Paris, France, and became ordained in 1974 in her own church, The Ecclesia Gnostica Mysteriorum in Palo Alto, California. Nor will these contemporary Gnostics omit, in their catalogue of modern influence and successes, the Ordo Templi Orientis, its international influence and rival claims to "apostolic succession."[11]

On and on the new Gnostics could go, citing names and locations of Gnostic churches and organizations, as myriad now as in the first four centuries CE before they were drummed into the desert. In short, ancient manuscript discoveries, plus popular film and fiction, have surely had an accumulative effect in creating more visibility and name recognition. But Gnosticism in this country was alive and well long before Dan Brown, Mel Gibson, and Elaine Pagels; long before the 1945 discovery of ancient Gnostic texts in the Egyptian desert at Nag Hammadi.

It is not a purpose of this book to resurrect old conflicts and question the presence and practice of Gnosticism in this country or abroad. Nor is there an intention to question the beliefs of Gnosticism or Gnosticism's right to exist and worship peacefully. It is the objective of this study, however, to probe deeper into the culture of American religion and investigate further the Gnostic phenomenon and ask the questions: Is that all there is? Are these the only manifestations of Gnosticism? Might there be one which has been around longer, covered more territory, attracted more converts? Is it possible that another medium of Gnosticism exists today, one not on the fringes of society but in its mainstream? One so ingrained and part of our culture we do not recognize it? One which is beamed electronically, daily, into our homes? One cloaked with all the righteous trappings of orthodoxy that we would never suspect, never pause and say, "Ah, now therein possibly lies a heresy." One some of us grew up with, studied, and would not see for forty years, even with theological credentials? "Is it possible," asked Philip Lee in his groundbreaking work "that by identifying a Gnostic thought pattern with those *outside* the Christian community, we have failed to locate it in its natural habitat?"[12] Is Harold Bloom accurate when he states, "We live now, more than ever in an America where a great many people are Gnostics without knowing it?"[13]

Since the first pilgrim set foot on American soil, there has been a growing continuity of religious phenomena within this country that has no resemblance to the mother church from which it sprang. For over two hundred years the God most Americans have sought has little or no resemblance to the God of European Christianity, the God of the great Reformers. Doctrinally, the old continental faith and the more recent belief systems of which I speak appear similar—"appear" a key word. Theologically, superficially, they appear the same; but behaviorally they are different. They share and participate in similar liturgies—baptism and Holy

Communion. They share the same source, the Holy Bible. But the interpretation and delivery of the more recent message parallels Gnosticism more than it does mainstream Christianity.

Though they are Gnostic cousins, I am not speaking of Jewish Kabbalists and Muslim Sufis, spiritualism and spiritualists. Nor am I am speaking of people with nonmainstream religious beliefs we hear about from time to time—the Scientologists, Moonies, Hare Krishna, Branch Davidians, the Rosicrucians, or Masons. Nor am I referring to New Age parodies of Shirley MacLaine and Arianna Huffington. Though there may be some resemblance to Gnosticism, this phenomenon is not intergalactic thinking, UFOolgy, cosmogonist speculation, or orgiastic cult mentioned in *The Da Vinci Code*. Nor am I suggesting the "new Gnosticism" that questions the reliability and authenticity of tradition and scripture.

This religion of which I am speaking is a form of Gnosticism that is very much alive and active in today's organized church, as it was in the early centuries after Christ. I am speaking of "Gnostics" who embrace the authenticity of tradition and scripture, worship every Sunday and attend Wednesday evening prayer meetings. On the surface, they are midstream, mainstream America. They sit on city councils and on administrative and corporate boards. They belong to the Parent-Teacher Association (PTA), garden club, Daughters of the American Revolution (DAR), and Junior Auxiliary. They volunteer for the United Way, Salvation Army, local hospital and library. They hold elected office, exercise considerable political clout, and have been arguably credited with swinging national elections. They are groups and individuals we know by varying names and denominations, but who, in more recent times, have fallen under the label of "religious right." According to Harold Bloom "they are scattered wherever our new southern and western Republican overlords worship: in Salt Lake City and Dallas and wherever else Mormon temples and Southern Baptist First Churches pierce the heavens."[14] These Gnostics of whom I speak are . . . the Fundamentalists.

Fundamentalism sounds . . . well . . . very *fundamental*. As its definition suggests, it is very basic, essential; nothing that would resemble anything unorthodox, nonessential, off the beaten path . . . heretical. With its emphasis on back-to-the-Bible theology and conservative values, one would not typically associate Fundamentalism with heresy. In fact, Fundamentalists would lead you to think the opposite: all others, except them, are the heretics.

But a closer examination raises questions: Are the basic tenets and practices of Fundamentalism not a mirror of those of ancient Gnostics? If they are not one and the same, are they not close enough to pass as branches from the same family tree? To answer these questions the first section of the book is devoted to a study and exploration of Gnosticism, followed by a second section of equal rigorous examination of Fundamentalism then concluded by a final segment in which the two are comparatively reviewed.

The primary aim of this work is to examine Gnosticism and Fundamentalism, make comparisons, and draw perspectives that will help others understand their own religious beliefs, the origins of those beliefs, and their implications for decisions in this modern world. A secondary aim is to help members of local churches understand that documents buried in Egypt centuries ago, and the faith they represented, do have something to do with their faith. The hopeful result will be more dialogue within the diversity of those two religious movements, more flexibility between their camps.

A few explanations are in order. Throughout the book I will follow the practice of Humphreys and Wise,[15] and others, by capitalizing Fundamentalism when referring to the original American movement and using fundamentalism (lowercase) when referencing the more general religious movements, which include other faiths such as Islam and Judaism. Unless otherwise indicated, all scriptural quotes are from the *New International Version (NIV)*.[16]

Orthodoxy is defined as "the practice of being orthodox," which means "conforming to the usual beliefs or established doctrines, especially in religion."[17] The definition for our purposes applies to those "beliefs or established doctrines" of the early Christian Church at the time of, and following, the formal acceptance of the Nicene Creed (325 CE). Because orthodoxy, or "right opinion," was not fully established in the Christian Church until the fourth century, the early adherents or forerunners of those teachings are referred to by many scholars as proto-orthodox (before orthodoxy).

For the purposes of this study, Classical Gnosticism is included among the Gnostic variants, but our major concern and focus is Christian Gnosticism, the product of the former. This was the form of Gnosticism considered by the early church apologists to be most threatening and the recipient of their vitriolic attacks.

Because most of us are creatures of habit, another issue that generates some concern among Christians is the shift in dividing time from BC (Before Christ) and AD (Anno Domini) to BCE (Before the Common Era) and CE (Common Era). We Christians must realize, and rally understanding, that for those of other faiths—Jews, Muslims, Buddhists, and so on—Jesus is not Lord and the abbreviations that work well for us, lack meaning and relevance for them. For this reason, most scholars have begun using the more inclusive abbreviations. Therefore "Common Era" means common to all people of all faiths who use the calendar of Western civilization and "BCE" means "Before the Common Era." The newer trend will be followed in this book.

For those who wish to pursue the historical issues in greater detail, in addition to the Bibliography, there is a list of books for suggested reading. Due to the nature of the study, some of the terms may be new to even the scholarly and academic reader. Notes are available for definitions and interpretations and there is a glossary of key terms and names (Appendices A and B respectively). Additional appendices include a chronology of key events and brief biological sketches of important early Church Fathers and Gnostic Christian leaders.

PART I

GNOSTICISM

CHAPTER 1

THE GNOSTIC GOSPELS

ONE EVENT MORE THAN ANY OTHER IN THE HISTORY OF THE CHRISTIAN CHURCH set the stage for the creation and preservation of the New Testament. That same event also spelled the beginning of the end of the early Church's key antagonist: Gnosticism. The event was the circulation and reading of the thirty-ninth Festal Letter of Athanasius, Bishop of Alexandria (326–73). Earlier happenings also played an integral role—Pentecost, St. Paul's mission work among the Gentiles, Constantine's granting legitimate status to Christianity. But because of this one pivotal event, today we are reading the Gospels of Matthew, Mark, Luke, and John rather than the Gospels of Peter, Mary, Thomas, and Philip. Instead of the Apostles' or Nicene Creed, we might be reciting other articles of faith from different books of worship. We might be worshipping a different Christ, a different God . . . or gods.

Athanasius was the one person responsible for the Church's creed and dogma as we have it today. At the Council of Nicaea in 325 CE, called by the Emperor Constantine, Athanasius triumphed over the Arians. The significance of this victory for contemporary Christians cannot be underestimated. Athanasius and the bishops siding with him believed Christ was of the same substance as God and eternal with God. A faction led by Arius of Alexandria proposed that Christ was created by God and similar to him but not of the same substance. The result of Athanasius' triumph was the Trinitarian and Christological doctrines as we know them today.

Athanasius was more than an experienced, seasoned bishop with a brilliant theological mind. He was *the* perennial comeback kid of early Christianity. Following Nicaea, he fell into political disfavor and was exiled several times from Alexandria into the North African desert. Yet he kept coming back, preaching his doctrinal word, and striking fear in the hearts of the unorthodox, which usually meant the Gnostics. This time, his thirty-ninth Festal Letter put them on notice:

> Since we have made mention of heretics as dead, but of ourselves as possessing the Divine Scriptures for salvation. . . . Forasmuch as some have taken in hand, to reduce into order for themselves the books termed apocryphal, and to mix them up with the divinely inspired Scripture . . . it hath seemed good to me also, having been urged thereto by the brethren, and having learned from the beginning, to bring before you the books included in the Canon, and handed down, and

accredited as Divine; to the end that any one who has fallen into error may correct those who have led him astray; and that he who continues steadfast in purity, may again rejoice, having those things brought to his remembrance.[1]

Athanasius goes on to list the twenty-seven books that were to be accepted as authoritative and divinely inspired, the same that would later become the established New Testament canon[2]: "These are the fountains of salvation, that he who thirsteth may be satisfied with the words they contain. In these alone is proclaimed the doctrine of godliness. *Let no man add to them, neither let him take aught from them.* For on this point the Lord put to shame the Sadducees, saying 'ye do err, not knowing the Scriptures.' And He reproved the Jews, saying, 'Search the Scriptures, for they testify of Me.'"[3] Athanasius left no doubt. He was not referring to just any apocryphal or unofficial text. In the historical context, his reference to those who "mix them up with the divinely inspired Scriptures" would have been clearly understood. He was referring to the writings of the Gnostics.

At this point one can only speculate what happened next at a small Coptic monastery in Upper Egypt (some five hundred miles down the Nile from Alexandria) when it received the Festal Letter.[4] The responsibility of translating, copying, and distributing the thirty-ninth Festal missive of Athanasius fell upon a monk named Theodore, the head of the monastery. Perhaps this Theodore was keenly aware of his community's vulnerability to the voice and weight of authority five hundred miles away in Alexandria.[5] Maybe there were orthodox communities not far away that received the same letter, with the same instructions. Possibly, in one of his forced exiles, Athanasius had hidden out in this area and these monks knew that he knew about them and an uncertain paranoia set in. Perhaps the inhabitants of this monastery interpreted Athanasius' words as the warning shot of a heresy "clear-out," and with all of their accumulated cache of heretical literature they had much to lose. We can only speculate.

What we do know is more significant. Athanasius's festal letter either signaled the beginning of the end of Gnosticism or hastened a decline already in progress. We further know that someone or some group of monks inserted at least thirteen codices[6] into a red earthenware jar approximately one meter high and hastily, stealthily, buried it in a place where it would remain hidden for almost seventeen centuries.[7]

In 1945, in the Egyptian desert near a cliff called the Jabal al-Tārif, seven Bedouin laborers were digging for *sabakh*, a bird-lime fertilizer rich in nitrogen, to use in their gardens.[8] Jabal al-Tārif is located along a curve in the Nile near the village of Nag Hammadi, approximately three hundred miles south of Cairo, forty miles north of Luxor and the Valley of the Kings. According to New Testament scholar James Robinson,[9] while digging one of the group struck something hard that turned out to be a human skeleton.[10] This sparked excitement, and after more digging near the skeleton, next to a massive boulder, they unearthed "a large earthenware jar, about two feet high, with a bowl over the top, sealed with bitumen."[11] Suspecting the jar might contain gold or some other precious commodity, they took their mattocks and broke it open. "A cloud of golden dust rose into the air and disappeared from sight," one witness reported.[12] Instead, all they found was a collection of old leather books that turned out to be thirteen Gnostic codices dating back to the fourth century, the time of Athanasius's Festal Letter. What followed was "an intriguing story of serendipity, ineptitude, secrecy, ignorance, scholarly brilliance, murder, and blood revenge"[13] that would rival any best-selling thriller.

The location of the discovery was just three miles from the site of the Cheno-boskion compound founded by Saint Pachomius. Most scholars believe these ancient books were previously part of the monastery library and hastily whisked away to safety around 367 CE. This is all conjecture. No one knows the reason the books were taken from the library.[14] The magical power radiated by these books is not conjecture. They were considered precious commodities of inestimable value, the most important assemblage of lost documents from early Christianity to surface in modern times. The thirteen codices included forty-six different treatises[15] with titles such as *The Coptic Gospel of Thomas, The Coptic Apocalypse of Peter, The Apocalypse of Paul, The Apocalypse of Peter, The Gospel of Phillip, The Gospel of Thomas.* The end result of the find was a much clearer and expanded understanding of Gnostic thinking.[16]

Though written in Coptic, the manuscripts are believed to have been originally composed in Greek. Their dates of composition and publication can be established because their spines were strengthened with scrap paper receipts dated in the 340s CE. They were probably written and bound, therefore, before 350 CE.

The entire Nag Hammadi Library, translated by James M. Robinson, is available in hardback and paperback versions and makes for interesting reading. In one treatise, *The Testimony of Truth*, the Garden of Eden story is told from the viewpoint of the serpent[17] that tempts Adam and Eve to partake of fruit from the tree of knowledge despite a threat from the Lord that they would die. Among the collection is an interesting poem, *Round Dance of the Cross*, and another strangely titled *Thunder, Perfect Mind*, in which a feminine deity suggests she is the "whore and the holy one . . . the wife and the virgin . . . the silence that is incomprehensible."[18] In some codices are secret gospels and stories of the origin of the cosmos and tales of myth, magic, and mystical exercises.

Prior to the Nag Hammadi discovery, only a handful of Gnostic texts had been located and identified. None were published before the nineteenth century. In the *Acts of John*, found in only fragmentary form,[19] Jesus is not a human but a spiritual person. In 1896 in Cairo, a German Egyptologist purchased ancient texts that turned out to be the *Gospel of Mary* (Magdalene) and the *Apocryphon of John*. Consistent with the Gospels of Mark (16:9) and John (20:11–19), the *Gospel of Mary* records Mary Magdalene as the first to see the resurrected Christ and describes his resurrection appearances as apparitions perceived in dreams or trances. Both were unacceptable to early Church theologians. The former was considered a threat to the authority of the emerging fledgling Church (an issue to be discussed more fully in Chapter 6) and the latter contradicted the physical nature of Christ. The *Apocryphon of John*, one of the treatises found at Nag

Hammadi, included stories of Jesus's resurrection appearances and the evangelist's mystical vision of the Trinity.

Aside from these few manuscripts, the only documentary evidence available to us was the writings of the proto-orthodox opponents of Gnosticism who, when Christianity gained Empire dominance in the fourth century, denounced Gnosticism as a heresy and destroyed every Gnostic text they could find. The burial of documents at Nag Hammadi during the fourth century in all probability is a testament to that campaign against heretical teachings, which was led primarily by the early bishops. Once hunted by the police, the bishops became the hunters.[20] Ownership of heretical books was condemned and became a criminal offense. Copies that could be found were destroyed. Those that were whisked away by a monk, or group of monks, from a monastery near Nag Hammadi were preserved.

The Nag Hammadi texts are a valuable resource on Gnosticism, or more accurately, Gnosticisms. The phenomenon was not a unified system of faith but widely diverse with many manifestations. "It is impossible to synthesize the views, presumptions, religious perspectives of these into one monolithic system," states Ehrman.[21] The various origins and sources of Gnosticism will be discussed more fully in Chapter 3.[22] Its adherents represented multiple views. Many of its writers were Christian. They used Christian terminology, worshiped with Christians, and did not consider themselves to be heretics. Noted church historian Henry Chadwick, in his scholarly time-tested work, *The Early Church*, describes Gnosticism as a "generic term used primarily to refer to theosophical adaptations of Christianity propagated by a dozen or more rival sects which broke with the early Church between A.D. 80 and 150."[23]

Prominent New Testament scholar Bruce Metzger provides this summary: "'Gnosticism' refers to a diverse set of views, many of them influenced by Christianity, that may have been in existence by the end of the first century but certainly by the middle of the second. Our best evidence for specific Gnostic groups comes from the second century, the period in which the proto-orthodox opponents of the Gnostics were penning their vitriolic attacks and many of the documents preserved at Nag Hammadi were originally produced."[24] The Nag Hammadi discovery adds to our limited knowledge of the Gnostic phenomena. Yet among all the treatises unearthed, none exists with a chapter heading "Basic Gnostic Beliefs." No catalogue of Gnostic tenets is unveiled. In fact, some of the documents are decidedly Christian with clearly articulated proto-orthodox themes. The Christian documents that attack Gnosticism "do not spell out the Gnostic system (or the Gnostic systems), but appear to presuppose it."[25] The principle tenets presented in Chapter 2 are based on inferences and presuppositions, which, in turn, are based on the contents of the Nag Hammadi texts along with other surviving ancient manuscripts that have survived.

SUMMARY

One of the most significant events to occur in the history of the Christian Church was the circulation in 367 CE of the thirty-ninth Festal Letter of Athanasius, Bishop of Alexandria. The letter was the first widely accepted listing of the twenty-seven books of the New Testament and also called for the proscription and destruction of all writings not in harmony with the teachings of these twenty-seven books.

A secondary outcome of Athanasius's declaration was an action at a remote Coptic monastery. To protect their valued manuscripts, they buried them in the desert. For seventeen hundred years, all we knew about Gnosticism was what scholars could glean from a handful of texts and filter through the heavily biased writings of the early Church fathers. The discovery of thirteen codices at the foot of the mountain Jabal al-Tārif, near the village of Nag Hammadi in Upper Egypt, changed all that. These forty-six treatises, often referred to as the *Gnostic Gospels* (though some are more Christian than Gnostic), have shed considerable new light on Gnosticism, a very diverse phenomena represented by many groups with myriad religious beliefs and practices. The task at hand, based on this new knowledge, is to condense all of this data into a core of basic tenets.

THE BASIC TENETS OF GNOSTICISM

IN ORDER TO ADEQUATELY EXAMINE GNOSTICISM AND FUNDAMENTALISM, we must first identify their basic concepts or hermeneutical keys. Important to understanding any belief system is grasping its hermeneutics or its underlying principles of interpretation.[1] Hermeneutics is the "science of interpretation, especially of the Biblical text." For the purposes of this study, hermeneutics is an important word and one we will encounter frequently.[2] One might view hermeneutics as a template or pattern of a particular set of beliefs. What are the dominant themes of a religion? When you peel back the layers of dogma and liturgy, what is the core? What ultimately drives this religion, fuels its meaning? What about it creates adoration, devotion, worship, sacrifice? What causes it to generate obsession, fanaticism? In other words, what are its basic concepts? What are the hermeneutical keys that open the doors to its interpretation of sacred texts?

The solution to delineating the basic concepts of Gnosticism, however, is not that simple. Gnosticism presents a very complex problem. As Bart Ehrman[3] points out, the Nag Hammadi texts do not present any Gnostic system(s), rather they help explain its nature only to a limited degree.

Theologian Kurt Rudolph puts it in a nutshell: "The question has been repeatedly discussed whether it is possible to reconstruct from the individual Gnostic systems which have come down to us, one 'original' system, which could then be considered the most ancient type of the Gnostic world view, from which all other systems were somehow developed, either by elaboration or by transformation. . . . [But] according to the present state of research it is still too early to posit a common 'original'" system."[4] He goes on to state the general rule of thought that there are certain concepts that characterize the essence of Gnosticism. These basic ideas were there from the first century. They were developed by early Gnostics, working independently, into theological systems and ideological frameworks. Over the course of time, these doctrines formed schools, which in turn spawned congregations and organized churches.

BASIC GNOSTIC TENETS

Though opinions differ among scholars regarding the origins of Gnosticism and its myriad manifestations, they do agree on several basic principles. These principles all interrelate, but one in particular dominates: *Gnosis*.

GNOSIS OR KNOWLEDGE

The early Church fathers called them *gnostikoi*, with the sarcastic innuendo that they knew something the rest of the world did not. The writer of 1 Timothy 6:20 takes a similar ironic swipe at them by warning his readers against *pseudo-gnosis*. Irenaeus, one of the first Church fathers, chose as a full title for his greatest work *Against Heresies: A Refutation and Subversion of Knowledge Falsely So Called*.

Though scholars tend to differ among themselves as to what the Gnostics actually meant by knowledge, they generally agree what the Gnostics did not mean. They did not mean the absence of ignorance. They did not connote general knowledge, a general fund of facts, such as those that generate entertainment with *Jeopardy* or Trivial Pursuit. This *gnosis* had nothing to do with rational knowledge or with philosophical reasoning and had nothing to do with technical know-how or philosophical wisdom. Though their writings and texts were important to them, these "scriptures" did not, in and of themselves, impart the knowledge that saves.

The Gnostics' *gnosis* was a type of secret information, something never before revealed and never to be revealed. It was a saving knowledge concerning the self; it was a form of self-knowledge, "an intricate self-understanding of who they were, how they came to be here, where they came from and how they could return."[5] Elaine Pagels translates Gnosis as "insight," a term suggesting a kind of psychological self-knowledge or a self-awareness that is intuitively attained.[6] She cites the Gnostic teacher Monoimus: "Abandon the search for God and the creation and the other matters of a similar sort. Look for him by taking yourself as a starting point. Learn who it is within you who makes everything his own and says 'My God, my mind, my thought, my soul, my body.' Learn the sources of sorrow, joy, love, hate . . . if you carefully investigate these matters you will find him in yourself."[7] Other examples abound in Gnostic literature: "I tell you this that you may know yourself"[8]; and "Everyone who seeks the truth from true wisdom will make himself wings so as to fly, fleeing the lust that scorches the spirits of men."[9] In the *Gospel of Truth*, Gnostic scholar Pheme Perkins notes how salvation, particularly in the writer's interpretation of the sheep parables and images, is associated with possession of insight. She elaborates: "For the Valentinian author of *Gospel of Truth*, for the author of *Dialogue of the Savior*, as well as for the compiler of the Coptic *Gospel of Thomas*, understanding the true teaching of the Savior is the key to salvation."[10]

For Gnostic believers the clue to the quest for immortality lay in the self-knowledge, or "insight," that comes to one only when the Kingdom of God is discovered within. One cannot discover the spirit unless one first possesses the spirit.[11] The center of gravity of this system is individual salvation. For the Gnostics, personal knowledge rather than behavior, is the focus of salvation. This is particularly demonstrated in the *Gospel of Thomas* where poverty is associated with those who dwell in the world without knowledge of wisdom and not a lack of material goods.[12]

However, this knowledge was only for an elite few, those who were *gnostic* or, as Ehrman so aptly phrased it, "in the know."[13] This knowledge was not for everyone and not available to everyone: "Blessed are the solitary and elect, for you will find the kingdom. For you are from it and to it you will return."[14] This secret knowledge was hidden from the populace and available only to those who were capable of receiving and understanding it. Since the material world was evil, this knowledge could not come from the world or from humans. This saving knowledge could come only from outside the material world. It could come only from God.[15]

To sum up, this saving knowledge came from God and only to certain elite individuals who were capable of grasping its esoteric content. This is, however, an oversimplification. There is much more to Gnosticism, which will be explained later. But in essence, the key concept is Gnosticism's saving knowledge available only to those capable of understanding. Those not possessing this saving knowledge are not saved, thus, they are damned. This understanding of salvation polarizes. It creates knowers versus unknowers, saved versus unsaved, a mindset of exclusion versus one of inclusion. Salvation is based upon one's understanding of knowledge (*gnosis*), how it came to earth, to whom it came, and who was qualified to receive it and pass it on. Only those with Gnostic credentials were candidates.

How could this be right? How could this knowledge be accessible only to certain special individuals? If it possessed the capacity to save, why could it not save more people? Would not a God of creation want more people saved? The answer requires analysis of other Gnostic principles.

Gnostic Worldview and Metaphysical Dualism

For Gnostics, reality was composed of two basic elements: physical (material or corporeal) and spiritual. There was no middle ground. Spirit was everything; anything material or physical was unessential. Any substance that was not spiritual was matter and therefore evil. This was called dualism. Dualism leads inevitably to more than one god.[16]

The Gnostic universe from the beginning was depressing. Creation was flawed: "The cosmos is an abortion; humanity, in the fleshly sense, along with all materiality, is a mistake."[17] The world was flawed because it was flawed when it was created: "For the Gnostic Christians, the material world itself was part and parcel of the human tragedy."[18] Like Buddhists, Gnostics portrayed human life as one filled with suffering and most of it comes from the defective cosmos. People are responsible for some of the suffering, but most of it comes from the original defects in an imperfect cosmos.

The source of metaphysical dualism will be discussed more fully in Chapter 3, "The Origins of Gnosticism." For summary purposes, some of it came from the probable source of all Western dualisms: Zoroastrianism of ancient Persia. Hellenistic interpretations of Zoroastrianism and of Plato are another source along with Apocalyptic Judaism.[19] Regardless of its origin, the physical world was evil and the spiritual was good and the two were locked in constant conflict.[20] For Gnostics, this was not a conflict that would continue forever. The material world came into being at a point in time, and at a point in time it would cease to exist.

THE GNOSTIC VIEW OF HUMANITY

Gnostic cosmic dualism permeates all facets of the system, thus it carries over into the sphere of humanity. The Gnostic creation story is complicated and will be fully developed in this chapter. For now, this simple version will suffice.

Humans were created by a Demiurge, or false creator. A "divine spark," older than the creation, resided within each human. It ultimately originated in Sophia or Divine Wisdom. Many humans are unaware that they possess the divine spark. To gain awareness and "insight" into this residual fragment of divinity, one must overcome a number of formidable obstacles. These obstacles, built in at the time of creation, are known as Satan, the Devil, the Evil One, and other names considered synonymous with all that is bad.[21] At death, the divine spark is released from its earthly incarceration. Unless those possessing the divine spark find illumination while still on earth, this release may be temporary.

Gnostic humanity was divided into three types:[22]

PNEUMATICS

Pneumatics (from the Greek *pneuma*, which means spirit) or *gnostikoi* were a small, select group comprised of the spiritual ones, the only ones worthy of understanding the mysteries. They were preselected, predestined on an individual basis. In Gnostic salvation, individuals were single units, not groups. This explains why they reject the Old Testament where the emphasis falls upon the salvation of an entire people: the Israelites.

According to Gnostic wisdom, these *gnostikoi* have been elected because they are worthy of election. Their divine spark was prepared for enlightenment, or Gnosis, which meant liberation. Gnostic Christians, for example, considered the teachings of Jesus reserved only for the elect, or pneumatics: "Only the pneumatics, the Gnostics themselves, could truly understand the revelation from God; on the basis of that revelatory knowledge, they were destined to escape the material world. . . . The writings of Jesus' own Apostles conveyed secret revelations not accessible to the literal minded psychics of the church. . . . Only true Knowers could unravel the meanings embedded in seemingly unrelated details of the text, meanings that comprised the secret teachings of the Gnostic system."[23] Due to their elevated spiritual status, the pneumatics engaged in a more flexible, symbolic interpretation of scripture. This form of spiritual teaching led to multiple interpretations, all of which seems incongruent with their inflexible understanding on salvation.

HYLETICS

Hyletics (*hylic*, meaning matter or earthly, fleshly): At the opposite pole from the *pneumatics* were the *hyletics*. These were the earthbound. All they could do was eat, drink, sleep, defecate, copulate, and die. They could see and recognize only the physical world and its tangible materials. They could perceive only objective, substantive reality; nothing beyond that; nothing spiritual. They were a lost cause.

PSYCHICS

Psychics (from Greek *psychē*, meaning soul). Between the *pneumatics* and *hylics* were the *psychics*, those who existed in a state of mental and emotional being. The psychics could go in either direction. If there is any evangelistic spirit within Gnosticism, it is in the pneumatic drive to help the helpable, save the savable: the psychics. Pneumatics took great pride in knowing they had rescued one from the edge of perdition and brought him back into the fold of the saved.[24] The psychic's path to liberation is not solely spiritual. More effort is required for these earthly denizens. Rather than seeking elevated, saving states of consciousness, they look to rules of conduct for their redemption. One might say they find their salvation through the law. The psychics accepted the literal meanings of scriptures.[25]

In these three categories of humanity, one can detect parallels in contemporary theology and religious expression. These same themes will be encountered when we examine the influence of Gnosticism on Christian theology and contemporary Biblical hermeneutics, namely, how certain Christian denominations interpret scripture. Some unknowingly associate these methods of interpretation with Gnosticism.

Gnosticism blurs the distinction between divinity and humanity yet asserts the basic nature of humanity to be divine. Orthodox theology categorically denounces this belief. The nature of humans is radically different from divinity. For Orthodoxy, there is no divine spark. No one possesses divine knowledge. Any divine spark that might have existed vanished at the Fall when Adam and Eve partook from the Tree of Knowledge of Good and Evil. Only God possesses this knowledge. Gnostics, however, partake of the fruit of the tree. The divine spark, therefore, allows them to escape the ignorance of their material body and this world.

THE GNOSTIC GOD

The Gnostic God was not only a creator God but also, as one scholar stated, a micromanager—"its lawgiver, policeman, judge, and executioner, and, moreover, performed these tasks in a capricious, often wrathful and illogical manner."[26] The

Gnostic God evolved during late Hellenistic Judaism when Jewish theologians struggled to solve the problem of evil. The Gnostics of that period were engaged in a similar struggle, which would color the rest of their theological system.

Steven Munciman in his book *The Medieval Manichee* captures the essence of Gnosticism: "It is a desire to solve the problem of Evil that lies at the base of Gnosticism."[27] The Gnostics were faced with the same dilemma as all religions: the problem of evil. If God is good, why does some evidence of his creation suggest he is evil? Given their intolerance for loose ends, the solution for the Gnostics was to get God off the hook, rescue him from the responsibility of the stigma of the evil contained in Creation. Therefore, they came up with an alternative god, the Demiurge. This God was *not* THE ultimate God, the First Principle, but a lesser God, a secondary or intermediary deity.[28] Beyond this intermediary God is ultimate reality, all that is ultimately real and good. This was called the Divine Realm.

THE DIVINE REALM

The story of Gnostic creation goes something like this: At a point far back in eternity before time began, the one true God had children. These divine children had their own divine offspring. Couples, sometimes called "aeons," began having their own couples, which eventually created a large happy extended cosmic family called a Divine Realm.

As with all families, something happened. In this case what happened was someone else's fault. The gods, too, are human. They have a problem claiming ownership for their errors. There was a cosmic catastrophe. A female deity or aeon, named Sophia (the Greek word for wisdom) somehow became separated or was kicked out—the mythical theories vary.[29] She ended up on the wrong side of the universe with the wrong crowd. One might draw an analogy of a child running away or being kicked out of the house then snubbing her nose at her parents and family. Such was the case with Sophia.

This was a hard fall for Sophia. She became terrified, filled with emotions of fear, anger, hate, abandonment, and despair. These negative feelings eventually took on a life of their own and became infused in other imperfectly formed offspring. These combinations resulted outside the union of Sophia and her consort, thus outside of the divine realm and therefore Evil.[30] It was in this manner that evil infected the earth. These evil children birthed their own evil darlings and with them created the evil material world.[31] As previously noted, this creator(s) of the material world in many Gnostic myths is called the Demiurge (Greek *demiurgos*, craftsman or maker). The term is found in a number of other religious and philosophical writings, most notably in Plato's *Timaeus*.[32]

Meanwhile, Sophia, who is knowledge and wisdom, is still trapped in this material world, separated from the divine heavenly realm. She is imprisoned in the material bodies of humans, thus providing the basis for the divine spark that resides within some humans. Those who have the divine spark seem to know or feel this spark and thus yearn to find its source. They have lost the memory of their true heavenly home, and regaining the spark will enlighten them and help them find the way. Those who do not have the spark are left out in the cold, doomed. When they die, they die. For them there is no hope of eternal life.[33]

We must pause a moment and recapitulate. Why was this elaborate tale so necessary in the first place? Why go to all the trouble? Why not just have one God and make things simpler? The answer lies in the age old problem of suffering, that is, why is there suffering in a world created by a good, benevolent God? These myths served primarily as a function to explain why good people suffer in a world created by a good God. Or rephrased, how a one true good God, all-powerful and omnipotent, permits evil to exist. The result: two or more gods.[34]

These myths were borrowed by the Gnostics and respun to fit their own theology. In this way, the Demiurge acts as a solution to the problem of evil. God did not create evil; someone or something else did. This takes God off the hook and keeps his (or her) slate clean. These myths also described the Gnostics' sense of alienation from the physical material world and explained how this estrangement occurred. Around 30 CE, a man named Jesus of Nazareth arrived on the scene. Through his death and resurrection he reframed the old problem of suffering. Their trapped sparks yearning for salvation, the Gnostics found a savior in this self-proclaimed Messiah. The final piece fell into place. Their system was almost complete.

SALVATION

In his introduction to Stanley Hall's *The Wisdom of the Knowing Ones*, Stephen Hoeller quotes a Gnostic statement defining the nature of Gnosis:

> What makes us free is the Gnosis of who we are of what we have become of where we were of wherein we have been cast of whereto we are casting of what we are being freed of what birth really is of what rebirth really is.[35]

The correct answer to each of these questions constitutes Gnosis and thus, liberation. Ignorance enslaves. Knowledge frees. When the gospel writer quotes Jesus as saying "The truth shall make you free," he was flirting with a fundamental Gnostic tenet. For orthodox Christians, Jesus freed humanity from sin and suffering and death. For Gnostics, Jesus came into this world to free them from ignorance. And toward that end he was to be their helper, their guide. This is, of course, no new theme. Far back in antiquity, Messengers of Light have figured into various schemes of salvation in a variety of religions systems.[36] The Gnostic way to the Light was escape from the world. Salvation thus constituted a form of escape from reality, a phenomenon evidenced today in Fundamental theology. (This will be more fully developed below in Chapter 9, "The Differences between Gnosticism and Fundamentalism.") With their true God set apart from the world and the Demiurge taking the rap for evil, Gnostics are free "to escape the world with impunity, for neither Gnostics nor their God have any stake in it."[37]

Salvation from sin, original or otherwise, was not a goal of Gnosticism. Their goal was release from unconsciousness and ignorance, or incomprehension. Humans who possess the divine spark can find their freedom only in learning of its source, how it came to be entrapped in the material world, and how it can escape to return to its original realm. This important theme of gnosis takes us back to the beginning of our search. Gnosis is the liberating knowledge that enables release from the material evil world. This knowledge was "special" and qualitatively different from, and transcendent over, the simple faith of the Church. But like the faith of the Church, it was a saving knowledge; and, like the faith of the Church, it required a savior. For the later discussion on Gnosticism and Fundamentalism, it is significant to note that salvation was potential in everyone. It was not vicarious, but individual. Individuals saved themselves.

DIVINE REDEEMER

Some scholars assert that the most important principle Gnosticism derived from Christianity was its core idea of redemption.[38] There are strong arguments to support this. However, by their own dualistic premise (spirit is good, matter is evil), anything material is alien to a supreme God. Thus, by default, Gnostics automatically dismiss any concept of incarnation.[39] Because flesh was inherently evil, their divine Christ could never come "in the flesh." It is important that this contradiction be fully grasped. If they do not become incarnate, born in the flesh, can a God or Redeemer save?

The Gnostics answer is the Redeemer. This Redeemer was not flesh but took on the "appearance" of flesh. To ordinary senses he looked real, seemed tangible flesh and blood. But Gnostics with the divine spark, with elevated insight, saw pure pristine spirit. Those without the spark saw a physical appearance, a semblance or *dokesis* (Greek for "appearance"), from which we get Docetism, an early form of Gnosticism that alarmed the early Church fathers.[40]

The Gnostic Redeemer was a divine being who came into the world to save his entrapped subjects. It was Christ himself, but what kind of Christ? It was not a real Christ. So how could the divine Redeemer come into the world and NOT be human. Gnostic Christians understood how this could happen in basically two different ways.[41]

The first was the docetic view previously introduced. Some scholars[42] consider the letters of John to be an attack on this form of Gnosticism. This was also the form of Gnosticism embraced by Marcion (about whom more will be said in Chapter 3.) To Gnostics, Christ represented only an appearance of being human. Not surprisingly, St. Paul became one of the Gnostic sources of support and they would often quote him. In *Romans*, for example, it states that Christ came "in the likeness of sinful flesh" (8:3). There were other aspects of Paul's letters, such as his animosity toward the law that Gnostics embraced.

An alternative view for Gnostics of God becoming human without actually becoming flesh was called the Separationist position. The man, Jesus, was a real flesh-and-blood person. Yet, another heavenly being inhabited Jesus' body for a period of time. This was the heavenly, divine Christ that entered Jesus's body at his baptism (the dove descending from heaven) but departed prior to his death. According to this theory, Christ did not suffer. Pain and death are foreign to Gnostic thinking. Following his death, the heavenly Christ returned and resurrected the earthly, human Christ, empowering him to spread the gnosis that his disciples and others would need for the heavenward journey home. Some Gnostics who held this theory had a particular fondness for the *Gospel According to Mark*. This evangelist depicts Jesus's ministry beginning with the reception of the Holy Spirit at his baptism and ending on the cross with his words: "My God, My God, why have you forsaken me?"(Mark 15:34). Considered by Gnostics to be Jesus's last words, their interpretation is unmistakable. The divine spirit departed his physical body. The spiritual Christ, who could receive no physical pain, would escape crucifixion.

Docetist and Separationist concepts were a threat to the proto-orthodox position that Christ only was the Divine Redeemer.[43] If He did not become human, He lacked power to save. The proto-orthodox fathers averred that God did empty himself and He did become human. This unique core belief of proto-orthodox theology could be summed up in four words: "The word became flesh." This was the dominant, guiding principle separating proto-orthodoxy (and later, orthodoxy) from the various Gnosticisms and religions of that era.

THE CHURCH

Because of its dualistic premise, the Gnostic Church was not inclusive, but exclusive. "No matter how we regard Gnostic thought . . . it is always an elitist faith."[44] It was an elitist body of elect.[45] Knowledge was the double-edged divider of the saved from the damned. The *gnostikoi*, because they were the enlightened ones and "in the know," were a cut above the rest. In most cases "the rest" were those in Christian congregations who were not *gnostikoi*.[46] Many Gnostics claimed to be Christian. They heavily populated early Christian churches. They comingled to a point that Christians could not differentiate them from their own. Similar to the earlier mystery religions, Gnostics kept their knowledge veiled behind a cloak of secrecy. Some Gnostic sects used passwords for passage through the various levels of saving knowledge.

Among the scholarly descriptions of this "Body of the Elect," Bart Ehrman arguably provides the best:

> According to some Christian Gnostics, the human race could thus be divided up into three classes: (a) the Gnostics themselves, possessors of ultimate knowledge, destined for a glorious salvation when they returned to the heavenly realm whence they came; (b) other Christians, who mistakenly believed that they had the truth, when they had nothing but a superficial knowledge of it through a literal understanding of the sacred writings of the apostles and the doctrines transmitted in the church; these persons would receive some form of salvation if they had faith and

did good works, but their afterlife would not be nearly as glorious as that of the true Gnostics; and (c) all other persons, who had no part of the divine within them and were destined for destruction along with the rest of the material world when the salvation of the divine sparks had been complete.[47]

Gnostic Christians perceived themselves as an elect group destined for salvation. They possessed a special mysterious ultimate knowledge. They read the same sacred texts as the "other" Christians and they participated in the same rituals (baptism and Holy Communion). They probably professed and recited, in unison with the congregation, the same creed (a truncated form of today's Apostles Creed). But they were a cut above the rest and saw themselves as a privileged, select body within the Church, a description similar to some current denominational positions.

Due to its ethereal nature, ultimate truth for Gnostics could not come from any earthly institution. This was intolerable and unacceptable. Gnostics were highly suspicious of anything resembling an institution. "All who had received gnosis . . . had gone beyond the church's teaching and had transcended the authority of its hierarchy."[48] Pagels also points out that Valentinians were not opposed to the institution. They just considered it irrelevant and had little to do with it. The individual, not the institution, was relevant to salvation. Most Gnostics were bored with the formalities, liturgies, recitation of creeds, and discipline of the Church. These same concerns will surface centuries later in the early American colonies when the cause of individualism burst on the scene in the Great Awakening and the "Old Lights" of the institution fought it out with the "New Lights" of the revival movement.

ETHICAL/MORALISTIC VIEWPOINT.

Early Church apologists and heresiologists accused Gnostics of being amoral, of having little, if any, concern for ethics. They described Gnostics as prodigal profligates who engaged in various and sundry acts of indecency and immoral sexual behavior, including murder and cannibalism.[49] In the third century, Clement of Alexandria accused the Gnostic Carpocrations of having "love-feasts for uniting" social events under the guise of religion in which gluttony and sexual orgies took place.[50] According to Irenaeus, adherents to the Valentinian system "fearlessly practice everything that is forbidden. . . . They eat with indifference food offered to idols . . . are the first to arrive at any festival party that takes place in honor of the heathen idols. . . . [S]ome secretly seduce women. . . . Others again who initially made an impressive pretense of living with (women) as with sisters were convicted in course of time, when the 'sister' became pregnant by the 'brother.'"[51]

The Carpocratians, Irenaeus said, "are so abandoned in their recklessness that they claim to have in their power and be able to practice anything whatsoever that is ungodly (irreligious) and impious . . . according to their scriptures they maintain that their souls should have every enjoyment of life, so that when they depart they are deficient in nothing."[52] The Heresiologist Epiphanius accused Gnostics of praying "with their whole bodies naked."[53] Tertullian's writings are filled with invectivess against them.

The Gnostic concept of salvation significantly influenced Christian opinion about their morality. Sole promotion of the "other world" meant severance from this world. With little interest in the physical world, Gnostics really had no ethic. The world had no value, so why not enjoy it. This form of libertinism applied especially to the "pneumatics." You will recall these are the privileged spiritual ones, the elect, possessed with more freedom than others. They were free from the law (in a very different sense than Pauline's freedom from the law).[54] Regardless of the reason, for most of the early Church fathers and heresiologists, libertinism defined Gnostic lack of ethics. Nothing in the Nag Hammadi texts supports this conclusion. Unfortunately, the only witnesses for that lifestyle are restricted to the Church fathers, and they used character assassination as a weapon of destruction. In the final analysis, they used it as a weapon of mass destruction.

So, what was the Gnostic ethic? Based on their denial of the material, physical, and earthly, it is more logical that in the beginning they adopted an ascetic ethic of self-denial. Documents indicate some were vegetarians and practiced sexual abstinence to the point of never marrying (another reason that they seemed to evaporate by the fourth century). Practiced religiously by more than just a few, this ethic was a tough competitor for the Christians. They also had problems with their own "love-feasts" getting out of hand (recall Paul's problems with the Church in Corinth mentioned in 1 Corinthians.) As late as the third century, Origen has to defend the Church against similar charges leveled by Celsus.

CONCLUSION

This chapter, I realize, requires considerable unpacking. The reader may still be saying "Okay, all that is helpful information, but, in a nutshell, what is Gnosticism?" That is a legitimate question. Limiting the amount of information was by intent for two reasons. First, Gnosticism is even more complex than the factors presented. And second, these factors will be needed later for comparison with Fundamentalism. Now to the nutshell. Harold Bloom, self-declared Jewish Gnostic, helps us cut to the core: "Gnosis is entirely the doctrine of the deep or deepest self . . . and the issue of Gnosis is indeed 'the true person.'"[55] This deepest self is the "divine spark." Through awareness the individual connects with, "knows," this "God within." At that point they are illuminated. That is the divine mystic moment. Bloom goes on to say that we are a nation addicted to finding "self-awareness."[56] One need only go to the psychology or religion section of a bookstore for confirmation. The hunt for true selfhood is what drives the Gnostic mind. It also drives other minds. Though they frame it differently, this type of thinking fuels the Fundamentalist mind.

SUMMARY

Until the discovery of the Gnostic Gospels in 1945, very little was known about the beliefs of the movement that challenged early Christianity. In their study of belief systems, scholars look for hermeneutical keys, that is, core beliefs that determine basic themes and subthemes. Their examination of the Gnostic Gospels has brought several to light.

Gnosis means knowledge, and it is knowledge that saves. For Gnostics, salvation lies in discovering the truth of their identity, their origin, how they came to this earth, and how they can return to the divine heavenly realm, which is their ultimate destination and goal. This is the knowledge, the truth that leads to salvation. But it is grasped by only an elite few who are "in the know."

Gnostic cosmogony, or worldview, is dualistic. Reality is composed of spirit and matter. Spirit is good. Matter is evil. Because there is evil in the world, it could not have been created by the one True Divinity, or God. Therefore, evil came about through a catastrophic cosmic disaster. As a result, the spirit became trapped in the evil, material world. In order for this spirit, represented as divine sparks in certain humans, to return to its heavenly divine realm it must acquire saving knowledge. This saving knowledge comes from a divine redeemer. This divine redeemer came into the world to save the lost sparks of the spirit.

So far, all of this sounds vaguely Christian. Then comes the significant factor, or hermeneutical key, that differentiates Gnosticism from Christianity: flesh is evil; therefore, the Gnostic redeemer is all spirit and never became flesh. For Christians, "the word became flesh." For Gnostics, the word became spirit. No flesh was involved. From the Christian perspective, the Gnostic divine redeemer was impotent. He (or she) lacked humanity.

Gnostic Christians were active in Christian Churches but did not believe all Christians would be saved, primarily because they did not have access to the saving knowledge. Because many belonged to the Church, and because of their insistence that the one true spiritual God could not have been human, Gnosticism posed a very real and major threat to the existence of the young struggling Church. Their ascetic ethic was another serious challenge.

CHAPTER 3

THE ORIGINS OF GNOSTICISM

THE QUEST FOR THE ORIGINS OF GNOSTICISM DATES BACK TO THE FIRST CENTURY CE when no systematic formalization of Gnostic theology existed.[1] Trying to find its source is analogous to trying to find the source of the Nile. There is no single point of origin, but many; because there is no single Gnosticism. Compounding the search is the ongoing research and archeological discovery. One scholar characterized the challenge in these words: "It is no exaggeration to number the problems of the genesis and the history of Gnosis among the most difficult. . . . Much is still in a state of flux and to write a complete history of Gnosis remains a task for the future."[2] Another reason for the difficulty of the task is the limitation of available sources.

Christianity, on the other hand, had the Acts of the Apostles, the four Gospels, the letters of Paul, and so on. Besides the numerous writings of the early Church fathers, there was Eusebius of Caesarea's *Ecclesiastical History.* Gnosticism had nothing comparable. Gnostic writings were handed down anonymously and lacked an interest in history. Unlike Christianity, the Gnostics "do not refer back to the life or revelations of a particular historical individual as the foundation for their faith."[3] The writers who were interested in a particular individual and history of a particular institution were the early Christian Church fathers, or heresiologists. They did write extensively about Gnostics and Gnostic theology and those sources are plentiful. But a heresiologist writing about Gnosticism would carry as much objectivity as would a Confederate general writing an unbiased history of the Civil War. The early Church apologists had one goal: wipe the Gnostics off the face of the earth. They almost succeeded.

Despite the discovery at Nag Hammadi, information regarding the history and the sources of Gnosticism remains limited. The texts uncovered at Nag Hammadi were inconsistent in their perspectives and, as Ehrman points out, "we have no assurance that all of these texts were ever seen as authoritative by any one community, in the way that the texts of the New Testament came later to be for orthodox Christians . . . they do not spell out the Gnostic system, but seem to presuppose it."[4] The Gnostic Gospels, therefore, do provide some insight into Gnostic thinking and theology but give little indication of origins.

The Greco-Roman[5] world where Gnosticism developed in the first centuries BCE and CE was a "melting pot of religious impulses from the eastern provinces like Syria and even beyond the boundaries of the Roman Empire, such as Iran."[6] Among the mix was the monotheism of the Jews and pantheism of Greeks and Egyptians. Greek philosophy was represented by Neo-Platonism and Neo-Pythagorism.[7] Hermeticism, a cult that would later give rise to alchemy in medieval Europe, had spread from Egypt throughout the Mediterranean basin. This was also a period of the Essenes, Nazarenes, and Osirian rites plus a variety of mystery religions. Primitive religious cults flourished along the perimeter of the Empire. On the fringe were the Manichaeans and Zoroastrians. Mystical cults of Persia and Arabia would later set the stage for the emergence of Islam. Everywhere there was "superstition . . . accompanied by paralyzing belief in magic, enchantment, miracle, astrology and witchcraft."[8] Professor Hall provides this compact summary: "There was a great mingling, mixing, blending, and confusing of faiths, which continued until the latter part of the third or early fourth century A.D."[9]

The period from 100 BCE to 100 CE was a time of prosperity and peace, a time of great decadence, and a time of moral and ethical confusion. Spiritual anarchy reigned. Ethics was left to the teachers of philosophy. The state ran many of the cults and appointed the priests. The norm was not one God but many gods, not monotheism but polytheism. Religious freedom and tolerance abounded. Variety of religious expression, not uniformity was common. People could worship whichever god they chose and as many as they chose. There was little, if any, formal organization and almost no hierarchy in the religions of that time. One word best captures the mindset of the majority: despair.

Emerging new religions thrive on despair and polytheism is usually a sign of despair, of a culture in the process of collapse. People felt alienated from an Empire in decline. There were predictions of world cataclysms. The Jews were despondent over the destruction of the Temple in 70 CE and their evacuation from Jerusalem. Had the minds of Nietzsche, Sartre, or Heidegger been around, they would have nailed the mood as existential and nihilistic. The populace was "in dull satisfaction with itself" and "seeking something new."[10] Whether relevant to their lives or not, people were hungering for something fresh. The cultural matrix was wide open and susceptible to change. From that confused and despairing mélange, Christianity was born. And so was Gnosticism.

Regardless of the source(s), it "evolved into an elaborate and complex philosophy, uniting within its own structure the essential factor of several great religions."[11]

JEWISH INFLUENCE AND JEWISH APOCALYPTICISM

Some scholars argue that any theory regarding Gnostic origins and evolution must include a Jewish background. The early Church fathers insisted that the first Gnostics came from the Samarian-Palestine area and that their teachings were from Jewish biblical tradition.[12] They may have been right. Several key figures of the Old Testament—Adam, Seth, Cain, Shem, and Noah—are claimed as ancestors by some Gnostic traditions. The supreme god of Gnosticism betrays features of Hebrew monotheism.[13] Gnostic mythology draws from the Old Testament and appeals to it as an authoritative text. Perkins, among other scholars, points out that "gnostic mythology exploited Jewish interpretations of the dual creation of Adam in Genesis 1–3."[14]

Bart Ehrman picks up the theme and raises it a level. In one of his recent works, *Lost Christianities*, he suggests that Gnosticism originated "not outside of Judaism, but *inside* it, as a kind of reaction movement to forms of Judaism that had developed by the time Christianity emerged, forms of Judaism that influenced Jesus and his followers."[15] Much of Jewish theology, he notes, goes back to Moses and the Exodus, the Hebrews crossing the Red Sea, the most significant event in Jewish history. God identifies with his chosen people and saves them.

In later times the Israelites suffered and were not saved by an intervening God. How could this happen? A large part of the Old Testament involves attempts to answer this question (Cf. books of prophets: *Isaiah, Jeremiah, Ezekiel*, and *Amos*). The suffering happened because God's people had sinned. They were being punished. But what happens when Jews do not sin, when they were on the right religious track? God should be good to them, right? But it did not happen. Bad things continued (suppression and hellenization under the Seleucid ruler Antiochus IV Epiphanes), provoking another question: why does a good God let good righteous people suffer and sinful people prosper? Attempts to answer this question can be found in other books of the Old Testament—*Job, Ecclesiastes, Daniel*—where new concepts began to infiltrate Judaism and ancient Jewish thought. One of those innovative ideas was Apocalypticism.[16]

The word apocalypse (from the Greek *apokalypsis*) means "unveiling" or "revealing."[17] Apocalyptic, therefore, is esoteric revealed wisdom, and the knowledge it reveals has an *immediate* relation to redemption. The notion of immediacy relates to mysticism, which will be discussed later.

Jewish Apocalypticism arose about 200 to 250 years before Jesus of Nazareth, in a time of great suffering among the Jewish people. The *Book of Daniel* is a prime example of apocalypticism. Enoch traditions are also probably the source of early Gnostic mythical speculation.[18] The books of Enoch were written between the third century BCE and first century CE. They are considered important Jewish writings but not part of the Old Testament.[19] In Daniel and the Enoch series we first encounter the apocalyptic figure "son of man" to which Jesus of Nazareth would often refer, and with whom, many avow, he identified.[20] The *Book of Daniel* is placed with "The Writings" in the Old Testament. Chapters 7 through 12 are apocalyptic revelations. Though no names are mentioned, "persons and events can easily be identified including Antiochus IV Epiphanes of Syria and the persecution of the Jews, which began in 168 BC."[21] The book, dated by most scholars to the Maccabean Revolt, is well known in the *Dead Sea Scrolls* and also found in a range of other Jewish writings not included in the Bible.[22]

The intent of the writer(s) of *Daniel* was to offer hope and consolation to the Jewish people in the midst of persecution. The resulting apocalyptic theology goes something like this: This punishment of the Jewish people could not come from God. It must come from another source, such as cosmic evil or cosmic powers or forces of evil. This world must not be a creation of the one true God who is All Good. Some other type of spiritual, or nonmaterial, god had a hand in it. Therefore he is linked to the world but beneath God the Creator. At some point in the future, God would intervene and overthrow these evil powers. Victory will be achieved at the hands of the Archangel Michael and the martyrs will be rewarded with resurrection.[23] In other words, the revered God of the Hebrews is taken off the hook.

Recall the Gnostic myth of Sophia in the preceding chapter. This Jewish make-over of God (Yahweh) is Gnosticism. From a Jewish concept of creation, of evil and suffering, a non-Jewish religion developed. According to this view, one or several Gnostic thinkers hijacked the Jewish myth and accommodated it to their own philosophical presuppositions. (Of course, the Jews had hijacked it from someone else.) The eschatological (end of time) slant the Gnostics gave it included a pronounced dualistic-pessimistic world, one no longer governed by God but by his enemy, the devil and his angelic powers. The world and history were left on an automatic course. Salvation from this material entrapment was achieved by *gnosis.* "The knowledge of God's mysteries guarantees salvation; knowledge and cognition, and redemption are closely connected."[24] This knowledge, or wisdom, was accessible only to the initiated . . . the saved. The mediation of revelation was through Sophia, goddess of wisdom. The influences of Jewish wisdom literature, Proverbs, Wisdom of Solomon, Ecclesiastes, and other wisdom writings not in the Old Testament, are speculated.

In summary, Gnostic sources strongly infer that the mythical elements of its development depended upon, and drew from, Jewish traditions, particularly Jewish apocalyptical traditions. The stories were changed to fit the philosophical presumptions, but the underlying themes remained similar. Additional research also suggests that some Gnostic groups may have been influenced by Jews disenchanted with their religious tradition and a God who did not deliver according to their expectations. Perhaps there existed a more reliable God (or gods) they could depend on when they were suffering. These Jews came to see the world as not only corrupted, but also inherently evil. They had to adjust their theology accordingly, which meant another deity: Satan. This was a perfect framework for Gnostic needs.[25]

GREEK-HELLENISTIC CONTRIBUTIONS

The vocabulary of most Gnostic systems was derived primarily from the language of Greek philosophy. "Without it Gnosis is unthinkable," states Rudolph.[26] During the first and second centuries CE, Gnostic thinkers drew heavily from Platonic and Neo-Platonic philosophy. Some of the following major themes and concepts were shared: God and the soul, the Demiurge, the "unknown God," origin of evil, the descent and return of the soul, fate, and freedom. Unlike Judaism, of considerable importance for Gnosticism was the Platonic dualism of spirit and matter, soul and body, God and the world. These dualistic concepts "gave Gnosis points of departure and of contact for the conception of its view of the world and bricks for its theology."[27] Gnostics emphasized a kind of dualism of shadow and reality, of matter and spirit.[28] Centuries later this would figure into Calvinistic theology and, in turn, contribute heavily to Fundamentalist origins and the Puritan emphasis upon work ethic.[29]

EGYPTIAN AND MYSTERY RELIGIONS

The Gnostics were heavily indebted to Egyptian religions. They were inspired by Egyptian religious artistry and the inscriptions on their gems were borrowed from Egypt. The redeemer figure Osiris came from Egypt. Hermetic philosophy, from which Gnostic thinkers borrowed, originated in Alexandria in first two centuries CE. Alexandria was a cultural center where the traditions of Syria, Chaldea, and Persia blended with Judaism, Christianity, and Greek philosophy.[30]

The demise of the antiquated mythological system of Roman and Greek gods and goddesses left a vacuum that was partially filled by a number of mystery religions.[31] Mystery cults focused on religious individualism. This resulted in confessional religions with a missionary character dividing believers and nonbelievers. Believers made up the inner circle, nonbelievers the outer. This feature is found in Christianity and may have been borrowed, in part, from the mystery religions where concentration was also on redemption and a savior. Salvation was sought in another world and occurred through direct participation in the life and example of the divinity. Favorite means of attaining this goal were faith, knowledge, wisdom—that is, intellectual attitudes. It is only a short step from these concepts to gnosis.

CENTRAL ASIAN AND ZOROASTRIAN INFLUENCE

Some scholars believe branches of Gnosticism generally followed the Syrian mystic doctrines and possibly the mysterious doctrines of central Asia. In this they were perpetuators of Babylonian stargazing and magic.[32] Gnostic systems with a dualism of opposing principles at the origins of the cosmos may have been influenced by the Iranian dualism of Zoroastrianism.[33] Because of the thriving trade routes and fluid commerce of the time, many Gnostics may have come in contact with this Persian metaphysical dualism.[34] Iranian (Persian) and Greek Hellenistic culture were a presence in the Syrian–Palestinian region centuries before Christ. Rudolph even ventures that "Jewish Apocalyptic religion did not come into existence without the contribution of Iranian-Zoroastrian religious ideas. . . . These include above all the idea of the eschatological judgment, resurrection of the dead, scheme of the ages and dualism."[35] Many redeemer figures came from the Mesopotamian area, notably Marduk and Mithra. Gnosis drew heavily from these

ideas. Many were introduced from, and passed through, a Jewish-apocalyptic filter. Considering the current state of world affairs, one might find it difficult to
conceive of Jewish religion as being heavily influenced by Iranian religious ideas.
But, in another era, at another time, it happened.[36] A touch of irony is added
when one considers that the same Iranian mysticism also influenced the origin
and development of Islam. That same Iran (Persia) was once, long ago, friends
and supporters of the people of Israel, the Jews. It was the Persians under Cyrus
who allowed the exiled Jews to return home and rebuild their temple.

There is considerable evidence Gnosticism derived from mysticism.[37] A common thread running through all of these religious expressions, concepts, and
worldviews is that of mysticism. Mysticism means direct spiritual experience with
God. This type of "knowing" transcends intellectual and cognitive understanding. Mysticism is *knowing* God directly and not through teachings or doctrine, or
even tradition. When Jesus proclaimed, "I and the Father are one," (John 10:30)
he was making the ultimate mystical statement. This type of spiritual knowledge
bypasses the normal channels of Orthodoxy. Mysticism is a highly visible and
important factor in the Fundamentalist movement of our time.

The importance of mysticism to this study is immeasurable. Mysticism provides an uncommon source for unique ways of "knowing" the word and will of
God. For both Gnosticism and Fundamentalism, mysticism is essential.

BUDDHISM

Lastly, there was the possible influence of Buddhism. Prominent British scholar
Edward Conze points out that the Redeemer of Gnosticism sounds more like the
Buddha than the Jesus of Christianity. He makes a strong case that Christians
of the *Gospel of Thomas* and Buddhists had contact in South India.[38] He argues
the trade routes between the Mediterranean basin and the Far East were opening
up at about the time of dialogue and conflict between Christianity and Gnosticism. He also notes that Buddhist missionaries had already been proselytizing in
Alexandria. No one can state with certainty that there was Buddhist influence on
either Christian thinking or Gnostic mythology, but the possibility is intriguing.

Buddhism maintains a dualistic base. Buddha taught his disciples and followers that the only way they could attain the Good was to disassociate themselves
from the world. Peace could come only with obliteration of materiality. If Conze
is right regarding the trade routes and infiltration of information, it is likely such
doctrines filtered into countries where Christianity was beginning to crystallize.
It is almost certain that Gnostics assimilated these ideas and equally "certain that
Buddhist tales and tales of Jewish origin were absorbed into Gnostic scripture."[39]
The Manichaean Church, basically a copy of Marcion's Church, maintained a
simple structure similar to Buddhists: division between monks and laity.[40]

CONCLUSION

When one carefully assesses the Roman world from which Gnosticism emerged, there can be little doubt that its ingredients came from Jewish apocalypticism, Platonism, Hellenized mystery religions, Zoroastrianism, and possibly a dash of Buddhism. Of Gnosticism's syncretistic origins, Gnostic scholar Hans Jonas omits little in this compressed description: "The Gnostic systems compounded everything—oriental mythologies, astrological doctrines, Iranian theology, elements of Jewish tradition, whether biblical, rabbinical, or occult, Christian salvation and eschatology, Platonic terms and concepts. Syncretism attained in this period its greatest efficacy."[41] Most of these elements were present before the advent of Christianity. But prior to Christianity, was Gnosticism a cohesive religious system? Or, was it still in a fledging stage, a fragmented phenomenon of disparate parts awaiting something to pull it together? Chadwick and others believe the latter: "it is unlikely that they had been blended into a systematic or organized body of doctrine . . . attached to any particular groups of people in space and time, or that a redemptive myth closely resembling Christianity was widely current already."[42]

At some point, did some representations of Gnosticism take a turn? Did they find in Christianity concepts that advanced the development of their own fledgling theology, taking it a step closer to something resembling an organized body of doctrine? Or did Christianity find in Gnosticism elements that advanced it closer to a cohesive body of thought? Many agree with Perkins that "one cannot presume that either Gnosticism or Christianity is a fixed entity that one can compare with the other."[43] Both religions were very fluid in the first century. Both borrowed, not only from each other but also from other diverse religious elements as well.[44] It is almost certain they drew from Judaism. Christianity and Gnosticism had a relationship and, through historical retrospect, it continues. This is not contested. What is contested is the nature and dynamics of that relationship and how much of Gnosticism, if any, has morphed into Fundamentalism.

There are strong similarities between Christianity and Gnosticism. Though their perceptions and descriptions vary, both believe in a transcendent being. For some Gnostics there are multiple deities, some feminine. There are some commonalities between Gnosticism and Christianity: the belief humans have fallen from a pure state; availability of a redeemer or savior; and a concept of salvation and a redemptory process. These two systems evolved about the same time in history, within the same cultural milieu, and almost surely influenced each other. The extent and the nature of that influence and their relationship will be explored in the following chapter.

SUMMARY

Metzger provides a good summary statement: "The systems of Gnostic teachings range from those that embody much genuine philosophical speculation to those that are wild amalgams of mythology, astrology and magical rites drawn from all quarters."[45] Because of this multifaceted diversity, pinpointing a single origin of Gnosticism is impractical, if not impossible. Compounding the problem is its own lack of interest in history or biography and the limited resources available. There does exist, however, considerable scholarly research on the Greco-Roman world in which Gnosticism evolved, and the multiple religions from which it probably borrowed. There is considerable evidence, both culturally and exegetically, that Gnosticism depended heavily upon Apocalyptic Judaism for much of its mythology and religious themes. Gnosticism was also a powerful link between the elaborate philosophical systems of Greek-Hellenistic philosophy (Neo-Platonism and Neo-Pythagorism), Egyptian Hermetic philosophy, and mysticisms of Central Asia (Zoroastrianism)and Syria. There is even evidence of possible contacts with Buddhism. And last, but certainly not least, there is Christianity.

Scholars are mostly in agreement that Christianity and Gnosticism both drew heavily from Judaism. How much they borrowed from each other is less conclusive.

THE INFLUENCES OF GNOSTICISM ON THE DEVELOPMENT AND GROWTH OF EARLY CHRISTIANITY

THE SCENE IS AN EASY ONE TO SET. IT IS THE SECOND CENTURY CE. THERE IS NO New Testament. There are writings called the Hebrew Scriptures, but nothing yet designated "Old Testament." There is no creed. There is nothing known as orthodoxy, no formulated doctrine. Only the faint chrysalis of a diverse, fragmented theology exists. Orthodoxy is just beginning to take shape and is not in full bloom as it would become in the fourth and fifth centuries following the Council of Nicaea in 325. In many locales there are organized congregations and churches. There is an inchoate structure of bishop, priest, and deacon but nothing resembling a universally entrenched ecclesiastical hierarchy that would emerge later. There are several metropolitan centers vying for control—Ephesus, Jerusalem, Alexandria, Rome, Cesarea—but no power center as Rome would eventually become. The teeming multicultured Greco-Roman world described in Chapter 3 is in place, but there are two new players who have yet to acquire names: Gnosticism and Christianity.[1]

Of the two religious phenomena, which came first? Because the two movements were represented in different forms, each diversified with many multiple personalities, some scholars say the question is impossible to answer. Others argue that they began about the same time, independent of the other. As previously noted, several scholars present strong arguments that Gnosticism predated Christianity, and both drew equally from various aspects of Jewish theology and myth and from the same sociocultural pools.[2] Gnostic beliefs in general varied sharply from those of the early proto-orthodox Church. At this point a brief review of those key differences might prove helpful:

- Gnostics were dualists and worshipped two (or more) gods; Christians were monists and worshipped one God.
- Gnostics focused on eradication of ignorance; Christian concern was the eradication of sin.
- Both had a redeemer. The Gnostic redeemer only *appeared* human; the Christian Redeemer *was* human, "the Word made flesh."
- For Gnostics, salvation came through knowledge of self; for Christians salvation was through faith in the risen Christ.
- In Gnosis, the focus was on the individual and individual experience; in Christianity, focus was on the community of believers
- Many Gnostics interpreted the scriptures literally; most Christians used allegorical interpretation.

Despite these sharp differences, Gnosticism and Christianity unquestionably influenced each other. Gnostic scholar Kurt Rudolph helps clarify the issue:

> The process which is plain from the New Testament itself is twofold, the Christianizing of Gnosis and the Gnosticizing of Christianity. The result of both processes is the canonizing of Christianity as an orthodox Church on the one hand, and the elimination of Gnosis as a heresy on the other. Gnosis as we meet it in the New Testament is understood less as an alien pagan religion; rather, it is dealt with so far as it is a phenomenon within Christianity. The Gnostics feel themselves as Christians and present themselves as such in the young Christian communities. Thus the danger is more from inside than outside.[3]

The premise of this book infers that Gnosticism not only influenced the organization, theology, and scriptures of the early Church but also made an indelible mark on Christianity discernible within a number of contemporary denominations. The Gnostic differences with proto-orthodox thinking previously catalogued were factors in this process. But it was the blurring, misunderstanding, and ignorance of those differences among average proto-orthodox Christians that allowed Gnosticism to exert its greatest influence over the young naive Church and make its strongest inroads into the heart of its emerging theology.

GNOSIS AS AN INNER-CHRISTIAN MOVEMENT

Gnostics operated within Christian congregations and considered themselves committed Christians: "You could not have found anyone in Corinth to direct you to a Gnostic Church: the overwhelming possibility is that there was no such thing."[4] Most Gnostics were members of the Early Church and present in the early congregations. They participated in the same rituals (Holy Communion and baptism), sang the same hymns, and often quoted the same scriptures. "The typical Gnostic was a member, often a pillar, of the local and recognized Christian Church."[5]

This incorporation or infiltration by Gnostics into Christian communities was not something that occurred overnight, or even within the first century when Christianity was not known as Christianity but as a reform movement within Judaism. The shift began some time in the mid-second century CE when those who held pre-Christian Gnostic beliefs began accepting Christian concepts into their own system and interpreting "the Christian mystery by means of their elaborate system of heterodox mythology."[6] At this point in Christianity, it may not have been a heresy to have Gnostic thoughts. (The Church's response to Gnosticism is covered in Chapter 5.)

This mythologizing process began in the first century, possibly earlier, and became part of a body of teachings that produced prominent Gnostic teachers in second century Rome and Alexandria.[7] Some of the names—Basilides, Heracleon, Valentinus, Ptolemy, Theodotos—were well-known Christians with strong followings. Early Church fathers knew them well. They were Gnostic Christians who became dangerous heretics only after their tendencies were identified and condemned. (For a biographical summary of some of those key Gnostic Christian leaders, see Appendix D.)

Subtly, at times not so subtly, these teachers would graft Gnostic and Christian concepts in a manner that drew the ire of Church leaders. Recast in their own mystical language of "hidden wisdom," these Gnostic concepts often echoed New Testament language and scripture with claims that the correct interpretation was decipherable only by the elect. Consider, for example, Mark 4:10–12: "When he was alone, the twelve and the others around him asked him about the parables. He told them, 'The secret of the kingdom of God has been given to you. But to those on the outside everything is said in parables so that, they may be ever seeing but never perceiving, and ever hearing but never understanding; otherwise they might turn and be forgiven.'" In this scripture, the parables are presented as serving the function of marking off insider from outsider, a clear Gnostic device.[8] The Gnosticizing of early Christian literature made an impact on the Early Church and it had to be countered.

THE WAR OF WORDS

Writings proliferated, but no accepted corpus of work sanctioned by the Church existed. Available for Christians to read was the Old Testament, usually referred to as "the Scriptures."[9] The first five books (Genesis, Exodus, Leviticus, Deuteronomy, and Numbers) were referred to as *The Torah*. Other divisions were called *The Prophets* and *The Writings*. The latter included the apocalyptic book of Daniel and Wisdom literature. Both would figure prominently in the development of Gnosticism. In addition to the Hebrew writings, there was the Greek Septuagint (LXX), the Hebrew Scriptures translated into Greek and abbreviated LXX. Also available was the Old Testament *Apocrypha*,[10] considered to hold secret doctrines and esoteric wisdom, a fertile field for Gnosticism. A wide array of writings included the "pseudepigrapha" or "false writing," "apocryphal" works, the Dead Sea Scrolls, and a plethora of Greco-Roman literature.

Stepping from BCE to CE and into the "New Testament" world, there were the letters of Paul. The general consensus places their order of composition beginning with Galatians (49 CE), followed by First Thessalonians (50–52), 1 and 2 Corinthians (53–55), Romans (56) Philippians (60–63), Colossians (55) and Philemon (61–62). Ehrman and others suggest that Second Thessalonians was a forgery,[11] a work claiming authorship by one person, yet written by another. Other books regarded as forgeries by some scholars are 2 Peter, 1 and 2 Timothy, and Titus.[12] These books are traditionally associated with Paul but based on internal evidence (a number of anachronisms) may have been composed by someone after Paul's death.

The four Gospels were available. They were probably not written by the apostles whose names appear on them but by other individuals or groups of individuals. These books are not classified as forgeries. Authorship is anonymous. The writers do not claim to be the Apostles; they just chose to remain unknown. Scholars seem more in agreement on their dates of composition. The synoptic gospels[13] came first: Mark, composed around 65–70 CE, followed by Matthew (75–80 CE) and Luke through Acts (90–95 CE). The Gospel of John, which thematically and structurally stands alone, is considered to have been written between 95–115 CE. Sometime between Luke–Acts and the Gospel of John came Ephesians, Hebrews, Revelation, and 1 Peter. The Johannine Epistles are dated roughly 110–115 CE, James 125–150 CE, Jude 125–150 CE, 2 Peter 150 CE, and Timothy/Titus 160–175 CE. Scholars generally agree on these time frames of origin. (For a review of varying opinions on the subject of New Testament dates of composition, see Appendix F.)

The chronological accuracy of textual composition is not as important as the fact that these manuscripts were in circulation. In today's technologically sophisticated world, sermons and religious presentations are instantly beamed electronically into our homes and offices. Are these messages traveling faster, over a larger area, to greater numbers, than did similar messages in the days of Empire? This is a question worth pondering. The infrastructure of that era was more sophisticated than we, in our hi-tech world, might think. The Roman Empire maintained a postal system for imperial use only, but private individuals made their own arrangements. Often mail was carried by family members, friends, slaves, or total strangers traveling to a certain destination. From ancient records, we know soldiers and traveling businessmen transported letters unrelated to their journey.[14]

In his book *Paul and First Century Letter Writing*, E. Randolph Richards provides a picture of ancient letter writing and dispatching.[15] Archaeological archives reveal an intricate and detailed method of postal record keeping, along with distances traveled (a tracking system similar to those used by FedEx and UPS). For example, it was not unusual for a Greek imperial letter carrier to cover one hundred miles a day. Of record is a Roman letter carrier who covered 125 miles to deliver mail dispatched the same day. Private individuals established drop-off points in a city—a shop or residence—for their mail to be picked up.[16] In Ephesus this might be a tanner's leather shop. (Remember, Paul was a tanner and worked his trade and set up shop in the cities he visited.) Letters have been found with the original recipient's address written on the outside of the envelope. Persons with financial resources paid professional letter carriers, an informal system much like our couriers of today.[17]

An empire ruled by law and order and an extensive imperial road system promoted the spread of manuscripts. Paul either carried his own letters or he sent them ahead by a secretary or scribe, possibly Timothy. In 1 Corinthians 1:11, his reference to receiving news from "those of Chloe," may be referring to Chloe's slaves as bearers of the letter. On occasions Paul probably sent his letters from congregation to congregation by members of the respective assemblies.

A prominent Church father, Origen of Alexandria (185–254 CE), through the resources of a wealthy convert, established an efficient book-producing organization consisting of seven shorthand writers, seven copyists, and an expert calligrapher.[18] Their output was voluminous. During the first three centuries, large numbers of letters, manuscripts, books, and all types of literary forms were crisscrossing the Mediterranean world.

Circulation of written materials was no guarantee they were being read. Letters, manuscripts, and books were delivered to an incorrect recipient or lost in transit. Often communication was between two people and the message went no further. Christian and Gnostic manuscripts were read multiple times. For example, Paul chose Timothy to deliver a letter to a congregation in Corinth. Upon arrival a bishop or elder would read the letter.[19] At their next meeting this literate person would read the written word to the congregation. The document would then be copied and forwarded on to another congregation, possibly Ephesus.

Christian documents were not the only genre in circulation. The Gnostics were aggressively doing the same. For every Gospel, Acts, and Apocalypse that proto-orthodox writers produced, the Gnostics produced five or more. Gnostic output was massive: *Gospel of Mary, Gospel of Philip, Gospel of Peter, Gospel of Thomas, Gospel of Nicodemus, Gospel of Truth, Gospel of the Nazarenes, Gospel of the Savior, Gospel of the Good Shepherd.* In addition to those were the *Infancy Gospel of Thomas, Proto-Gospel of James,* and *Secret Gospel of Mark.* Gnostic "Acts" were also available in print: *Acts of John, Acts of Paul, Acts of Pilate, Acts of Thecla, Acts of Thomas.* Other Epistles and related literature included *The Letter of Ptolemy to Flora, The Preaching of Peter,* and *Treatise on the Resurrection.* Apocalypses abounded: *Apocalypse of Paul, Apocalypse of Peter, (Coptic) Apocalypse of Peter, First Thought in Three Forms, Hymn of the Pearl, Origin of the World, Second Treatise of the Great Seth, Secret Book of John, Shepherd of Hermas.*[20]

Although these documents are not now available, we know about them by the barrage launched against them by the heresiologists. These early Church fathers were not firing at phantom targets but at a body of thought they perceived threatened their organization and spiritual existence. Gnosticism was a formidable enemy they felt inspired to expunge from the earth.

Despite this massive production of religious propaganda, there were no recognized formal Christian communities and organizations. The words *Gnostic* and *Gnosticism* did not exist. The word *Christian* barely existed. Christian baptismal initiates recited a creed upon their entry into the Church, a precursor of *The Apostles' Creed* as we know it today, but there was no carefully constructed, formalized creed. There was no doctrine, no cohesive theology. In one of its many manifestations, Gnosticism was an inner-Christian movement. Its elements and voices permeated the early Church communities and blurred the line of demarcation between Gnostics and Christians.

How then was heresy identified? Often it was not. There were times early Christians did not "catch on" and were duped. The nuances of theology seemed only a burning issue with the educated elite, who were far removed from the smaller towns and rural communities of the typical churchgoing parishioner. These latter were concerned about food for the table, physical ailments, family quarrels, birth and death, and day-to-day living, which was why they had flocked to Christianity in the first place. They had been attracted to the simple faith promising eternal life, something better beyond the drudgery where they were stuck. The Gnostic propagandists knew any message offering hope or solace, anything associated with the resurrected Christ, would be appealing.

An example of the ready acceptance of these Gnostic writings is told by fourth-century historian Eusebius. He writes of Serapion, a proto-orthodox bishop of Antioch and his experience with a questionable writing. While visiting Rhossus, a small town within his jurisdiction, Serapion learned of a gospel from which the people were drawing inspiration and guidance. This popular document was the Gospel of Peter. According to some scholars, it was as popular as the Gospel of Mark.[21] After all, if it had Peter's name on it, it must be authentic. When the book was read by the bishop, he quickly noted the strong docetic heretical leanings denying the reality of Christ's crucifixion and death. He promptly responded with his own pamphlet, "The So-Called Gospel of Peter." Though much of the gospel was theologically sound, its "additions" could be used to support a docetic view. That was anathema. The book, concluded to be a fake that could not have been written by Peter, was declared nonapostolic and promptly banned.[22]

The *Gospel of Peter* was discovered in the nineteenth century, but whether it was the same gospel related to the previous story is unknown. This is one example of the subtle manner in which prolific Gnostic literature infiltrated the loosely defined and porous early Christian community. Had it not been for passages reflecting a Gnostic bent, or susceptible to Gnostic interpretation, *The Gospel of Peter*, and other similar writings, might have made it into the New Testament canon. Ehrman has appropriately called these "Lost Christianities," not because they were not canonized[23] but because the theology disappeared with the orthodox destruction of their writings.

Forgeries were not uncommon in that era. Many early Gnostic intellectuals considered themselves to be Christians with good intentions and knowingly hatched forgeries. Christian writers did the same. Books were often given a false name with the intent to mislead. There was no legal structure to protect one's copyright. Early Church fathers had to be guarded and vigilant. Based on today's diagnostic criteria, a few might have qualified as paranoid.[24]

Prolific Gnostic output contributed to the emergence of the New Testament. The seminal case is the voice of Marcion. The very existence of Gnostic writings, whether forgeries or authentic, strongly influenced the creation of the New Testament as a canon of Christian theological writings. These false beliefs had to be countered; they could not go unchecked. A Christian hierarchy was emerging; centers of power began developing. There was more at stake than defending the faith. Bishops and priests were guarding home base. This was a turf war, one fought with the power of pens.

By causing negative reactions from proto-orthodox theologians to anything resembling heresy, Gnostic ideas and writings indirectly influenced Christian texts and doctrine.[25] Reaction was often in response to concerns over interpretation. Editing was required to cleanse some words and passages of any potential heretical interpretation. Christians were also concerned that Gnostics had hijacked their redeemer. Jesus was an attractive and powerful figure. By using their redeemer, Gnostics were beating Christians at their own game. The Church's reaction was a spontaneous and sporadic outpouring of manuscripts. There was no central office, no war room of operatives orchestrating production. A Gnostic would write a pamphlet and a Christian would respond. A Gnostic gospel might appear in Alexandria, make its way across the Mediterranean to Rome and there be countered by a Christian writer. Or the reverse would occur.

At some point, this percolation of wild and uncontrolled ideology became more controlled. During these early centuries of literary output, certain Christian documents came to be accepted as having equal authority as the Old Testament. Various churches collected these documents. "At first a local church would have only a few apostolic letters and perhaps one or two Gospels. During the course of the second century, most churches came to possess and acknowledge a canon that included the first four Gospels, the Acts, thirteen letters attributed to Paul, 1 Peter, and 1 John."[26]

Into the third century CE there was bickering among churches about the authenticity of various documents. It was during this time that Gnosticism posed its greatest threat to proto-orthodox Christian beliefs. About this time Gnostic heretical sects emerged with their own collection of "sacred" books and forced the Church to limit its own canon and bring it to a close.[27] Toward this urgent goal, the Church was aided by a very significant event.

In 312 CE Constantine became Emperor. Though he worshipped a pagan sun god, he attributed the military victory that made him emperor to Jesus Christ and combined the two religious expressions. The result was a cessation of persecution of Christians and the legitimization of Christianity throughout the empire. This placed the bishops, who were the Church power brokers, in a stronger position to eradicate their opponents. Backed by local and regional authorities, suppression of the Gnostics began. In 367 CE Athanasius sent his famous 39th Festal Letter strongly endorsing twenty-seven books of the New Testament and monks in the Egyptian desert hid their Gnostic texts. Athanasius's letter was more than an endorsement. It was a declaration that the twenty-seven books be declared sacrosanct. In 393 CE, just twenty-six years later, a synod at Hippo Regius accepted Athanasius's list as canon and followed by two other synods, both at Carthage, in 397 and 419 CE.

When the literary dust of this ideological warfare settled, Christianity reigned victorious. But did it? How complete was its victory? The Gnostics may have been on the run and nearly extinct. But was their departure complete? What did they leave behind?

GNOSTIC INFLUENCE ON THE SYNOPTIC GOSPELS

Of the Synoptic Gospels, [28] Mark is generally considered to have been written first (65–70 CE), followed by Matthew (75–80 CE), then Luke (90–95 CE). These dates of composition and chronological order are generally accepted by scholars. (See Appendix F, "Composition Chronology of New Testament Books.") There are several theories regarding the sources of the synoptic gospels but one, highly regarded, is worthy of attention. The "Two Document" hypothesis places a priority on Mark. Patzia[29] presents a simple diagram illustrating that 90 percent of Mark is found in Matthew and 57 percent of Mark is found in Luke. What then is the source of the material common to Matthew and Luke? German scholars were of the opinion that there was a missing literary source. They named this hypothesized collection of logia "Q" for the German word for "source" ("Quelle").[30]

By cross-textual analysis and comparison, scholars have been able to isolate those passages common to "Q." Gnostics could relate to many of the sayings in Matthew and Luke that came from Q, this earlier source. For example, sayings with references to secret teachings and knowledge to be revealed, such as Luke 12:2: "There is nothing concealed that will not be disclosed, or hidden that will not be made known." A theme intrinsic to Gnostic interpretation is "secret" knowledge that can be learned. Similar parallels to the sayings found in the *Gospel of Thomas*, considered a Gnostic document, are found in the Synoptic Gospels.[31] The question and answer format of Q, a technique utilized by Gnostics, can be found in *The Sophia of Jesus Christ* in the *Nag Hammadi Library*.[32]

Parts of the Gospel of Mark are considered to be derived from Q and some of these bear Gnostic influence. In Mark, Jesus is often portrayed as making reference to secret teachings and secrets. An example is Mark. 4:11–12: "The secret of the kingdom of God has been given to you. But to those on the outside everything is said in parables. They may be ever seeing but not perceiving, and ever hearing but not understanding." In Mark, Jesus's messiahship is alluded to tangentially but Jesus never states overtly that He is *the* Messiah. To assert that some teachings should be kept secret and deliberately obscured could be interpreted as having a Gnostic origin.

GNOSTIC INFLUENCE IN THE GOSPEL OF JOHN AND THE JOHANNINE LETTERS

In its writing style and, in places, its dream-like quality, the Gospel of John presents the clearest similarity to Gnostic thought. It represents a daring departure from the synoptic tradition and reflects, more than any other New Testament book, the influence of Gnosticism and Gnostic mythologizing.

Though they are in comparative agreement that more than one person had a hand in its composition, scholars are not in agreement on the source of John.[33] It is unlike Matthew, Mark, and Luke, which had common sources and harmonize in a number of passages, at times verbatim. Many of the Synoptic stories do not appear in John. The majority of John's stories that take place outside of the lengthy Passion narrative are not in the Synoptics.[34]

The Gospel opens with a prologue in which Jesus is identified with the Word, or *Logos*, echoing usages of the Hebrew "Word of God," which was contemporary with Jewish Wisdom speculation and contemporary Hellenistic philosophy. In a decidedly Gnostic tone, it also describes a figure who will mediate between God and the cosmos.

The dualism of darkness and light, flesh and spirit, were pronounced Gnostic themes and pervade this gospel. The motif is introduced immediately in the Prologue: "In him was life and that life was the light of men. The light shines in the darkness but the darkness has not understood" (1:4). This passage could be cut from its context, pasted onto a Gnostic page, and a Gnostic reader would not miss a beat. Nor does the writer let the light extinguish; it surfaces over and over: "Light has come into the world, but men loved darkness instead of light . . . everyone who does evil hates the light . . . whoever lives by the truth comes into the light" (John 3:19–21). In John 8:12 Jesus says. "I am the light of the world. Whoever follows me will never walk in darkness, but will have the light of life." Later, prior to his crucifixion, Jesus states: "You are going to have the light just a little longer. Walk while you have the light, before darkness overtakes you. The man who walks in the dark does not know where he is going. Put your trust in the light while you have it, so that you may become sons of light" (John 12:35–36). There are other passages. As with many Gnostic works, the Gospel of John radiates with light. Could the writer(s) be using Gnostic terminology in order to oppose Gnosticism?

Christian Gnostics believed in a descending revealer and John's Gospel revolves around one. Gnostics believed the material world was evil and that salvation came only through the acquisition of knowledge (*gnosis*), which was the pathway to freedom. Christ became the divine being who came to the evil earth to teach and in his teaching reveal the secret knowledge necessary for salvation.

Unlike the more balanced Christ of the Synoptic Gospels, John's Christ tilts significantly toward the divine. The author (or authors)[35] captures the incarnation theme early in the Prologue: "The word became flesh" (John 1:14). After that, however, we hear little else of an earthly Christ. There are a number of stories in the Gospel of John portraying Jesus as human. But basically, from the Prologue on, John's Redeemer is a heavenly, Godlike figure. Only in this Gospel does Jesus speak of himself, and equates himself with the Godhead: "you do not know him but I know him because I am from him and he sent me" (John 7:28–29); "I and the father are one" (John 10:30); "If you really knew me you would know my father as well" (John 14:6); "Anyone who has seen me has seen the Father" (John 14:9); "I am in the Father and the Father is in me" (John 14:11).

Ehrman notes the similarities in their Christologies of the Gnostic Redeemer and the Redeemer of the Fourth Gospel. Though John does portray Jesus in places as human and as chosen by God to be the Messiah, He is God Himself and His ultimate goal is to share the liberating knowledge necessary for salvation: "You will know the truth and the truth will set you free" (John 8:32).[36] In addition to the dualism of light and dark, spirit versus flesh appears in the Gospel of John: "I tell you the truth, no one can enter the kingdom of God unless he is born of water and the Spirit. Flesh gives birth to the flesh, but the Spirit gives birth to the spirit" (John 3:5–6); "The Spirit gives life, the flesh counts for nothing. The words I have spoken to you are spirit, and they are life" (John 6:63).

For a Gnostic, the goal of salvation is perfect knowledge. Similarly, the fourth Gospel insists that Jesus, who is the way and the truth, reveals the Father. In the fourth Gospel only does Jesus say, "I am the way and the truth and the life" (John 14:6); and, "For this I came into the world to testify to the truth. Everyone on the side of truth listens to me" (John 8:37). The first passage (John 14:6) might stand on its own without Gnostic association. But what follows is unequivocally Gnostic: "No one comes to the Father except through me. If you really knew me, you would know my father as well" (John 14: 6–7). One Johannine quote seems blatantly Gnostic: "You will know the truth and the truth will set you free" (John 8:32). The passage immediately before sets it more in a Gnostic context: "If you hold to my teaching, you are really my disciples" (John 8:31). Key themes permeating the Gospel of John are truth, knowledge, and Jesus the Redeemer as embodiment of truth and knowledge. There are even moments when knowledge seems synonymous with faith.

As *The Da Vinci Code* reminds us (and on this issue was accurate) Gnostics were fond of puzzles, and in this gospel Jesus presents a series of "riddles:" The "I am" sayings, being reborn from above, living water, eat my flesh and blood. Even the disciples, until after the resurrection, are left with riddles.

As with most Gnostic documents, in John, there is a lack of ethical exhortation. Perkins points out that the gospel, "contains none of the ethical teachings except 'love one another' . . . [and] even that appears only at the last supper . . . clearly directed inward toward those in the cultic community."[37]

In summary, Gnostics of the second century would find John's Jesus acceptable. Its emphasis on revealed mysteries caused some Christian Gnostics to revere the gospel as a sacred text. Indeed, one of the first commentaries written on the Gospel of John was by one Heracleon, a Gnostic of the second century.[38] The Fourth Gospel was so convincing to one group of Christian Gnostics that they took it with them when they broke from a Johannine community.

Most scholars believe that the three Letters of John originated from the same community that produced the Gospel of the same name and were written by an individual concerned about a group of Christians who had broken away from his Church.[39] The views held by this breakaway group were probably Gnostic, since they believed Jesus was not human, but divine.

Similarities exist between these letters and the Gospel of John. Some contain Gnostic images and symbols. Light and darkness are one example (1 John 1:5–7 and 2:9–11). In writing about a Christian Gnostic group that had broken away from a Johannine community, one would think the writer would avoid any images suggesting Gnostic sympathies that might undercut his message. The author of 1 John, however, comes close to a Gnostic position when he admits that those who are "born of God" cannot sin, because God's "seed" remains in them (3:9).[40]

As previously indicated, some scholars are convincing in their arguments that Paul was not relying on Gnostic elements but almost entirely upon Jewish Apocalyptic sources. There are others, however, who contend that Paul was influenced by Gnostic concepts. Rudolph speaks for many scholars when he states: "Through him (Paul) Christianity became a religion of salvation in late antiquity, and Gnosis played its part in it."[41] He goes on to outline the following Gnostic concepts prevalent in Paul's letters:

- There is an attitude of world rejection.
- Dualism is the antithesis of the flesh and spirit; those who belong to the Spirit no longer belong to the flesh.
- Dualism is darkness and light.
- The world is a fallen creature dominated by Satan and demonic powers.
- Marriage is discouraged.
- Sin is the result of Adam's fall, which also brought death into the world.
- Redemption occurs only through Christ, the Redeemer.
- Faith is accompanied by knowledge of the truths of salvation.
- Some passages suggest Christ's resurrection is a mystery.[42]

Perkins agrees. She cites 1 Corinthians' uniqueness among Paul's letters in its preoccupation with cultic behavior and notes: "Paul's perception of the flesh as the entry point for the sinful desires that ultimately bring death to humans unless they receive the Spirit of Christ comes very close to what one finds in Gnostic mythologizing."[43] Another element of Gnostic origin relates to the "other law" of sin found in one's members (Romans 7:14–25), which is similar to a two-spirit tradition found in *The Apocryphon of John*, a notable Gnostic work discovered among the Nag Hammadi texts and thus dated around the mid-fourth century.

Marcion, the chief architect of Gnosticism, hijacked Paul's theology and compiled his own canon around his letters. Some of his themes also surface in the Synoptic Gospels. Elaine Pagels suggests that Paul *was* a Gnostic who developed his early congregations as a mystery religion couched in Jewish elements. His writings, she contends, were misunderstood when the Church abandoned its Jewish foundations and began employing more literal interpretations of texts.[44] From a theological perspective parts of her theory are plausible. But the overwhelming issue for Paul is salvation by faith, not knowledge, a faith rooted in Jesus Christ who was flesh and blood. In his Christology (a teaching or understanding regarding the nature of Christ), Paul tends to fall more into the adoptionist school, not that of the preexistent Logos. There is no virgin birth in Paul. There are few references to Jesus's birth and all indicate an earthly, not heavenly, origin. This would be enough to argue against a Gnostic leaning.

SUMMARY

Though theories abound that Gnosticism had little to do with the origin and development of Christianity, the evidence suggests otherwise. There are indications that Gnosticism predated the emergence of Christianity; both influenced each other and both probably drew from Jewish apocalyptic traditions. Gnosticism's influence on Christian theology can be seen in the particular themes of salvation, mystical dualism, concepts of humanity, divine realm or heaven, eschatology, and the divine Redeemer. There are significant differences in these, but there are points of convergence that will be discussed when we explore the relationship between Gnosticism and Fundamentalism.

Gnostic influences appear occasionally in the Synoptic Gospels. The Gospel of John and the letters of Paul reflect a number of Gnostic themes. It is a fact that Gnosticism made an impact on the early Church and its adherents. Their manner of response to it set the course for Christianity for the next two millennia.

CHAPTER 5

THE RESPONSE OF THE EARLY CHURCH TO GNOSTICISM

READ AND REFLECT ON THE PASSAGES 1 THROUGH 10. Can you distinguish between the orthodox Christian and the Gnostic Christian sources?

1. "Do not make the kingdom of heaven a desert within you. Do not be proud because of the light that illumines, but be to yourselves as I myself am to you. For your sakes I have placed myself under the curse, that you may be saved."
2. "The kingdom of God does not come with your careful observation, nor will people say, 'Here it is,' or 'There it is,' because the kingdom of God is within you."
3. "When a blind man and one who sees are both together in darkness, they are no different from one another. When the light comes, then he who sees will see the light, and he who is blind will remain in darkness."
4. "He himself was not the light, he came only as a witness to the light. The true light that gives light to every man was coming into the world."
5. "For when they had seen him and had heard him, he granted them . . . to touch the beloved Son. When he had appeared Instructing them about the Father . . . when he breathed into them what is in the mind, doing his will, when many had received the light, they turned to him."
6. "I am the light of the world. Whoever follows me will never walk in darkness, but will have the light of life."
7. "I am the light which exists in the light, I am the remembrance of the Providence—that I might enter the middle of darkness and the inside of Hades."
8. "The knowledge of the secrets of the kingdom of heaven have been given to you, but not to them."
9. "The kingdom of the Father is spread out upon the earth, and men do not see it."

10. "If you hold to my teachings, you are really my disciples. Then you shall know the truth and the truth shall set you free."

The odd number passages are from the following Gnostic works in the Nag Hammadi collection, respectively: *The Aprocryphon of James, The Gospel of Philip, The Gospel of Truth, The Apocryphon of John,* and *The Gospel of Thomas.* The even number passages are from the following New Testament Gospels, respectively: Luke 17:21; John 1:8–9; John 8:12; Matthew 13:11; John 8:31. These are a few samples of the voluminous Christian and Gnostic Christian scriptures circulating in the early centuries.

What did Tertullian, Origin, Justin Martyr, Clement, and Hippolytus, intelligent and educated Church fathers, find offensive about Gnostic passages written by intelligent and educated men—Marcion, Basilides, Valentinus, Saturninus? What was so threatening about these writings that a band of monks, probably hastily and under cover of night, buried them in the Egyptian desert, far from the long arm of the Orthodox Church? Many of these Gnostics' ideas resembled a young developing Christian theology. They caused a furious barrage of Christian publications and decrees that, within a relatively short time, virtually expunged them from the Western civilized world. Henry Chadwick makes the following observation: "The conquest of Gnosticism may be counted the hardest and most decisive battle in church history."[1]

As noted in Chapter 4, although there were ideological and theological differences between the two groups, their similarities created some confusion and made it difficult for Christians to "spot" Gnostics. In their overall makeup, Gnostics were as diverse as Christians. Even on important issues, Gnostics could not agree. According to Irenaeus, they were frauds who produced "something new everyday . . . enormous fictions,"[2] which made it "a difficult matter to describe all their opinions."[3] Later, in that same work, possibly alluding to Acts 20:29, Irenaeus stated, "such persons are to outward appearance sheep . . . but inwardly they are wolves."[4] Diverse as they were, Christian leaders saw them filtering into the Church as a monolithic threat.[5]

Many Christians were theologically naïve. They did not understand that Gnostics could worship, sing, and recite the same scriptures with them while simultaneously their "knowing" minds were moving at a deeper symbolic level. Other Christians were not as naïve. They detected the nuances and fine distinctions. These Church fathers would educate their flock.

REACTION TO GNOSTIC HERESIES

As we have noted, the process of New Testament canonization was spurred along by the emergence of heretical sects with their own sacred books. Pressure was on the Church to set limits to its own growing voluminous literary corpus. Metzger expands on the problem: "The full extent of the Gnostic threat to the church was not fully grasped until recently because our documentary evidence came from refutations by orthodox authors, who destroyed all the Gnostic writings they could get their hands on after Christianity came to 'dominate the Empire in the fourth century.' Our knowledge of Gnosticism has grown rapidly since the discovery at Nag Hammadi."[6]

Part of this prodigious output included a massive eruption of ideas, polemics, apologia, attacks, and defenses. One of the reasons for the outbreak was a clearer understanding of the Gnostic message on the part of the proto-orthodox Church fathers. Gnostic dualism's multiple gods was troublesome to them. One Gnostic sect had 365 gods, one for every day of the year. Gnostics were also saying that the Christian God was not the God who created the universe. The Christian God was a lesser god called the Demiurge. For Christians, this proclamation was unacceptable heresy; only one God created the world. And this Gnostic god was unknowable and approached only through secret knowledge. The Gnostics were taking a simple God and a simple theology and clouding it up with divine and malformed aeons and other beings.

According to Gnostic belief, light came from the heaven within rather than heaven above. It is the spark of divinity that needs to be awakened within each person to create enlightenment. This theory broke the first commandment. For Christians, God was "wholly other," apart. He did not reside within humans. Humankind was "a little lower than the heavenly beings" (Psalms 8:5). When Jesus said the "kingdom is within you" (Luke 17:21), he was not referring to some preexisting spark of God but to the spiritual presence of God that comes within the person, though the source is from without. Gnostics said everyone has part of the unknown god within them, a "divine spark." That spark of God existed with God before time began. There was no time it did not exist. This meant everyone had part of God within them. Some were actualized through "insight" or "self-knowledge," which came from their own little god within.

Then there was *gnosis*. The Gnostics were saying a person could be saved through knowledge, not from sin but from ignorance. This *gnosis* involved understanding the true teachings of Jesus. This knowledge, however, was hidden, secret, and known only by the elect, or *pneumatics*, or spiritual ones. This was not Christianity. Christianity was an egalitarian and democratic faith, open and available to all. At least, it began that way. The Church fathers took their cues from Paul, in what was probably his first letter to them: "You are all sons of God through faith in Jesus Christ. . . . There is neither Jew nor Greek, slave nor free, male nor female, for you are all one in Christ Jesus" (Galatians 3:26–28). The knowledge of salvation was available to all, regardless of status, intelligence, gifts, and so on.

Gnostics were saved by a divine redeemer, which sounded in-line with Christian beliefs. But in a further departure from proto-orthodoxy, this divine redeemer was *all* divine, with no human qualities. This God only "appeared" to be human. If God did not become human, he had no saving power. The implications for resurrection are obvious. If God did not die, there could be no miracle of resurrection.

The nature of the Redeemer was the keystone of proto-orthodox theology: "The Word (Logos) became flesh" (John 1:14). It not only became flesh, but also "made his dwelling among us." This was a new and radical theology, something entirely different from anything the world had seen or heard. It differed from Judaism, from Greek Neo-Platonism, and from Neo-Pythagorism. There was nothing like it in the mystery religions, in Persian Zoroastrianism, or in Egyptian fertility cults.[7] All had redeemers, in many cases redeemers resurrected from the dead. But none had a redeemer who "became flesh" and made his home, "tented," among them. This was the crux of Christianity, and the accumulative effect Gnostic literary output had on its leaders was a multiple broadcasting of ideas to congregations all over the Roman–Christian world. Little wonder their response amounted to an all-out attack.

If these Gnostic ideas caught on, the consequences for the infant Church and its leaders would be severe. If you were a believer who thought personal salvation depended upon a risen savior (resurrected from the dead) then the very idea of a Christ only in spirit would be a totally unacceptable belief. It did not take long for the proto-orthodox fathers to assess the impact these concepts would have on Christianity. It threatened not only their theology but also their institutional and political existence.

Two significant effects of Gnosticism on Christianity were the way in which it forced lines of authority within the early Church and how those lines of authority were linked to apostolic succession and the resurrection of Christ and "proved critical in shaping the Christian movement into an institutional religion."[8]

The Gnostic belief in two or more gods influenced organizational concepts. Instead of one leader, Gnostic congregations were democratic with multiple leaders. For the young Christian Church in its early development, this was unacceptable to those in ascendant positions of power, namely, the bishops. There was one God; there was one authority, thus one bishop. Early on, the importance of the resurrection became apparent.

THE RESURRECTION AND REACTION TO GNOSTIC DEMOCRACY

For what I received I passed on to you as of first importance; that Christ died for our sins according to the scripture, that he was buried, that he was raised on the third day according to the Scriptures, and that he appeared to Peter, and then to the twelve.

—1 Corinthians 15:3–5

In this brief passage from one of Paul's letters to the Church at Corinth, penned around 53–55 CE, the apostle encapsulates his early theological position and engages the battle of beliefs with the Gnostics. He further states that the risen Christ appeared simultaneously to more than five hundred "of the brothers, most of whom are still living . . . then he appeared to James, then to all the apostles and last of all he appeared to me also" (1 Corinthians 15: 6–8). But he is not finished. What follows is a lengthy discourse on the resurrection of Jesus and the nature of the resurrected body.

There are several significant aspects about this passage. First of all, it is important that Paul establish the historicity of Jesus, that he was a real person existing in time, and that he actually died and was buried. Similar phraseology appears in the Apostles' Creed, and for the same reason, that is, to combat Gnosticism.

Second, Paul is moving his reader toward a hard issue of faith: "And if Christ has not been raised, our preaching is useless and so is your faith" (1 Corinthians 15:14). In 2 Corinthians he offers a description of the resurrected body and how it will change into a spiritual body (5:1–5). This resurrection theme is also sounded in Acts on the Mount of Areopagus in Athens (17:31–32).

Third, the context of this segment in Corinthians is the key to its interpretation. As biblical scholars remind us, context is first and foremost the first principle of textual interpretation. In this case, context helps explain why Paul positioned this passage on resurrection immediately following a discussion about worship and collection of money for the poor; "but everything should be done in a fitting and orderly way" (1 Corinthians 14:40).

Paul's authority may have been the key issue here. Those who had authority in the Church were those who had seen the risen Lord. An apostle was one who had witnessed the presence of the risen Christ. Not only was the proclamation of Jesus's physical resurrection from the dead the Church's clarion call and criterion of faith,[9] but it also became a litmus test for authority.

There are those, including myself, who hold the position that faith in the resurrection was the primary force that shaped the early Church. The Church came into existence because of faith in the risen Christ, not political machinations. This belief, not the politics, was the moving motivating force. Others hold different views. From a practical, political science perspective, the passage from Corinthians previously referenced may be the most important in the New Testament. Pagels presents a study of this concept and its linkage to authority in the early Church:

> Why did orthodox Christians in the second century insist on a literal view of resurrection and reject all others as heretical? I suggest that we cannot answer this question adequately as long as we consider the doctrine only in terms of its religious content. But when we examine its practical effect on the Christian movement, we can see, paradoxically, that the doctrine of bodily resurrection also serves as an essential political function: it legitimizes the authority of certain men who claim to exercise exclusive leadership over the churches as the successors of the apostle, Peter.[10]

She goes on to describe how this doctrine served to legalize the apostolic succession of bishops, which is the core of papal authority: "The controversy over resurrection then, proved critical in shaping the Christian movement into an institutional religion."[11]

Due to its need to maintain the belief in Christ the God–man and the Incarnation, Orthodoxy insisted on a literal interpretation of resurrection. However, there may have been other reasons, political expediency among them. To assert otherwise might undercut the authority of the early apostles, particularly Peter. Even though the gospels of Mark and John record Mary Magdalene as the first to whom the resurrected Lord appeared, another tradition maintains that it was James, the brother of Jesus. Peter has been upheld by tradition as being the first to witness the resurrected Lord.[12]

Early Church fathers such as Irenaeus and Tertullian understood the importance of this interpretation of the resurrection and the effect it would have on Gnostic beliefs. The Gnostics, with their mystical conception of communication with the deity, needed no authoritative channel of progression in order to worship. "God talk" with them was individual, subjective, and immediate, not intermediate as the Church preferred with its ecclesiastical hierarchy of intermediaries. The Gnostics had direct access to their deity (or deities), direct contact with the Holy Spirit. After all, the Holy Spirit dwelt within them. It was a part of them and had been since time began. Why should they not have direct contact?

The Gnostics were loosely organized and radically democratized. In worship services they drew lots to determine ritual and clerical roles, that is, who would preach, read, pray, serve, and take up collection. It was Paul's "priesthood of believers" taken to its ultimate conclusion, which may be another reason Marcion probably liked the Apostle. Within this loose structure were the "pneumatics," the elite "spiritual ones." With a divine spark and spiritual knowledge, they could understand revelations from God. Gnosticism offered "nothing less than a theological justification for refusing to obey bishops and priests."[13] These types were problematic for the Church. Throughout the Church's checkered history that followed, these same charismatics would spawn uprisings and reformations.

The Church fathers were aware of the presence of these "pneumatics." They were concerned about their theology. They saw the implications regarding ecclesiastical authority. A physical resurrection would check this type of freewheeling spiritualism. It validated a "chain of command" through which church members must move to have access to God.

At the peak of the proto-orthodox–Gnostic conflict, in the second century CE, the Church had a three-tiered hierarchy: bishops, priests, deacons. In some local congregations a single bishop was in charge; in others, a body of elders. The power structure, though incomplete, was beginning to fall into place. During this time Ignatius of Antioch writes about monarchical bishops at Antioch and in other churches of central Asia.[14] This was the beginning of stationary clergy subordinate to apostolic succession.

Clement of Rome, generally accepted as the third bishop of Rome,[15] introduced the term layman (*laikos*)[16] and established lines of authority. He wrote a letter to the young Church in Corinth where there had been an upheaval over leadership. The letter is available and, based upon internal evidence, dated 94 CE.[17] In the letter he established precedence for two distinct orders of ministry: bishop (also called presbyter) and deacon. Anyone who was in disagreement on this line of authority he branded a heretic. Other bishops joined in. This hierarchical arrangement mirrored the hierarchy of heaven. Ignatius took the pronouncement a step further: "Without these, there is nothing which can be called a church."[18]

In summation to this point, Gnostic dualism forced lines of authority within the early Church. Those lines of authority became linked to the development of apostolic succession and the resurrection of Christ. Gnostic dualism posited two or more gods, which meant split authority to the early Church fathers. If God was not One, there was not one head of the Church or congregation, there were many. Monism, the resurrection, and apostleship were not the only means of securing and validating authority in the early Church.

During this early period of time, the Eucharist (Holy Communion) and baptism were beginning to anchor the ritualistic life of the Church. Some viable and plausible theories assert that the Church's hierarchy evolved from leadership functions in the Eucharist liturgy. Chadwick proposes that the two-tiered ministry of bishop and deacon was centrally related to the Eucharistic celebration.[19] A ladder of recognized authority was quickly becoming a more implacable chain of command. The Church was organizing along lines of authority based upon apostolic succession, which were based upon the risen Christ and those who had been in his presence or had seen him.

Theological concepts translated into organizational concepts: proto-orthodox vertical authority versus a Gnostic linear view of authority. In the latter, authority spread throughout the congregation. The Gnostics evaluated each person by a highly subjective process based upon one's "spiritual maturity, insight or personal holiness . . . level of understanding of its members and quality of their relationship with one another."[20] Theodotus "taught that only those who received direct spiritual inspiration belonged to the 'spiritual church.'"[21]

The early Church proto-orthodox fathers viewed this as spiritual anarchy. In the late second century, Irenaeus successfully argued for strict lines of apostolic succession along with universal requirements for Church membership: confession of the creed, acceptance of the ritual of baptism, participation in worship, and obedience to the clergy.[22]

Recall the opening epigram: "The heresy of one age becomes the orthodoxy of the next." Was one heresy generating another? Did elitism breed elitism? In laying down sharper outside–inside lines than the Gnostics, was the Church reacting to an enemy within its own congregational walls to the point of overcompensation? Did the presence of the Gnostics within spawn a theology of salvation that discriminated?

During the post–Jesus apocalyptic era, Christians were in a different situation. The end was imminent. There were no lines of authority or conduits of salvation. The Church was more open. If you believed in the resurrected Christ, your sins would be forgiven and you would be saved. There was no doctrine; no ironclad creed, no entrenched sacramental liturgy. But the end did not occur. It was delayed. In that interim, doctrine began to take shape. Loose structure began to form and a ladder of hierarchy began to develop.

The Christian Gnostics within the Church established a reputation for openness and democracy. In opposition to this loose structure, the Church began to close ranks, tighten the rules, and draw clear lines of authority. In this response to Gnosticism some scholars believe the Church allowed an organizational development at odds with its own principles of inner faith and theology. Regardless, it is apparent that the hierarchy of the Church was shaped by opposition to Gnostic polity.

CAMPAIGN AGAINST HERESY

THE WRITINGS OF PAUL

The first references to Gnostic intrusions into Christian congregations and communities occur in the letters of Paul. Paul was aware of the dangers of Gnosticism and its existence among his constituents. Rudolph Bultmann and others are convinced Paul was referring to Gnostics in Acts when he warns, "I know that after I leave, savage wolves will come in among you and will not spare the flock" (Acts 20:29). Bultmann also considers a similar reference in 2 Corinthians: "for such men are false apostles, deceitful workmen, masquerading as apostles of light" (11:13).[23] Gnostics are the targets of Paul's polemics in the Corinthian letters, as well as in Galatians, Philippians, 1 and 2 Thessalonians, and Romans. Paul is warning against elitism (cf. Gal. 2:6; Gal. 3:28; Phil. 2:3).

Paul's authentic letters, the ones most scholars agree were authored by him, contain repeated expressions challenging false doctrines. This included Gnostic doctrines. It is apparent in his letters to the young Church (or churches) at Corinth that he was referring to Gnostic doctrine. Based upon an analysis of his writings, he probably founded a church there around 41 CE. His letters were composed around 53–55 CE.[24]

As early as 1 Corinthians, Paul is aware of "pneumatics" and Gnostic influence in that Church (1 Corinthians 8:1–3, 12:3). He is also aware of the difference between "pneumatics" and "psychics," which is that the latter are new creations, participants in the coming glory and free of the law (1 Corinthians 2:10–3:18). In Philippians 3:8–10, Paul states that faith is associated with knowledge. This knowledge is about salvation and that salvation is always for our sins, not to combat ignorance. Christians who receive the Spirit gain freedom and power that are linked to obedience and love.[25]

THE PSEUDO-PAULINE EPISTLES

There are numerous references in the Pseudo-Pauline letters of Ephesians, Colossians, 1 and 2 Timothy, and Titus. A major concern in these letters is the Christianizing of Gnostic ideas. At Ephesus, Gnostic images have made their way into Church doctrine (Ephesians 5:25–32, 1:10; 2:14–18; 4:8–11).

Paul's authorship of Colossians is questionable, but it does possess the tone and content of Pauline writings. Colossus is considered to have been founded by

Epaprhas, a Colossian Paul had converted at Ephesus.[26] He was aware of false teachings at Colossae, another testament to the flow of communication in that era. Metzger describes the Colossian Heresy as "a syncretistic movement, combining Jewish ritualistic observances (2:16) with features drawn from pagan mythology and philosophy (2:8, 18). The Christian religion was in danger of being transformed into a theosophical or Gnostic speculation concerning 'the elemental spirits of the universe' (2:8, 20)."[27] To combat the compromise of Christ's supremacy as Mediator and Redeemer (2:18), Paul emphasizes the uniqueness of Christ as the authentic fullness of God and his victory over death, sin, and all other opposing forces (implying Gnostics). In 2 Timothy 2:16 the pursuit of *gnosis* is depicted as hopeless. "The heretics . . . are deceivers, liars and avaricious men" (2 Timothy 4:20) whom Paul has already admonished (1 Timothy 4:1; 2 Timothy 4:3) and expelled from the community.[28] With only a basic of knowledge of Gnosticism, one can read these letters and see that the Christian attack on Gnosticism is certainly there within those pages.

THE JOHANNINE EPISTLES

In the opinion of Rudolph, the Johannine Epistles represent an unmistakable attack against Gnostic tendencies within the Church: "for in them such a polemic can be clearly recognized, and in them ecclesiastical interests become more prominent (unless this is caused by a later redaction)."[29]

One aspect of Gnosticism that caused Christian leaders great concern was the belief that Jesus was not human and suffered no pain; he only *appeared* to be crucified. An early challenge to this is found in 1 John: "They went out from us but they did not really belong to us" (1 John 2:19). "They" refers to a group of Christian Gnostics who broke away from a congregation over this issue. In this letter, Christians are warned against heretical teachings by those claiming to have special insight and denying "that Jesus is the Christ" (1 John 2:22) and not acknowledging that "Jesus Christ has come in the flesh" (1 John 4:2). The letter of 2 John warning against hospitality to false teachers is believed by scholars to mean the adherents of Gnosticism. There is a similar admonition by the writer of Paul's Letter to the Colossians.[30] Also striking about the Johannine letters are their admissions that Gnostics considered themselves Christian and belonged to Christian congregations. In spite of the influence of Gnosticism on John, the Epistles are clearly opposed to Gnosticism.

THE APOLOGISTS

They were defenders of the faith and called "apologists." [31] The word does not mean today what it did in ancient times. Then, an apology was a well-thought-out, logical defense of one's behavior. An apology could be a defense of an individual or group that faced false allegations. The *Apology of Socrates* would be a good example. Other examples might be the New Testament books of Luke and Acts, which some scholars feel belong to the apology genre of their time.[32] Centuries later, when the Church was faced with justifying its existence and its theology, a new breed of apologists would appear. They would come to be known as heresy hunters and centuries later, heresiologists.

These heresiologists included Ignatius, Bishop of Antioch (d. ca. 110), Justin Martyr (ca. 100–ca. 165), Irenaeus, Bishop of Lyons (ca. 130–ca. 200), Tertullian of Carthage (155–230), Hippolytus (ca. 170–ca. 236), Origen of Alexandria (ca.185–ca.254), and many others. They picked up where the contributing writers of the New Testament left off and escalated the pitch of the attack. Their intense and passionate writings give the impression that Gnosticism was a dire threat to the Church. Irenaeus complains, "a multitude of Gnostics have sprung up, and have been manifested like mushrooms growing out of the ground."[33]

The early heresiologists shared positive common themes that were associated with *apologia*. Besides an uncommon "common" enemy (they perceived the fractured world of Gnosticism as a monolith, much in the way some Americans did Communism in past decades), the writers touted the Christian faith as superior to any other religion. Look around you, they would say, at all the Christians when only fifty or one hundred years ago, there were none. It had spread so fast, they asserted, because their God, Providence, was behind it.

For further proof of the power of God, they pointed to the bravery of their martyrs. They linked Christ to the Old Testament prophecies, in existence for millennia. Christian citizens were portrayed as law abiding, good citizens. Another slant of the apologists' argument included a challenge to the other religions: if they were that good, why did they have to persecute Christians? But Christians seemed blind to this perception by the adherents of other religions. The Christians' claim to have the One True God and the *only* way to salvation impressed other religions as condescending.

Later apologetic literature, which involved much letter writing, could scarcely be characterized as simply a defense. The intent of these apologists was obvious. They commenced an all-out frontal attack, a war fought simultaneously on two fronts. One was against Judaism, particularly sectarian Judaism that shared beliefs common to Gnosticism. The Christians had overtaken the Jewish Scriptures and claimed them as their own. They had inherited and altered some of their sacraments and feasts. Judaism was still very much of a presence and many early Christians were Jews. The other front was against Gnosticism.[34]

In their war against Gnosticism, the early Church fathers adopted a primary strategy of proving that its heretical beliefs were not only essentially non-Christian but also stemmed from Greek philosophy and mythology, astrology, magic, mystery religions, and even included Indian sources. They were not averse to significant magnification, alterations, and adding a touch of fiction to their literary skill. They had a tendency, as do contemporary spin doctors, of focusing on the bizarre elements of their opposition and satirizing their theories and personalities.

Key players in the early Church's battle against Gnosticism were its scribes. Their careful alteration of texts kept the written word in line with emerging proto-orthodox teachings. Scripture was not sacrosanct. Had the early scribes avowed inerrancy and literalism, there might not be a Christian Church today. They frequently tampered with texts to rid them of traces of Gnosticism. Utility was the watchword. If a particular word, phrase, or passage did not fit the Church's acceptable concepts, it was altered, replaced, or expunged entirely. The two examples that follow reflect how editing, redactions, interpolations, and other changes occurred in New Testament manuscripts. (Chapter 10, "The Case against Inerrancy," also addresses this issue.) Both center on the birth of Christ, an important, and essential, element of early Christology.

The first scripture is Matthew 1:16: "And Jacob the father of Joseph, the husband of Mary of whom was born Jesus who is called Christ." Ehrman points out that this verse appears as written here, in the majority of manuscripts. Then he notes the variants: "Several witnesses however lack the participle (and its article), making the text now refer to the birth of 'Jesus Christ.'[35] The variation appears also to be attested to by Tertullian, who, in his only citation of the verse, uses it against Valentinian Gnostics and their Christology."[36] By deleting the participle, the scribe improved the theological meaning so that the birth is *Jesus Christ* rather than someone "called the Christ." He is *Jesus Christ*.

According to scholars of textual criticism, the second disputed scripture where there were indications of manuscript tampering is Luke 22:43–44: "An angel from heaven appeared to him and strengthened him. And being in anguish, he prayed more earnestly, and his sweat was like drops of blood falling to the ground." This is the passage in its current translation.

Considerable textual evidence suggests the verses were secondary and "interpolated by second-century scribes who found their emphatic portrayal of Jesus experiencing real human agony useful for repudiation of docetic Christologies."[37] Ehrman and other scholars agree that a majority of the early manuscripts, including some that are highly respected and reliable, do not contain the two verses ending with his sweat falling like great drops of blood. The fragment is also incongruent with the tone of Luke's description of Christ. Again, context is an important factor. The Jesus of Luke is portrayed as facing his final moments with patience, calm, and emotional control. Mark's Jesus is described as distressed and agitated: "he began to be deeply distressed and troubled. 'My soul is overwhelmed with sorrow to the point of death'" (Mark 14:33–34). New Testament scholar Philip Comfort concludes: "In Luke 22:39-46, the account of Jesus' agonizing prayer in the Garden of Gethsemane prior to his crucifixion, several early manuscripts . . . do not have the words traditionally printed as Luke 22:43–44. ('And an angel from heaven appeared to him, strengthening him. In his agony he prayed more earnestly, and his sweat became like drops of blood falling on the ground.')"[38]

Based upon additional evidence, some scholars conclude that the two verses were probably interpolated mid-second century. Justin (died circa 165 CE) and Irenaeus (died early third century) confirm the existence of the early unaffected text, as do early Latin and Syriac witnesses.[39] Comfort also points out that Marcion, Clement, and Origin did not include the verses in the Gospel of Luke, yet "other early church fathers (Justin, Irenaeus, Hippolytus, Dionysius, Eusebius) acknowledged this portion as part of Luke's Gospel."[40] He goes on to add, in agreement with Ehrman, that the fragment passage is probably a second mid-century interpolation, taken from an earlier oral tradition.[41]

In summary, to insure that texts could not be used to justify a Gnostic interpretation, the early Church fathers changed them. The practice became so widespread that it drew this complaint from Origin (died 235 CE): "The differences among the manuscripts have become great, either through the negligence of some copyists or through the perverse audacity of others; they either neglect to check over what they have transcribed, or, in the process of checking, they make additions or deletions as they please."[42] The Christians were not the only ones complaining. One prominent Gnostic, Celsus, who was relentless in his attack on Christian ideas, filed this objection: "Some believers, as though from a drinking bout, go so far as to oppose themselves and alter the original text of the gospel three or four or several times over, and they change its character to enable them to deny difficulties in the face of criticism."[43] Marcion, a literalist, complained of the apologists' use of allegory to interpret any text as they chose. The Church fathers grumbled about Gnostics applying similar tactics. Irenaeus attacked Gnostic treatment of scripture: "They destroy the narrative order of the Gospels and Acts and reject the revealed four-Gospel canon."[44]

Scripture would not be considered sacrosanct until the fourth and fifth centuries, following the post–Nicene era and Synods of Hippo Regius (393) and Carthage (397, 419), when the canon was locked. Ironically, during that period of ecclesiastical domination, the scribes were more professional and thorough, resulting in fewer flaws in their work. The inerrancy of scripture would not arrive on the scene for almost two millennia.

EARLY CHURCH REACTION TO
FEMININE ELEMENTS OF GNOSTICISM

Theologians have been puzzled by the changing role of women in the Church. They were very involved in the beginning, with leadership positions. At some point they were relegated to minor roles; then no roles at all. By the year 200 CE, "virtually all the feminine imagery for God had disappeared from orthodox Christian tradition."[45]

In Dan Brown's *The Da Vince Code*, were Mary Magdalene and her secret a threat to the disciples as they scrambled for leadership in those early days? Since she was closer to Jesus than other disciples, was she a threat even without a secret? Or is there a bigger picture? Did the early Church fathers' response to Gnosticism have anything to do with the vanishing role of women in the Church? If so, what was it? When did it occur?

It would seem logical that the Christian religion, stemming from Judaism, would be male-oriented. There is an absence of feminine symbolism in Jewish tradition (and in Islam). Jesus of Nazareth changed that, at least initially. Numerous scriptures attest to his liberating attitude toward women. He is portrayed as violating Jewish convention by being seen openly with them and by including them among his companions. They are frequently mentioned in Gospel passages. They are the first to arrive at the tomb and the first to spread the news of Jesus's resurrection. The Church produced a tradition stating otherwise, but according to scripture, Mary Magdalene was the first at the tomb and the first to see the risen Christ. Was she, therefore, a threat to apostolic succession?

In the words of Paul, women are given equal status. The scripture is a familiar one: "There is neither Jew nor Greek, slave nor free, male nor female, for you are all one in Christ Jesus" (Galatians 3:28). Paul recognizes the importance of women and makes frequent reference to them. Their names are prominent in the lists of greetings and farewells. On one occasion he elevates them above himself in terms of seniority (Romans 16:7). While acknowledging their importance and allowing them much more participation than they would find in traditional Jewish synagogues, at times he seems ambivalent. One of the scriptures often cited is 1 Corinthians 14:34–35ff., where it says women should keep silent in church and not be permitted to speak. This scripture has been challenged by scholars as an interpolation.[46] Not surprisingly, this interpolation probably occurred during the peak time frame of the conflict with Gnosticism. In Ephesians, Colossians, 1 and 2 Timothy, and Titus, women are clearly subject to the authority of men. These letters are now considered by most scholars to be pseudo-Pauline. They were written by someone else using Paul's name. These documents were also composed during the second century at the height of the Gnostic challenge. The results of this scholarly research clear Paul of woman bashing.

The question is renewed: When women were making social and employment advances throughout the empire,[47] what in Gnosticism caused the downfall of women in the Church?

Indirectly, the anti-Gnostic literature spawned by the Church fathers was an important factor. Directly, however, it went straight to the heart of Gnostic theology and a concept of deity that was androgynous, possessing both male and female attributes, a concept early Christianity opposed. In *The Apocryphon of John*, for example, the Holy Spirit is equated with the Divine Mother.[48] In *The Gospel to the Hebrews* Jesus refers to "my Mother, the Spirit."[49] *The Gospel of Philip* refers to the Spirit as both Mother and Virgin: "Adam came into being from two virgins, from the Spirit and from the virgin earth. . . . Christ, therefore, was born from a virgin."[50] In Gnostic literature, Sophia (in Greek, *sophia* means wisdom) is interpreted in a twisted fashion to be the divine wisdom through which God created the world. Wisdom is responsible for the Demiurge, the God who created Israel. "Among such gnostic groups as the Valentinians, women were considered equal to men. They were revered as prophets, teachers, traveling evangelists, healers, priests, and even bishops."[51] According to Tertullian, Marcion appointed women on an equal basis with men as priests and bishops. Though there were a few exceptions, the general rule among Gnostic cells was one of sexual equality, an egalitarian attitude stemming from their androgynous theology.

The natural impact of this theology diminished the female role in the Church. Orthodox Christians struck back: "A woman should learn in quietness and full submission. Do not permit a woman to teach or to have authority over a man; she must be silent" (1 Timothy 2:11–12). Public opposition to women in leadership roles occurred simultaneously with the writing and circulation of the pseudo-Pauline letters—Ephesians, Colossans, 1 and 2 Timothy, and Titus. A common theme in these epistles was the subordination of women to men as evidenced by the previous quote and echoed later by Tertullian. In Titus where the pseudo-Paul provides guidelines for the selection of bishops, women are excluded: "An elder must be blameless, the husband of but one wife, a man whose children believe and are not open to the charge of being wild and disobedient "(Titus 1:6).

Elaine Pagels also cites from the *Apostolic Church Order*, which appeared toward the end of the second century and was being circulated through congregations in order to retaliate against the idea that women could be divinely ordained. She sets the scene with the apostles engaged in a controversial discussion. Mary and Martha are present. John speaks first:

> When the Master blessed the bread and the cup and signed them with the words, "This is my body and blood," he did not offer it to the women who are with us. Martha said, "He did not offer it to Mary, because he saw her laugh." Mary said, "I no longer laugh; he said to us before, as he taught, 'Your weakness is redeemed through strength.'"[52]

Pagels summarizes the conclusion of the episode: "But her [Mary's] argument fails; the male disciples agree that, for this reason, no woman shall be allowed to become a priest."[53]

Following closely behind these epistles were The Apostolic Fathers. Tertullian, a prime architect in the devaluation of women, saw the adoration of females as a rebellion against discipline. He was especially concerned about "those women among the heretic," who shared positions of authority with the men.[54] He referred to a woman who led a congregation in North Africa as "a viper."[55] One of his strongest statements was possibly paraphrasing one of the pseudo-Pauline epistles:

> It is not permitted for a woman to speak in the church, nor is it permitted for her to teach, nor to baptize, nor to offer [the eucharist], nor to claim for herself a share in any masculine function—not to mention any priestly office.[56]

In reference to husbands, Clement, Bishop of Rome, declares "women are to remain in the rule of subjection."[57] During this time of Gnostic struggle, congregations began the practice of segregating the sexes. Toward the end of the second century, the participation of women in worship was condemned and groups that continued to place women in leadership roles were apostatized and labeled heretical.[58] In 1997, Pope Paul VI issued a proclamation declaring the priesthood off limits for women. His justification: "Our Lord was a man." As we have learned, the history of an all-male priesthood is more complicated. Several factors fed that evolutionary process. The Church's reaction to Gnosticism was one of those factors.

LONG-TERM EFFECTS OF CHURCH'S RESPONSE TO GNOSTICISM

Gnosticism did not create the dogma of the Church, but it made an impact. It challenged the incipient Church to rethink its theology, which affected its hierarchical structure and its political place in the world. Sooner or later, some other esoteric theology would have challenged the early Church fathers.

Despite its conflict with Gnosticism, the early Christian Church made adaptations, accepted Gnostic themes it deemed appropriate and,

> developed into a forward-looking ideology and community structure, which ultimately made it heir to the religions of antiquity. By avoiding extremes and by transforming the radical traits of the early Christian message into a form acceptable to the world, thus not persisting in mere protest but at the same time accepting the cultural heritage of antiquity, it increasingly reduced the influence of Gnosticism until it ultimately, after having been invested with the authority of the state (in the 4th century), succeeded in mobilizing the physical power against it which the remaining adherents could not resist for any length of time.[59]

After a prolonged battle, Gnostic thought seemed to die out. In actuality, it did not. The old problems of origin of evil, nature of body and spirit, redemption, and spiritual knowledge surface throughout the history of the Church. Elements that suggested continuity with the Gnosticism of old would burst forth from time to time. Lee makes the observation that "because a certain number of people at every stage of history are caught up in despair, Gnosticism of one sort or other always has a following . . . every great religion has variations on this theme."[60] One example of Gnostic rebirth occurred in the tenth century in Bulgaria, the Bogomils.[61] Later in the twelfth century, the presence of the Cathars or Albigensians (1150–1300) of southern France was so prominent that it took a crusade sanctioned by the Pope to throttle them. Cathars were also present in northern France, northern Italy, and Germany. Sabanism, a form of Hermetic Gnosis, can be found today in segments of Islam, especially in the current news-prominent Shi'ite sect, which has been called Gnostic Islam by modern Gnostic scholars.

The presence of Gnosticism in our own modern time is indisputable. According to Rudolph: "One can almost say that Gnosis followed the Church like a shadow; the Church could never overcome it, its influence had gone too deep. By reason of their common history they remain two—hostile—sisters."[62] Harold Bloom boldly states that "authentic spirituality in the United States, for nearly two centuries now, is essentially Gnostic."[63]

THE ENEMY WITHIN

Many opponents of the Jewish tradition have not been enemies outside its system but rather within. The false prophets of the Old Testament dwelt among the Israelites. The golden calf came not from some alien movement but erupted within the dissatisfaction of the Hebrew people. Some of the greatest violators of the Mosaic Law were the rulers themselves.

In the life of Jesus, the enemies were not some opposing religion. He does not attack the mystery religions or pagan gods and practices. His harshest words are reserved for those within the organized structure: Pharisees, fellow believers, and churchmen who were the core of the established Church representing the orthodoxy of his time. The ones to be feared are those within the Church: "Be on your guard against the yeast of the Pharisees, which is hypocrisy" (Luke 12:1). The Pharisees are characterized by Jesus as a concealed danger: "Woe to you [Pharisees] because you are like unmarked graves which men walk over without knowing it" (Luke 11:42; Matthew 23:22–29).

The Gnostics are no exception. Throughout the history of the Christian Church the force that has challenged orthodoxy has been an enemy within. Rarely, have the verbal attacks—of Church fathers or later apologists—been against other threats. Jewish theologian Martin Buber, in his work, *The Eclipse of God*,[64] states that "the perpetual enemy of faith in the true God is not atheism (the claim there is no God), but rather Gnosticism (the claim that God is *known*.)"[65] Buber portrays Gnosticism much in the way Camus depicts the plague in his novel of the same name, like something that "never dies or disappears for good; that it can lie dormant for years and years . . . and that perhaps the day would come when, for the bane and enlightenment of men, it would rouse up its rats again and send them forth to die in a happy city."[66] To shift metaphors within Camus, the Church is analogous to Sisyphus, continually pushing his stone up the mountain only to have it roll back and have to begin anew. Gnosticism, in other words, is a phenomenon that is always with us.

SUMMARY

One reason Gnosticism was a threat to Christianity was its pervasiveness through the infiltration of its adherents into Christian congregations and through Christian scriptures. Gnostic theology was veiled in the garb of Christianity. The early Church fathers had to respond.

At the top of their list was the Gnostic concept of deity. Their dualism or multiplicity of gods challenged not only the Christians monotheism from a theological perspective but also their early developing political organization. The early apologists could not tolerate the idea that part of this divinity resided within humans and that knowledge of the deity was privilege for a few elect. Because of their "divine sparks," they could partake and learn. The fact their redeemer was all spirit, with no human qualities, stood in sharp opposition and contrast to the Christian Christ Redeemer, who was both spirit and human, which gave him saving powers. This understanding of Incarnation was unique with the Christians. No other religion could touch it.

To further complicate matters, early Church thinkers considered Gnosticism a philosophy, not a theology or religion. In this respect it clothed Christian concepts with foreign imagery, symbols, and myths. One of these was the Gnostic Redeemer, which was all spirit and only "seemed" to be human, flesh, and blood. If people believed the Gnostics were right, the concept of resurrection would be drained of its significance. A real person would not have risen from the dead. This would have further implications for church politics. Ecclesiastical authority was based upon Apostolic succession, which, in turn, was based on those who witnessed the presence of the resurrected Christ. The Gnostic idea of two or more gods was another threat to church unity and the authority of the bishop, This fragmented lines of authority at a time when the early Church was creating structure by laying down organizational lines. "As the doctrine of Christ's bodily resurrection establishes the initial framework for clerical authority, so the doctrine of the 'One God' confirms, for orthodox Christians, the emerging institution of the 'one bishop' as monarch ('sole ruler') of the church."[67]

The campaign against heresy began with Paul and the writers of the early pseudo-Pauline letters and Johannine Epistles. They defended Jesus as a human, touted the spirit, and attacked anything that smacked of dualism or docetism. Following them came the Apologists or Heresiologists—Tertullian, Irenaeus, Origin—hammering on the same issues. Working parallel with the heresiologists were scribes that ensured the authenticity of the doctrines and the writings. Through their editing, redaction, interpolation, alteration, and deletions, texts were revised and brought into doctrinal line. Much of that is evident today when available manuscripts from those times are compared with each other.

One group affected by Gnosticism was the women of the early Church. Initially, an unusual openness was extended to them, but that suddenly ended as a result of the tenets of Gnosticism. Its emphasis on female deities, which filtered down into its sociology and equality of women, drew the ire of the heresiologists. This was bad theology and, by consequence, bad church politics. Women, therefore, lost their previous status and were banned from assisting in worship. Another side effect of Gnostic influence was the segregation of sexes in the congregations.

The long-term effects of the Church's attack on Gnosticism were unexpected. Gnosticism was thought to have been annihilated. Yet, vestiges of its ideas and theology have surfaced surfaced over the centuries in the Bogomils of the tenth century, Cathars of the Middle Ages and the Islamic Shi'ite sect. One reason Gnosticism was never obliterated related to its locus of operation. Like many other opponents of the Judaistic–Christian tradition, it did not attack from outside of the system but bored from within. Its current resurgence is traceable among the most unlikely of candidates: Fundamentalists.

PART II

FUNDAMENTALISM

CHAPTER 6

THE ORIGINS OF FUNDAMENTALISM

WHAT IS FUNDAMENTALISM?

FUNDAMENTALISM IS DEFINED AS "FORMING A FOUNDATION OR BASIS,"[1] yet the word today resonates with destruction and annihilation. It evokes strong emotions and impulses. Originally characteristic of American conservative Protestantism, Fundamentalism is now associated with violence and terror. In her bestseller, *Battle for God*, Karen Armstrong underscores the meaning of *Fundamental* and the power it evokes:

> One of the most startling developments of the Twentieth century has been the emergence within every major religious tradition of a militant piety popularly known as "fundamentalism." Its manifestations are sometimes shocking. Fundamentalists have gunned down worshipers in a mosque, have killed doctors and nurses who work in abortion clinics, have shot their presidents, and have even toppled a powerful government. It is only a small minority of fundamentalists who commit such acts of terror, but even the most peaceful and law-abiding are perplexing, because they seem so adamantly opposed to many of the most positive values of modern society. Fundamentalists have not time for democracy, pluralism, religious toleration, peace-keeping, free speech, or the separation of church and state.[2]

Because of the stark realism of these words, Fisher Humphrey and Philip Wise hesitated quoting them in their recent book entitled *Fundamentalism*.[3] Though disturbing, the realism does reflect the power and passion of a concept far from its roots and intended mission, one driven to its extreme.

In its original context, which is relatively modern, Fundamentalism was called "a Twentieth Century name for historic Evangelism."[4] In *Webster's New World Dictionary*, Fundamentalism is defined as "religious beliefs based on a literal interpretation of the Bible".[5] This definition falls short of the total picture. Literal interpretation of scriptures and biblical inerrancy are given primacy over other tenets of Fundamentalism and continue to be the lynch pins of its theology. But Fundamentalism represents more than just a way of interpreting scripture.

Martin Marty and Scott Appleby in their landmark study *The Fundamental Project*, discovered common factors among various movements that would qualify as "fundamental":[6]

- *Religion*: Religion is the source of all forms of fundamentalism; each form usually manifests a religious compulsion that drives a religious faction.
- *Traditionalism*: Fundamentalists are traditionalists but discriminating and selective in what "works" for their tradition.
- *Anti-Modern*: Fundamentalists react negatively against modernity and modern ideas.
- *Siege mentality*: Fundamentalists possess a siege mentality with an air of paranoia; they perceive the world as a specific threat to individual and corporate identity.
- *Militancy*: Fundamentalists exhibit a militant attitude, fed by a paranoia that their back is to the wall and that they are fighting for their very existence.
- *Perception of History*: The Fundamentalist perception of history is distorted. Fundamentalists live in a glorious past, to which there is a felt need to return if the future is to survive. History is viewed as a conflict between evil and good, and evil is the modern world.
- *Authoritative male leadership*: With very few exceptions, fundamentalist movements are led by authoritative males
- *Exclusionists*: Fundamentalists stereotype and label. Clear lines are drawn between believers and nonbelievers, insiders and outsiders. There is no middle ground or gray area.
- *Totalitarian*: Consistent with their dualistic view of reality (good versus evil), everything is seen in absolute terms. Their totalitarian system would replace the old.

At the conclusion of their work, the two authors make this excellent summation:

> In these pages fundamentalism has appeared as a tendency, a habit of mind, found within religious communities and paradigmatically embodied in, certain representative individuals and movements, which manifests itself as a strategy or set of strategies, by which beleaguered believers attempt to preserve distinctive identity as a people or group. Finding this identity to be at risk in the contemporary era, they fortify it by a selective retrieval of doctrines, beliefs, and practices from a sacred past.[7]

In an additional attempt to locate a viable and comprehensive definition of "Fundamentalism," this author could locate only a handful of reasoned, well-researched references. The remainder was diatribes against the American "religious right" or Muslim Fundamentalism and reflected the extent of current worldwide religious and political polarization.

From his Bob Jones University web site, prominent Fundamentalist leader, Bob Jones III, gives this definition:

A genuine Fundamentalist is a man who does four things: First, he believes the Bible—accepts it without question as the divinely, verbally inspired, authoritative and inerrant Word of God. Second, he defends the Word of God without equivocation, hesitation, or apology. He does battle for the Faith. In the third place, a fundamentalist declares the whole counsel of God . . . recognizes that the same Book that says, "preach the gospel," says, "Preach the word . . . reprove, rebuke, exhort with all long-suffering and doctrine. . . . He rebukes unscriptural attitudes, actions, and alliances." Fourth, a Fundamentalist obeys the Scripture, seeking in every point to confirm not only by his way of life but also by his own alliances, affiliations, and connections, his belief in the inerrancy of the Word of God. To be a Fundamentalist one must be a complete separatist, fully in compliance with scriptural standards, and an example of obedience to the commands of God.[8]

In his book *Stealing Jesus: How Fundamentalism Betrays Christianity*, noted Episcopalian author Bruce Bawer provides a summary of points that represent the Fundamentalist viewpoint:[9]

- Jesus's death on the cross paid for the sins of believers and won for them eternal life.
- Jesus's primary purpose was to carry out this act of atonement.
- Eternal life is understood as a heavenly reward after death for "True Christians," namely, "The Elect" or "saved."
- Therefore, God loves only "the saved" and they are exclusively his children.
- Satan is a very real creature, "a metaphor for the potential for evil that exists in each person, Christian or otherwise, and that must be recognized and resisted."
- Individuals should be skeptical about trusting their own thoughts and emotions, which can be exploited and manipulated by Satan. Conscience should rule in the fight against Satan.
- Truth is established in the Bible, literally, and "known for sure by true Christians."
- The Bible is the literal and inerrant Word of God and the ultimate source of truth.

After an extensive search for a working definition of Fundamentalism, I came to this conclusion: there are two fundamentalisms. There is a type of generic worldwide fundamentalism, a phenomenon not limited to one particular country or culture but one that finds expression across multiple cultures and geographical areas. We might call this "fundamentalism," with a lowercase "f."[10]

The other type is specific. It targets a specific group with specific geographical boundaries. This "Fundamentalism," with a capital "F" represents a religious movement that surfaced in the late nineteenth and early twentieth centuries in the Protestant culture of the United States and manifests most of the attributes previously categorized by Marty and Appleby. It arose among conservative members of a variety of Protestant denominations. Its primary goals included preserving traditional biblical interpretation and Christian doctrine in protest to Darwinianism (or evolutionism), secularism, and liberal theology.

This Fundamentalism and its comparison with Gnosticism is the topic of this study.

ORIGINS OF FUNDAMENTALISM

Though several names are associated with its evolution, there is no single founder of Fundamentalism. American Evangelist Dwight L. Moody (1837–99) and British preacher and father of dispensationalism[11] John Nelson Darby (1800–1882). Also associated with the early beginnings of Fundamentalism were Cyrus I. Scofield, Moody understudy and publisher of the now famous Scofield Reference Bible.

The Fundamentalism of today began as a form of Anglo-American millennialism in the prewar (World War I) years from 1875 to 1914. The term Fundamentalism was coined after World War I and is linked with several key events. The first was the publication of *The Fundamentals: A Testament to the Truth*, which contains ninety essays or tracts in twelve pamphlets compiled and written between 1910 and 1915. Sixty-four conservative British and American conservative Protestant theologians joined hands in a common effort to challenge what they considered a liberal encroachment on their faith. The key elements of that liberal infringement have been summarized as follows:[12]

- *The Enlightenment*: Individualism, freedom, reason, and progress led to a modern liberal democracy and freedom of church and state.
- *Biblical criticism*: Christians "have never denied that human beings wrote the Bible. . . . However, Christian churches have not always been attentive to the historical character of the origin of the Bible."[13]
- *Evolution*: The *Origin of the Species* (published 1859), with its theory of evolution and life issuing forth from accidental random mutations dealt a crushing blow to the argument for God's design of the universe.
- *Liberal Theology*: For conservatives this emerged from academia and took many forms. It always had a theme of modernism, which later became known as liberalism.

A $250,000 grant from Californians Lyman and Milton Stewart, heads of Union Oil Company, allowed for three million sets of these tracts to be distributed to English-speaking Protestant leaders throughout the world.

The second event was the use of the conservative slogan "the fundamentals" at the 1910 General Assembly of Northern Presbyterian Church in which five items were specified as "the fundamentals of faith and evangelical Christianity":[14]

1. Inspiration and infallibility of Scripture
2. Deity of Christ

3. Christ's virgin birth and miracles
4. Christ's penal death for our sins
5. Christ's physical resurrection and personal return

Humphreys and Wise encapsulate the event:

> In summary, the original Fundamentalism was A movement of traditional Protestants in the United States who set aside their denominational differences in order to form a united front against a common enemy, liberalism, which was understood to be the thin edge of the wedge of secularism and a serious threat to the faith of the Christian church. Fundamentalism began as a religious impulse to protect traditional beliefs by opposing liberalism, the impulse led to a movement, and the movement created a network of institutions that embodied the impulse.[15]

A third event occurred July 1, 1920, when Northern Baptist newspaper editor, Curtis Lee Laws wrote the following in a long-remembered column: "We here and now move that a new word be adopted to describe the men among us who insist that the landmarks shall not be removed . . . We suggest that those who still cling to the great fundamentals and who mean to do battle royal for the fundamentals shall be called 'Fundamentalists.'"[16] "From that time on, it seems to have become habitual for American Evangelicals to refer to these articles as 'the fundamentals.'"[17]

But Fundamentalism was part of the American religious landscape long before the turn of the century, long before the word "Fundamental" came into vogue. Many scholars say its roots extend back to Puritanism and the Pilgrims. Others would not disagree but quickly contend that without an extraordinary event on August 6, 1801, there would be no discussion about Fundamentalism as we know it today. It simply might not exist. A revival at Cane Ridge, Kentucky that lasted a week and was attended by an estimated twenty-five thousand people would launch the Second Great Awakening and insure the future of Fundamentalism for decades, possibly centuries, to come.

EARLY BEGINNINGS IN AMERICA

"Why did this kind of religion develop in America, of all places?" Bruce Bawer asks.[18] He points immediately to the Pilgrims. The Pilgrims, along with most early settlers, were Puritans. True to their name, purity was a primary goal. The Puritans' objective, and one of their reasons for seeking a new world, was to free the Covenant people from contamination and error. Initially they believed Calvin's teachings. They thought they were bringing his brand of Reformation to America—predestination, an omnipotent sovereign God, fighting the same foes of papism, and the Anabaptists. They succeeded in keeping the trappings of structure and sacraments. They also maintained emphasis on the Old Testament and the people of Israel, their covenant with God and journey to the Promised Land.

But the Promised Land they encountered was a new world, in a new time, with new and different problems. Along the way something happened to Calvinism in colonial America. It became twisted and shaped into something else. The primary reason was the Great Awakening of 1740–770: "With Jonathan Edwards and the experience of the Great Awakening, the American preoccupation was dramatically shifted from the mighty acts of God to the religious experience of the Christian person."[19] The emphasis upon a people-oriented corporate covenant shifted to an individualized covenant. This transferal of emphasis to self and the elitism that often accompanies that focus caused the "we generation" of Calvin's congregational theology to become a "me generation." A personal experience of salvation was required for one to claim to be Christian. Assurance could be found only in being "born again." Individual knowledge of Jesus and conversion became the focal points of American religion. In the process, Calvinism was turned into a hardy pioneer mix strongly resembling the first heresy of the Church: Gnosticism. "Despite its orthodox beginnings . . . New England and . . . most of North American Protestantism was to fall into other hands which were neither catholic nor charitable. An evangelical elite was to gain ascendancy and make the question of individual conversion the central question of Christianity."[20] To understand how Fundamentalism today resembles the Christian Gnostics of old, it is important to grasp this pivotal point in the history of American religion. What began in New England would spread throughout the American colonies. Other denominations—Baptists, Methodists, and Pentecostals—became infected with the contagion. Because of their pioneer networking and their ability and courage to move beyond the safe towns and communities of established religion, these new brands of theology could more quickly expedite the message, which spread like wildfire. John Wesley would not recognize this new brand of Methodism with an overemphasis on subjective feeling and the loss of the more objective rational component.

Consistent with the capitalistic spirit, religion became based upon a divine calling of the individual. Individual achievement and divine calling went hand-in-hand; "religion and ethics both become a matter of private enterprise."[21] Parallel with industrial development, conversion became analogous to a technique, or vehicle, to escape from earthly entrapment and to gain spiritual salvation.

Prior to the Great Awakening, the Church of England, or Anglican Church, was dominant in the colonies. It was a state church supported by taxes. Most believers stayed away but followed the call of the spirit. The sacraments aroused disagreements and opposition. With the Great Awakening, much that had been conventional about Protestantism was shattered. Baptists became divided into two different groups: "separate" and "regular." The Great Awakening called for reform with Protestant standards. Whether or not those reforms improved or advanced the Christian cause depended upon who was asking the question. Values of individual experience were revived, which threatened the traditional church as an organization.

During this period a struggle began between groups called the "Old Lights" and the "New Lights." The historical and political background is not important. Originally they had no political cast. But who they were and what they represented is important and ushers up that old shadow of Gnosticism. Congregational democracy, similar to what happened in the ancient Gnostic churches, began to take hold.

The New Lights were the supporters of the Great Awakening or the revivalists. The Old Lights, or traditional orthodox, were its opponents.[22] Some of the New Lights were caught up in the spirit and given to great convulsions, while the Old Lights were frightened by all this strange irrational religious behavior. In Connecticut, statutes were pushed through the legislature to bar itinerant preachers from local pulpits and a long standing statue for religious toleration was repealed. This forced the New Lights into becoming a political force.[23]

The Great Awakening had a divisive effect upon the colonies and the people. The New Lights splintered the Congregational establishment in New England and multiplied Baptists in the South. Anglican and Presbyterian Churches lost large numbers of members. Denounced by Old Lights as madmen and apostates, the New Lights succeeded in founding several Ivy League Universities (schools to train their own ministers) and set the stage for the next century's evangelical revivals, which would be led by Baptists and Methodists.[24]

Was this the return of Gnosticism? Was it another recurring vestige of Gnosticism? The American colonial phenomenon manifested enough similarities with Gnosticism to legitimize the question.

The European Reformers' insistence and emphasis on a transcendent supreme deity veered close to Gnosticism. Their fundamental doctrinal truth was the sovereignty of a God who was unknowable and ineffable in his transcendence. This theological emphasis eclipsed the Incarnation where God is near and knowable. The logical outcome of this belief was absolute determinism. This was the omnipotent God the Puritans brought with them to the New World. This was a Gnostic God. A primary tenet of Gnosticism was belief in a transcendent deity who dwelled in his own realm, totally separate from the mundane, sordid, and "all over dirty" world of humans that Jonathan Edwards described: "Everywhere it is covered with that which tends to defile the feet of the traveler. Our streets are dirty and muddy, intimating that the world is full of that which tends to defile the soul, that worldly objects and worldly concerns and worldly company tend to pollute us."[25] This deterministic view of sin, which was blatant dualism and a tenet of Gnosticism, "became a feature of the extreme form of puritanism that dominated American evangelical religion."[26] The great literature of that era, particularly the works of Calvinistic disciples Herman Melville and Nathaniel Hawthorne reflected a continual search for God's grace. With humanity's fate sealed in omnipotent and absolute determinism, a world totally inundated in evil, there were only two choices: humankind had to deal with a distant, uncaring, and malicious God; or God was partitioned and there were two separate Gods. The outcome of either was a typical dualistic Gnostic split between creation and redemption.[27] The early heresiologists leveled a similar charge against the Gnostic heretic Marcion. By denying the existence of a Creator, in essence, Marcion partitioned God the Creator from God the Redeemer. Dispensationalists would accomplish the same feat.

The strict Calvinistic concept of "the elect" propounded by Edwards, along with his emphasis on the power of immediate personal religious experience, echo the Gnostic "pneumatics" (the elect with "divine sparks"). This was a repeat of spiritual immediacy with the deity (mysticism) and individual salvation of the soul versus the greater spiritual good of the community. The emphasis on spiritualism was partially rebellion against the Enlightenment and served to cast suspicion over intellectuals. (This same battle will be fought a century later between the Fundamentalists and Modernists.)

Another key principle of Calvinism was original sin. When original sin and total depravity are used as tools to increase the thanksgiving of the faithful, the concepts are orthodox.[28] But when the concept of original sin is taken literally, that is, *literally* evil entered the cosmos from an outside source, "a barrier has been broken and those profound but perilous doctrines of the Church have been Gnosticized."[29] Whether Gnosticism borrowed the concept of predestination from the early Church or vice versa, a deterministic concept of sin became, through a rather circuitous route, a dominant theme of American evangelical religion.[30]

The Gnostic concept of original sin includes, by definition, belief in divine selection. Remember the *pneumatics* or *gnostikoi*, one of the three types of Gnostic humanity (*hylics* and *psychics* were the others). According to Gnostic wisdom, the *pneumatics* were an elite corps that possessed insight and were elected to salvation because they were worthy of election. The *psychics* had a remote chance. The *hylics*, who probably made up most of the masses, were doomed.

For the Gnostic or Fundamentalist, the responsibility for sin shifts. With an omnipotent God and original sin, humankind was off the hook. Creation was the problem. Humanity is not held accountable for sin. Sin entered the world at creation, at the inception of the cosmos. Adam's sin was caused by another source: the devil made him do it. There is no need for the salvation of humans from sin, because they never sinned. From the Gnostic point of view, they are ignorant and unable to comprehend the truth. This logic, therefore, made Gnosticism unable to assimilate any serious meaning of the *Incarnation* and the cross.[31]

From this perspective, ultra-Calvinism and Gnosticism are similar. The esoteric saving knowledge of the Gnostics also returned to the theological scene in colonial America: "Very soon after Calvinism was transplanted to New England . . . the importance of *what* is to be known was eclipsed by the importance of *knowing*."[32] God's act in converting the sinner took center stage. Some theologians theorize that this shift in Puritan theology was to combat charges of Arminianism (the belief that individuals achieved salvation through their own will). Regardless of the reasons, individuals now received a divine call consistent with a surging capitalistic economy that encouraged individual achievement.

Mirrored in the colonial controversy is the same struggle, along similar power lines, between the emerging authority of the early Church and Gnosticism. In America, the emphasis upon individual salvation and individualism diminished clerical authority and hierarchy. In some areas the laity took over. In some townships they demanded authority to select and elect their own pastors. Fear of an identical outcome energized the early Church fathers in combating similar Gnostic tendencies. The New Lights of the Great Awakening fed democracy.

Fundamentalists today are ancestors of this earlier movement, which had its roots in Gnostic concepts and created a good mix for today's legalistic Christianity. Helping it along was a pragmatic and materialistic pioneer attitude that respected hard work along with skepticism of unproductive intellectuals unconnected to the real world. The result was success for faiths that involved measurable works, minimal or no mental reflection, and reward in the form of a substantial heaven.[33] America was also considered by many to be the New Eden. This notion was a short step from a primitivism that accepted the Bible as the only guide one needed to make it in the world. The result was a primitive literalism among naïve, uneducated rural types with a dislike of elitism. Also, the effect of not having ordained clergy on the frontier tended to promote individualism. All of this played out in an insistence on biblical inerrancy and literalism. "The generation that made the Revolution were the children of the twice-born, the heirs of this seventeenth century religious tradition."[34]

Following the First Great Awakening of the eighteenth century came the Second Great Awakening of the nineteenth century.[35] It was a Protestant phenomenon that lasted about fifty years and touched every geographical area of the country. During this period, through the use of itinerant preachers and emotionally charged revivals, Methodist and Baptist membership swelled, mostly at the expense of Presbyterians and Episcopalians. With excessive emotionalism impersonating religion, as some perceived the phenomenon, the age of evangelicalism had arrived. Whereas the First Great Awakening focused on those who were "churched" or already members, the Second sought to attract the unchurched. The Second Great Awakening was the time of the famous Cane Ridge Revival, frontier camp meetings, and the spread of Methodism.

The long-term effects of the Cane Ridge Revival cannot be underestimated. Harold Bloom called it "the first Woodstock."[36] Barton Stone, a Presbyterian minister and one of the leaders of the revival, hailed it as a significant occurrence of Enthusiasm.[37] The Cane Ridge Revival may have been the beginning of Fundamentalism as we know it today; a revival of Gnosticism as it was known millennia ago.

This Second Great Awakening was a time of crisis in New England Congregationalism, which saw the rise of Unitarianism. This period also witnessed the creation of the American Bible Society, American Home Missionary Society, American Temperance Society, and Abolitionism. Traditional rigid Calvinism was toned down and stripped of its harsh predestinarianism and innate depravity and one's individual soul was redeemable through free will. One result of this time of high emotionalism and revivals was a "competitive marketplace of religion" within the country.[38] Another was a surge of moral and social reform.[39]

During the Second Great Awakening, Baptists burst upon the scene. The Baptists are currently the largest Protestant denomination, and beneath their umbrella are numerous offshoots who claim the name. According to religious critic Bloom, the "American Baptists descend from two rival sects of Inner Light Puritans of the early seventeenth century: General Baptists, who believed that everyone in general could be redeemed, and Particular Baptists, who held on to the Calvinistic convictions that only those elected in particular would be saved."[40] In 1801 at Cane Creek, the two groups merged and compromised, but the distinction between General and Particular redemption was blurred. The Particular form is still prevalent among some Baptist circles. The Southern Baptist Convention began in 1845. They have been called "the Established Church of the old Confederacy" and the "Catholic Church of the Confederate States."[41] In the 1870s the Baptists joined a growing premillennialist drive that denounced progress and industrialization and reaffirmed supernaturalism. It was during this time that the term "inerrancy" was introduced with regard to scripture and today's style of Fundamentalism began to take shape.[42]

The First and Second Great Awakenings of the eighteenth and nineteenth centuries foreshadowed religious movements of the twentieth and twenty-first century. Given the historical and sociological course of religious development in America, Fundamentalism was a logical outcome.

Fundamentalism in the twentieth century was launched by two events: the 1910 General Assembly of the Northern Presbyterian Church, and the publication of "The Fundamentals" from 1905 to 1910. In the initial stages of its development, Fundamentalism was a loose diversified alliance with no definite core leadership. There were significant differences. Early proponents, such as James Orr, author of the first article in *The Fundamentals*, refused to accept inerrancy of the scriptures.[43] Dispensational premillennialism and an emphasis upon piety were rejected by others involved in the movement.

Despite its differences and slack organization, Fundamentalism was off to a strong start but soon faced big battles. First, despite strong continuous efforts, was the failure to dominate any major denomination. The national radio broadcast of the Scopes Trial in 1925 became a negative. Scopes was found guilty, but public opinion turned against Fundamentalism. Another battle hardily fought and lost was the repeal of the prohibition amendment in 1933: "During the 1930s, the movement more or less disappeared from public view, and many Americans assumed that, except for a few benighted people in isolated locales, it had died. . . . In fact, Fundamentalism had not died, but rather was flourishing."[44] A print and telecast industry was established along with a system of para-church groups, whose goal was to meet the spiritual needs of targeted groups. A system of day schools, missionary agencies, colleges, and seminaries was founded. Fundamentalists modified their message to appeal more to the average working person.

The next splash made by Fundamentalists was in the 1940s with the emergence of Billy Graham and the birth of *evangelicalism*. Evangelicalism was less rigid, more open to intellectual stimulation and debate, and less rejecting of other Christians. With Evangelicalism came a higher level of cooperation among Christians with varying viewpoints.

But old style Fundamentalism returned in the 1970s with the Moral Majority founded by Jerry Falwell (1979). It became more visible in the 1980s with Pat Robertson's Christian Coalition. This new Christian Right comprised a majority of the electorate that elected Ronald Regan to the White House. With the impact that Fundamentalism made in the 2004 election under the generalship of Carl Rove, it appears to be here to stay. There are no signs of atrophy, no indications that it might be disappearing. President George W. Bush and others have called it the Third Great Awakening, and there are no signs it is going back to sleep: "The nation may implode financially, and our new Roman empire may collapse suddenly, with no intervening decline. . . . What will not subside is the ongoing exfoliation of the American Religion, whose Pentecostal wing expands daily, both here and abroad."[45]

SUMMARY

Today, Fundamentalism is a polarizing "buzz word" that often evokes strong emotion from most sectors. It is more than just a set of religious beliefs that focus on biblical literalism and inerrancy. Because of its many facets, Fundamentalism is more easily described than defined. The landmark work of Marty and Appleby developed nine attributes, or factors that characterize Fundamentalism: religious origins, antimodern, tradition-oriented, persecution complex, glorification of the past, authoritarian male leadership, discrimination, and totalitarian. There are two types of fundamentalism: one is generic, spelled with a lowercase "f"; the other is the more specific American phenomenon spelled with a capital "F."

The Fundamentalism of our focus has roots extending back to ancient Judaism and Gnosticism, but it actually began in this country with the First and Second Great Awakenings, particularly the Cane Ridge Revival of 1801. Formally, it emerged shortly after World War I when a group of Protestant clergymen and theologians decided to challenge a modernity threatening their religious faith. Gnostic elements, which may or may not relate directly to classical Gnosticism, are detected in each of these movements.

CHAPTER 7

THE BASIC TENETS OF FUNDAMENTALISM

> The authority of the holy scripture, for which it ought to be believed and obeyed, dependeth not upon the testimony of any man or church, but wholly upon God (who is truth itself), the author thereof; and therefore it is to be received, because it is the word of God.
>
> —Westminster Confession, I. iv.

LIKE GNOSTICISM, FUNDAMENTALISM IS A PHENOMENON OF LOOSELY confederated groups with no established creed and a range of differing beliefs. Therefore, defining its theology proves as difficult as defining the theology of Gnosticism. Fundamentalism had the benefit of an organized press and several scholars working in concert to publish their view. With their resources, Gnostics produced prodigiously, but they had no doctrinal base of authority. Fundamentalism had a recognized assembly to stamp its beliefs and give them authority. Gnosticism was a loose collection of disparate groups that lacked organization.

A summary of Fundamentalist beliefs and the two events associated with their creation was discussed in Chapter 6. The first of those events was a publication of a series of pamphlets entitled *The Fundamentals*.[1] The second was the "Five Points of Fundamentalism," generated by the 1910 General Assembly of the Northern Presbyterian Church. Each will now be discussed separately and in greater depth.

THE FUNDAMENTALS

The Fundamentals, though compiled almost a century ago, are still popular among conservative Christians and available today in a four-volume set. They comprise ninety articles written by different individuals and cover a wide area of theological concerns and issues that include the following: "The Reasons for the Incarnation," "The Personality and Deity of the Holy Spirit," "Proof of the Living God," and "The History of the Higher Criticism."

The most prominent of those themes in the ninety tracts is the divinity of Christ. Very limited emphasis is given to his humanity. This imbalance regarding the doctrine of Incarnation is not taken lightly by fellow Christian critics: "The lack of attention to Jesus' humanity is serious, for if Jesus was not fully human, then, of course, there was no Incarnation."[2] This lack of attention to the humanity of Jesus is the clearest similarity of Fundamentalism to Gnosticism. The Fundamentalist defense against this omission is that the humanity of Jesus was not challenged; only his divinity necessitated a defense.

Consider the attention to Jesus's humanity in the Apostles' Creed: "suffered," "crucified," "dead," "buried." One might ask why the early Church Fathers, in a similar situation as the Fundamentalists, emphasized the humanity of Christ. This was because, unless the Word became flesh, there would be no salvation. Compounding this imbalanced presentation of the Incarnation in these essays is lack of attention to the Trinity, which is the principle Christian doctrine. This glaring omission has prompted some to state that "one problem with The Fundamentals is that they were not fundamental enough."[3]

The writers vigorously defended the inerrancy of Holy Scripture, including Moses' authorship of the Pentateuch, or first five books of the Bible. Following the logic of direct connection between the Spirit and the person, one of the contributors argued that Jesus, based on the presupposition that certain persons were divinely selected, concluded that Moses wrote the books. One dare not challenge the deified thought processes of the Christ. The adherents of The Fundamentals seemed less focused on the divine inspiration behind the scriptures and overly focused on who wrote them. On this type of minutiae, Humphreys and Wise make the following comment: "In our judgment, it is misleading to treat a matter like this as if it were a fundamental of the Christian faith. One problem with treating non-fundamental matters as if they are fundamental is that you begin to treat people who disagree with you about nonfundamental matters as if they disagreed about fundamental ones; you may even begin to assume that such people are not really Christians at all."[4]

THE FIVE FUNDAMENTALS

This list of beliefs, or "the five fundamental beliefs" as they have come to be called, have a compelling and convoluted story beyond the scope of this book.[5] Though their version has been altered from time to time and shaped to fit the controversy of the hour, they still remain the guiding principles of the Fundamentalist school:

BIBLICAL INERRANCY

The concept of inerrancy of scripture floated nebulously around the Christian world for a couple of centuries without any clear articulation or definition. Then came the Niagara Bible Conference of 1895 and a statement by a group of antimodernist ministers (mostly Baptist and Presbyterian) declaring there was no true Christianity where there was not complete and total acceptance of Christ's divinity, his birth from a virgin, and his physical resurrection. To this list they also demanded belief in the inerrancy of scripture, that is, belief that the Bible was free of error and every word was literally true.

This was a new doctrine that had never really been considered important or carried doctrinal weight. One of the reasons for its lack of significance was due to the many prima facie contradictions and inconsistencies.[6] Charles Hodge, a prominent conservative preacher of the 1870s, expressed that the Bible could have errors and inconsistencies and still be divinely inspired. A generation later his son, Archibald Alexander Hodge, along with fellow colleague Benjamin Warfield, took the concept to the next level stating God not only inspired the Bible but also dictated it word-for-word. In response to their opponents' logic regarding flaws and contradictions, they declaimed that the original autographs were inerrant and flawed later by copyists in their reproductions. This required a blind faith beyond reason.

For Fundamentalists the Holy Bible *is* the word of God. The word of God is Truth. Completing the third leg of the syllogism, the Bible is Truth. The New Testament is the perfected form of religion of the Old Testament and is the final authority. James Innell Packer, one of the strong voices of Fundamentalism states,

> As the Westminster Confession puts it: "The supreme judge, by which all controversies of religion are to be determined, and all decrees of councils, opinions of ancient writers, doctrines of men, and private spirits, are to be examined, and in whose sentences we are to rest, can be no other but the Holy Spirit speaking in the Scripture." . . . Anything short of unconditional submission to Scripture, therefore, is a kind of impenitence; any view that subjects the written Word of God to the opinions and pronouncements of men involves unbelief and disloyalty towards Christ.[7]

The basic principle of the Fundamentalist view is that the Bible, or written Scriptures, is the inerrant Word God spoke and continues to speak to his churches. It is the final authoritative word for faith and life. If one wishes to learn what God was, or is thinking, one must consult the scriptures, that is, His written word. "The Bible is inspired in the sense of being word-for-word God-given . . . and contains all that the Church needs to know in this world for its guidance in the way of salvation and service."[8] Fundamentalists are further convinced that the Bible is in need of no further amendments and should suffer no deletions. In this respect, and others, they are descendants of Athanasius, who, it will be recalled, fought for the divinity of Christ.

From its modern inception early in the twentieth century into this new millennium, the battle cry of Fundamentalists has been the unerring word of the Bible. The Bible is the Word of God without exception. This Word is the absolute Truth, letter of the law, binding for all time. It is the absolute authority and is completely closed to any further additions. On this one fundamental, all the others rest. Without it, they fall. Literal interpretation is the hermeneutic. We have not only no further additions but also no further interpretations.

Two terms associated with this Fundamentalist position, inerrancy and literalism, warrant further clarification. Though very closely related, they are not the same. In *Webster's New World Dictionary* the definition of *literalism*, "the tendency or disposition to take words in their literal sense" is based on the definition of the word *literal*: "following or representing the exact words of the original; word-for-word; as a literal translation."[9] Most biblical literalists who believe the Bible is *the* literal Word of God—that is, they read it just *as it was written*—also believe it is flawless or inerrant. For them, the two concepts go hand-in-hand. In this sense, inerrancy implies literalism, therefore there is no interpretation. Because if one begins to ask, "What does this mean?" they are headed down the path of denying literalism.

Fundamentalists distinguish between infallible and inerrant. Regarding the former, they cite a lengthy pedigree of religious giants and treatises of the past that have made similar claims. By "infallible" they mean something that can be trusted, will not deceive or betray or mislead. Something that is infallible is trustworthy. By "inerrancy," they mean without error or flaw. The two words are often used together and in a manner suggesting they are synonymous and interchangeable. This statement from Packer is an example: "The infallibility and inerrancy of biblical teaching does not, however, guarantee the infallibility and inerrancy of any interpretation, or interpreter, of that teaching."[10] Not only do the statements illustrate the preceding point but they also present the Fundamental hermeneutical, or interpretational, key: faith (in God's trustworthiness) is the guarantor of inerrancy and correct interpretation, the latter of which is based upon a literal and inerrant Word or text. This leaves the interpretation wide open. From a nonfundamentalist perspective, exegesis and interpretation invalidate literalism. Exegesis (the interpretation of written passages) is a hermeneutic and is therefore not needed by those who take the scripture literally.

There are other Fundamentalists, however, who take the literalist position and allow for the involvement of human hands in its production. They admit there are human flaws, but the errors are minimal and do not cancel out the primacy of divine meaning. The Bible is the *inspired* Word of God, to be read and understood within that frame of reference. Many of these individuals are unconcerned about theological sophistication, exegetical research, or archaeological discovery. They usually know exactly what the scriptures mean. The Bible interprets itself, but they self-interpret. Over time, biblical inerrancy and literal interpretation, though dissimilar in meaning, have become synonymous. The nuances, however, should be noted. All those who believe in biblical inerrancy are also literalists. The converse does not apply. All those who are literalists are not necessarily advocates of inerrancy.

When many Fundamentalists speak of the inspired writings of the Bible, they use the term God-breathed. Conservative theologian Packer states that, within this context, "inspiration is defined as a supernatural, providential influence of God's Holy Spirit upon the human authors which caused them to write what He wished to be written."[11] What do the Fundamentalists have to say about "dictation," or as some have called it, the "typewriter" theory of inspiration? Packer is unequivocal: "it is not so. This 'dictation theory' is a man of straw. It is safe to say that no Protestant theologian, from the Reformation until now, has ever held it."[12] Instead, God adapted his inspiring thoughts to mold and frame of the mind of the writer, taking into consideration the idiosyncratic writing styles and habits of each.

The unity of the scriptures is of utmost importance to Fundamentalists. Scripture is the sum total of God's revelation, which means all that is revealed in both Old and New Testaments. Though complex, the message is considered single and God-given, one that was spoken and still speaks. This is one reason for the singular Word of God, rather than Words of God. It is a written testimony to God Himself. When Fundamentalists call the Bible the Word of God, they mean a single statement or expression, utterance or declaration, which originates from God. This is an inexhaustible Word. Exegesis and interpretation never end. Exegesis presupposes a hermeneutic. The Fundamentalist presupposes a hermeneutic that does not need interpretation, which is another way of putting words into God's mouth. Errors within the scriptures are nonexistent, "textual corruptions are no part of the authentic Scriptures. . . . Faith in the consistency of God warrants an attitude of confidence that the text is sufficiently trustworthy not to lead us astray. If God gave the Scriptures for a practical purpose—to make men wise unto salvation through faith in Jesus Christ—it is safe inference that he never Permits them to become so corrupted that they can no longer fulfill it."[13] Fundamentalists admit that the autographs, the original biblical manuscripts, are no longer available for scrutiny. But those autographs were faultless and unflawed. As previously stated, faith accepts that God will be true to his intention. Despite that creedal presupposition, Fundamentalists rally scholarly support for the principle of inerrancy. Packard quotes Frederick Fyvie Bruce, a noted New Testament scholar: "the Bible has come down to us in such substantial purity that even the most uncritical edition of the Hebrew or Greek . . . cannot effectively obscure the real message of the Bible, or neutralize its saving power."[14]

These connotations will be discussed in Chapter 8. They are important for a principle thesis of this work, namely, that the Word, though divinely inspired, was nevertheless composed and written by humans. It is flawed and consistent with the Church's understanding of Christ: "The Word became flesh."

Fundamentalists further clarify what they do and do not mean by inerrant. The position does not restrict them to a pure literal exegesis of scripture. They understand that real events may be interpreted symbolically as demonstrated in the story of Adam and Eve.

In May of 1987 the problems with technical inerrancy became paramount to Fundamentalism. At a conference on biblical inerrancy sponsored by the Southern Baptist Convention, one of the key spokespersons made the statement that biblical inerrancy "has eroded our confidence that the Bible which we now have is the Word of God."[15] The response was predictable. Today's Bible, without regard for original manuscripts, is literally the Word of God. And the Bible to which most refer is *The King James Version*.

Many within the Southern Baptist Convention and other Fundamentalist denominations are abandoning technical inerrancy. There are still many who cling to the belief that the Bible is the pure unfiltered Word of God and the authority of the Church.

THE VIRGIN BIRTH OF CHRIST

Over the centuries Christians of varying convictions have held this second Fundamental conviction. At the Niagara Bible Conference in 1895, belief in the Virgin Birth was declared a requirement to be a true Christian. The Virgin Birth has been particularly embraced by Fundamentalists as scriptural and supported by the first Fundamental belief of inerrancy. More importantly, it establishes the divinity of Christ.

The first treatise of volume 1 of *The Fundamentals* by James Orr of Glasgow focuses on the virgin birth. The virgin birth is affirmed in the Gospels of Matthew and Luke. It is revered by the Eastern Orthodox, Roman Catholics,[16] and a plurality of Protestant denominations.

THE SUBSTITUTIONARY ATONEMENT

The penal substitutionary atonement of Christ is the belief that when Christ died on the cross, he experienced God's punishment for the sins of the world. In its present form, this theory is one developed by John Calvin in the sixteenth century. There are numerous passages in the New Testament referring to the suffering and death of Christ and his subsequent resurrection, but the proof texts for penal substitutionary atonement are limited or questionable. As in the sacrifice of the Passover and Atonement in Jewish rituals, Jesus gave his life. Others, too, must follow his example and take up their crosses. There are numerous references comparing him to the Suffering Servant of Isaiah 53.

For Christians and Jews, atonement is basically a description of how sin can be forgiven. It is the process of forgiving or pardoning a wrong or transgression. In the Jewish faith, Yom Kipper was the Day of Atonement.[17] It is one of the holiest of Jewish holidays, and its attendance and participation by even secular Jews is comparable to attendance in Christian Churches on Easter Sunday.

Despite this definitive concept of atonement from the "mother church," it is lacking in the Christian Church that began as a reform movement within Judaism. Over the centuries, the Church has generated no uniform dogma or doctrine of atonement. Several theories have been advanced over the centuries by different individuals or groups, and some have been adopted by various denominations:

- *Ransom Theory of Atonement*, also known as the Classical Theory, was introduced by Origin in the third century CE and asserts that God was deceitful and bribed and paid off Satan with the death of Jesus. According to Origin, sin began with Adam and Eve. Since that time sinners were held in captivity, then released when God paid the ransom: Jesus Christ. This view was held by the early Church two centuries after Christ and is still honored today by the Eastern Orthodox Church and Protestant Movement.

* *Satisfaction Theory of Atonement*, introduced by the eleventh century theologian Anselm, expresses the belief that God is appeased through the human sacrifice of Jesus. The concept has its roots in the ancient Hebrew ritual of animal sacrifice. Though not raised to the level of dogma, the Catholic Church and some Protestant denominations embrace this theory.

* In the *Substitution Theory of Atonement*, Jesus takes our place and bears the penalty for our sins.

* *Sacrificial Theory of Atonement*, introduced in the Reformation era circa 1520 CE, states that following the sacrifice of Jesus, God's wrath was replaced with his mercy. This is the theory held today by Conservative and some mainline Protestants.

* *Moral Theory of Atonement*, introduced by Peter Abelard in the twelfth century portrays the death of Jesus as an act of humanity, which should be emulated.

There are other theories, but these are the ones most recognized and used today.[18]

Most Fundamentalists uphold the Sacrificial or Penal Substitution Theory. Individuals wishing to be classified as true believers must adhere to this theory. The concept is not verifiable in scripture, which has resulted in opposition to it within conservative ranks.[19] The idea that God must punish Jesus, father punishing son, is reprehensible to some Christians, particularly from a moral viewpoint. They ask, was it necessary for God to do this? The theory suggests problems between father and son, disharmony within the heavenly family.

THE BODILY RESURRECTION OF CHRIST

> I believe in the Holy Spirit, the Holy catholic Church, the communion of saints, the forgiveness of sins, the resurrection of the body.
>
> —The Apostles Creed

The importance of the physical resurrection of Christ to the early Church and its leaders has been noted. The key word is "body": If Christ did not physically rise from the dead then "our preaching is useless and so is your faith" (1 Corinthians 15: 14). To combat the Gnostic belief that Christ was not a physical entity, emphasis on his bodily resurrection was important for the early Church. At the time conservative theology was being forged in the late nineteenth century, some liberal theologians were denying the physical resurrection of Christ. The physical resurrection of Christ gained importance primarily as a counter tactic. Like the ancient Gnostics, these liberals used scripture to make their case. The risen Jesus was not recognized by his own followers. His body could not have been physical, because he is portrayed as magically appearing and disappearing and walking through walls. Most of these examples appear in the Gospel of John that was suspect of being a Gnostic testament in the early days of the Church.

Regardless of their classification, most Christians today accept the bodily resurrection of Jesus. Without it, Christianity becomes another religious house of cards and quickly collapses. After all, this was the "good news," the Gospel. For the Fundamentalists, any threat to the resurrection is a threat to the supernatural aspect of Christianity.

THE HISTORICITY OF MIRACLES

Basic to Fundamentalism is the supernatural element of Christianity. The primary support of this tenet is inerrancy of scripture. The miraculous stories in the Bible happened because "the Bible tells me so." It is one thing to say that miracles cannot or can happen, and yet another to say that certain miracles did not or did happen: "The assumption that miracles can't happen makes sense only if one assumes either that there is no God at all or that, if there is a God, God cannot act in this world in ways at variance with the orderly processes or laws of nature."[20] If Christians begin reading their Bible with the underlying belief that miracles do not happen, they begin in contradiction. It is, however, simply good Bible study to ask questions about stupendous miracle stories (Jonah and the whale, for example). Did the writer intend an allegory or symbolism? If it is a story rooted in history, is it accurate?

These five concepts are the "Fundamentals" of Fundamentalism. However, Bawer reminds us that not all legalistic Protestants are Fundamentalists. Fundamentalists are elitists, he states and "keep themselves apart from the evil mainstream culture and thus pure."[21] William Loader also cautions against viewing Fundamentalism as a monolithic system of thought.[22] Many who are fundamentalist in their thinking are not fundamental in their demeanor, outlook, or behavior. They possess Fundamental beliefs because they were raised in a Fundamental milieu and knew nothing else. Their spirituality, however, functions on a different level. They are not ideologues. They manifest an openness, compassion, and flexibility not usually associated with their more rigid and purist cousins. "Their approach to the Bible is just an element of their spirituality."[23] He advises this additional caution: "Some assume all too readily that to espouse anything other than a fundamentalist stance towards the Bible means to devalue it."[24] The Bible is not an all-or-nothing proposition. In spite of its flaws, it is appreciated and valued. There are many differences and variations within the multiple Fundamentalist denominations. Some espouse themes and concepts not included in the Five Fundamentals.

SIMILARITIES BETWEEN EARLY
CHRISTIANITY AND FUNDAMENTALISM

The attitude of early Christianity toward other known world religions is as rigid and intransigent as the unyielding position taken by most Fundamentalists. In the Roman world, all gods and religions were respected; they thrived side-by-side. Judaism was even allowed its one God, but they did not proselyte. This harmonious cohabitation changed with the advent of Christianity. When Christians came upon the scene, the drive for the one true right religion commenced; all others were wrong. Six centuries later, borrowing from Judaism, Christianity, and Gnosticism, Islam would pick up that theme.

Another defining characteristic of a fundamentalist mindset is its perception of history and preoccupation with a "golden" past that should be maintained and relived at some future point. In fact, survival of the future depends upon return to this glorious "golden" time. This perspective is obvious in the names of certain denominational branches or sects: Primitive Baptist Church, Primitive Christian Church, Primitive Advent Christian Church, Primitive Methodist Church, and so on. Some do not use the defining prefix "Primitive," but their name implies an association with that pristine era of Christ and the Apostles: Apostolic Lutheran Church of America, Apostolic Christian Church, Anabaptists, Mennonite, Amish, Strict Baptists, Old Order German Baptist Brethren, Biblical Way Church of Our Lord Jesus Christ, Church of Christ, and so on.[25]

Most of these sects emulate the state of original primitive Christianity in doctrine, liturgy, structure, and lifestyle. Some, such as the Apostolic Christian Church, disallow musical instruments in worship, and all singing is a cappella. The Amish, Mennonites, and others eschew modern conveniences and modern clothing styles. The Old Order German Baptist Brethren split over the use of the automobile. A small branch of them still use horse and buggy, as do the Amish. A large number of the primitive order emphasizes born-again experiences, the literal interpretation of scripture, and speaking in tongues.

At some point in the development of early Christianity, a policy of exclusion was adopted. Only "true Christians" could belong. The baptismal creed was taken seriously. Backsliders were basically kicked out of the congregation. Along with this exclusive policy was the doctrine that Christianity was the only true Church and outside of it there was no salvation. Fundamentalists have similarities with the early Christian Church. With early Christianity they share a similar view of time and history. Survival of the future depends on a return to the primitive church of the glorious past. A policy of exclusion of nonbelievers practiced by the early Church is very similar to that practiced by many Fundamental branches of Protestantism.

SUMMARY

Today's Fundamentalism is a relatively modern phenomenon that began as a reaction to modernity. The basic tenets of Fundamentalism were first generated in a series of pamphlets written between 1910 and 1915 entitled "The Fundamentals," which were reduced to the "Five Points" generated by the 1910 General Assembly of the Northern Presbyterian: biblical inerrancy, the virgin birth of Christ, substitutionary atonement of Christ, bodily resurrection of Christ, and the historicity of miracles.

It is significant that the first tenet is biblical inerrancy. Without it, the others would not be tenable. Of the five, the one less commonly held is the substitutionary atonement that portrays God as punishing his Son. There is linkage among the remaining four to the extent that they all rely on each other. If one falls, the others fall with it. This reasoning suggests that, for Fundamentalists, salvation comes from "right belief" and not grace, a concept that aligns them with Gnosticism.

One is cautioned against lumping Fundamentalists into one theological mold. Not all Fundamentalists share every principle. In cases where they unanimously agree, emphasis often falls unevenly across the spectrum. There are differences and variations among the multiple denominations. Some have dominant themes that are not included in the "Five Fundamentals." Examples of those differences include snake handlers of Appalachian notoriety and foot-washing Baptists.

In some ways, current Fundamentalism is similar to primitive Christianity. Early Christianity, in a short period of time, understood its beliefs and practices as representative of the one true religion. All others were excluded from the circle of salvation. Some Fundamental denominations and sects are preoccupied with the "golden past" of the Church's history. This "golden" time should be maintained and relived at some future time.

PART III

GNOSTICISM AND FUNDAMENTALISM

REVIVAL OF THE GNOSTIC HERESY

FUNDAMENTALISM

DESPITE THE NEARLY TWO MILLENNIA SEPARATING THEM, Gnosticism and Fundamentalism evolved in similar sociocultural matrices. Though much has changed, technologically speaking, the human condition has changed very little. This has been the general consensus in the numerous books and papers researched for this project. One book in particular caught my attention. It contained portions of a dialogue between Tobias Churton and Hans Jonas, names that might not resonate with the reader but are well known in religious studies.

Churton is a Gnostic scholar, writer, and film producer. Author of *The Gnostics*, he is best known for his documentary on Gnosticism for British television. Professor Jonas has been called the "old master" of Gnostic studies. He was writing about Gnosticism when he was a student of existentialist Martin Heidegger and New Testament scholar Rudolph Bultmann. This was in the 1920s, before Hitler came to power, long before Nag Hammadi. Because he was a Jew, Jonas's writings were restricted. Below is a segment of that lengthy interview Churton conducted in 1986 with Professor Jonas in his home in New Rochelle, New York:[1]

> *Churton*: I have been putting forth the thesis that we live in times with remarkable parallels with this period . . . the fear of cosmic catastrophe, apocalyptic expectation, boredom with institutional religion and alienation from the business of running the Empire and being part of that.
>
> *Jonas*: Oh yes, certainly they are the main ones. . . . There is certainly widespread disease in the modern mind concerning this age-old question of what it is all about. . . . Are the concerns of the day, the pressing needs of day-to-day existence, is that all there is to it? . . . a kind of nihilism . . . of not knowing what the standards are . . . a sign that something is out of joint . . . and we hear these old voices which tell us that the out-of-jointness is not just the accident of a particular situation but belongs to man's being in the world, but that our roots may be somewhere else—that we may be exiles.
>
> *Churton*: What was there in the historical situation of the second century Empire which might have promoted this feeling?

Jonas: major dislocations of national cultures. From the conquest of Alexander the
Great (334–323 B.C.), the establishment of cosmopolitan Hellenistic (Greek-
influenced) civilization . . . national traditions driven underground but in their
subterranean survival they underwent certain changes . . . which bred also the
spirit of rebelliousness. The official dominant culture which was then taken
over by the Roman Empire . . . did not express the indigenous spirit of the
conquered in its new urban civilization.
Churton: So the individual became a part of the machine.
Jonas: Yes.

"The individual became a part of the machine." That one sentence caught my eye.
That same individual is the individual of today: rootless, overwhelmed, fearful of
losing identity. In that same interview Churton made the following statement:
"All over the Empire, people were going beyond the received culture in search of
a penetrating vision of life which made sense to them."[2] Unsurpisingly, there was
a scramble for meaning among a multitude of religions and sects. People were
trying to latch onto anything with half a promise of hope and salvation. They
needed something more than the bare "isness," the out-of-jointness to which
Jonas refers. This is the cultural matrix from which Christianity and Gnosticism
sprang. Another polyglot cultural milieu produced a similar theological defense
against a different machine, a different brand of modernity: Fundamentalism.

The fact that all three—early Christianity, Gnosticism, and Fundamentalism—were diverse and broken into myriad representations is another reflection of the fragmentation of their cultures. Gnosticism had as many schools of
thought as devotees, certainly teachers. Christianity was more complex then it is
now. Pagels underscores this range of mixture: "Contemporary Christianity, as
diverse and complex as we find it, actually may show more unanimity than the
Christian churches of the first and second centuries."[3] Ehrman presents a similar
perspective:

> It may be difficult to imagine a religious phenomenon more diverse than modern
> day Christianity . . . all this diversity of belief and practice, and the intolerance
> that occasionally results, makes it difficult to know whether we should think of
> Christianity as one thing or lots of things, whether we should speak of Christianity
> or Christianities. What could be more diverse than this variegated phenomenon,
> Christianity in the modern world? . . . Christianity in the ancient world . . . the
> practices and beliefs found among people who called themselves Christian were
> so varied that the differences between Roman Catholics, Primitive Baptists, and
> Seventh-Day Adventists pale by comparison.[4]

A product of this more recent swirling theological mix is Fundamentalism, which
emerged in response to the onset of Darwinism, liberal theology, and a growing
secularism due primarily to the Industrial Revolution. The machine was back.
And so was Gnosticism . . . though in a different form.

In a recent prominent national publication, Anglican Bishop Nicholas Thomas
Wright is quoted as saying, "the Gnostics were more like contemporary American

fundamentalists than most liberal-minded of Gnostic supporters would like to acknowledge."[5] Religious critic Harold Bloom makes similar comments: "Mormons and Baptists call themselves Christians but like most Americans they are closer to ancient Gnostics than to early Christians."[6] Then again: "Gnosticism, the most negative of all ancient negative theologies, emerges again in the Southern Baptists."[7] Protestant theologian Philip Lee joins the chorus: "Despite the vast cultural differences between North American Protestantism and ancient Gnosticism, parallels of the two innovations can no longer be ignored."[8]

Are these accurate statements? Do they truly characterize current religious expressions of Fundamentalism? Are the comparisons with Gnosticism, ancient or modern, justified? If so, what is the nature of the relationship between Gnosticism and Fundamentalism? Is there any historical cause and effect? Is Fundamentalism part of an ongoing, though dormant, form of religion, one that has surfaced from time to time over the centuries with dogmas and behaviors that suggest a linkage to classical Gnosticism? Or is it a unique religious phenomenon endemic to the American scene, a product of its rugged pioneer individualism?

These are all legitimate questions and drive us back to the core concepts of Gnosticism and Fundamentalism previously outlined in Chapters 2 and 7. The material in this book will demonstrate not only that Gnosticism is back but also that it is back with a Fundamentalist persona, clothed in Fundamentalist themes and terminology.

SIMILARITIES BETWEEN CHRISTIAN GNOSTICISM AND FUNDAMENTALISM

Why are so many people, Christians or otherwise, interested in the Nag Hammadi texts, which are writings considered hostile and destructive to the Christian faith? Philip Lee posed that rhetorical question a few decades ago: "Perhaps the answer is that modern readers find in this literature an immediacy which claims their attention. These Gnostic ideas strike a familiar chord for modern ears: we sense that we have heard something before—or something very much like them."[9] We have heard it before and continue to hear it daily. Surf television or radio stations daily and you will see and hear the message of the fastest growing religion in Christianity: Fundamentalism. People are listening. They feel rootless, caught in a mood of despair, fearful of losing their identity . . . angry . . . trapped in a machine. The message of their denominations no longer interfaces with their needs. The words and rituals no longer resonate. That formal institutional church they had depended on has become a dinosaur. They are looking for a sudden infusion of hope, an espresso cure, straight IV therapy, an injection that goes straight to the spiritual heart and revives instantaneously.

Little has changed in the history of American religion: "Since the time of the first Great Awakening, there has been within North American Protestantism a tendency to seek a quick religious *fix*, so that in one brilliant moment a single solution may be found to all the problems of life."[10] This is the American way.

This is the message we have heard before, the reason ancient texts resonate to our modern ears. It seems to be intellectually satisfying for some people to divide life and the world into the "good" and the "evil" and "right" and "wrong."

DUALISTIC REALITY: SPIRIT VERSUS MATTER

The cradles of Gnosticism and dualism were Persia (Iran and Iraq) and the deserts of Syria and Egypt—Mithraism, Zoroastrianism, Jewish Apocalypticism. The philosophical orientation of these systems is not reality-oriented. Their myths and patterns of behavior are not reflective of reality. Their ontology (philosophy of being) is grounded more in fantasy, flights of fancy, illusion, and make-believe. In Gnostic literature and theology, this simplistic worldview is persistent and universally expressed. There is no attempt to veil its imagery or symbols. Matter, or flesh, is evil. Spirit is good. There was no in-between. It was a clear-cut way of making sense of a congested world.

For some, dualism and Gnosticism are synonymous.[11] Dualism is certainly not a foreign concept to Christianity. It is ever present in the New Testament and in some parts of the Old Testament and the Apocrypha. That is hard scriptural fact. Themes in the Gospel of John and Letters of Paul are unmistakably dualistic. They are conspicuous in the Gospel of John. When the writer (or writers) speaks of light and darkness, the spiritual versus the physical world, he is in the realm of dualism. Though he does not speculate about the divine or lower worlds, Paul's letters are replete with the antithesis of flesh and spirit, where "flesh" represents fallen humanity. Perkins expresses that "Paul's perception of the flesh as the entry point for the sinful desires that ultimately bring death to humans unless they receive the Spirit of Christ comes very close to what one finds in Gnostic mythologizing."[12] This dualism of evil and good, flesh versus spirit, surfaces in the synoptic gospels and Johannine epistles, which, most scholars agree, were targeted by the writer specifically against a Gnostic group or sect that had broken away from the Church.

These dualistic themes within the New Testament, however, are within the context of an incarnated Christ, "The word became flesh" (John 1:14). They are pulled together, gathered into that singular event and person, so the polarities, the contradictions, are subsumed and held in balanced tension. Except in parts of the Gospel of John, a theological dialectic is maintained between the humanity of Christ and His divinity. Conflicts would rage about this issue for centuries. The strife continued through the Councils of Nicaea (325 CE) and Chalcedon (451 CE) where the two natures of Christ, the divine and the human, were hammered out and articulated in creedal form.[13] The dualism of Gnosticism and Fundamentalism, of the physical world versus the spiritual world, is another matter. Most scholars contend that they are not only imbalanced but also significantly skewed toward the divine pole of the theological spectrum.

Where is dualism, the splitting of reality into physical and spiritual (evil and good) compartments, evident in Fundamentalism? On the surface it is not openly manifested. Nothing in its creedal statements, resolutions, or "Five Fundamentals" overtly states that the Spirit is good; matter is evil. There are no seminary classes in conservative schools of theology labeled, "Dualism 101." It is neither an obvious theme preached from pulpits nor sung specifically from hymnals. Dualism is not among the Fundamentalist "formulas" one hears—sin, salvation, judgment, redemption, atonement, and so on. But dualism is there. It is imbedded in the themes of evil flesh and saving spirit. Dualism is evident when one speaks of the bad world and the need to set oneself apart from that world by leading a spirit-filled, or spiritual, life . . . by *knowing* Jesus. It is implied in any messages one hears about a God who is good and a Satan or devil who is bad.[14]

Gnostics and Fundamentalists agree that the material, physical world is evil and irredeemable. Matter cannot be justified or remedied. Materiality is denounced; spirit is good. Only the spirit can overcome evil. Only by *knowing* the Redeemer, says Gnosticism, can one escape the dark world of ignorance and incomprehension and be saved into the world of Eternal Light. In Fundamentalism, only by *knowing* Christ and accepting Him as savior can one abide in His spirit and be saved from the evil world.

This conceptual framework and nomenclature are identical with Gnosticism. However, Gnostics are not saved from sin, as Fundamentalists are, but from ignorance and incomprehension. (The case could be made that "knowing Christ" and "knowing" and "believing" for Fundamentalists are signs of comprehension. The Fundamental concept of knowing Christ comes very close to Gnostic comprehension, which places salvation in control of the knower or believer.) The Fundamentalist's sin is of the flesh, of the world. The spirit is of the other world. We are back to the two operant spheres of evil and good. The spiritual guide, or Redeemer, will save us and deliver us to the heavenly realm.

The renunciation of the world—of worldly ambition, appetites, and goods—is indispensable for Gnostic and Fundamentalist spiritual salvation. Separation from the concerns of humanity and manifestation of a new heavenly identity is inextricably bound up with their view of humanity.

DUALISTIC HUMANITY: SPIRITUAL VERSUS PHYSICAL

Gnostic and Fundamentalist dualism splits reality, which affects their understanding of humanity. An alternate Webster's definition for "dualism" is "a doctrine that man has two natures, physical and spiritual."[15] The theme recapitulates: flesh is evil; spirit is good. In Gnosticism this division is more complicated, primarily because there were different types of Gnosticism. Two types were predominant within Christian Gnosticism: Docetist and Separatist. These two forms of Gnosticism have been previously discussed and are important for any comparison with Fundamentalism's understanding of humanity.

The Docetist portrayal of humanity logically follows from its dualistic view of the world and absolute divine Christology. Humans are made of flesh, which is evil. Yet residing in the elect is the divine spark that connects them with the divine redeemer who reunites them with the Divine Light from which they have been separated. This can happen only through the attainment of *gnosis*, knowledge necessary for salvation.

The Separatists, on the other hand, advanced a Christology in which the Godhead partially entered Christ at baptism and left him at his crucifixion. This form of dualism, an attempt at compromise with the proto-orthodox Christian concept of two natures, allowed them to have it both ways. They could portray Jesus and Christ as distinct entities, yet maintain Jesus's humanity without sacrificing Christ's divinity. Previously noted, the Separatists divided humanity into three groups, two that are precursors of Fundamentalism: (1) the *pneumatics*, or spiritual ones whose spirituality placed them superior to others, and (2) the *psychics*, guided by literal interpretation and by legalism. Both of these are characteristic of conservative theology. Theoretically, they articulate a theology of grace. But in actuality, salvation is through "knowing" Jesus and a personal decision related to that "knowing." The operant of salvation is the "knower," not the One known. The grace of God is a dominant theme of Fundamental theology, but behaviorally it is deemphasized, soft-pedaled. Each person "works out," that is, evokes, his or her own personal salvation.

A "theory of humanity" is not explicitly stated in the "Five Fundamentals," and little is expressed in *The Fundamentals*. Like Gnosticism, there is no particular document Fundamentalists can identify as their "theory of humanity." Fisher Humphreys and Philip Wise briefly address the Fundamentalist understanding of humankind in the segment on "The Substitutionary Atonement." Otherwise limited information was available about Fundamentalist orientation toward humanity.[16] The issue is not addressed in J. I. Packer's book entitled *Fundamentalism and the Word of God*.[17] One of the reasons might be an apparent obsession with Fundamentalists in their defense of the "Five Fundamentals" with emphasis on the inerrant, literal scripture and the historicity of miracles. Another might be a theological imbalance. Their primary doctrines are the "Five Fundamentals." Even in *The Fundamentals*, written between 1910 and 1915, there is a heavy emphasis on Christ but little about his humanity and there was nothing about the Trinity. Based on our limited knowledge, what is the Fundamentalist view of humanity?

The Fundamentalist understanding of humankind is less complex than the Gnostic positions, but it is unmistakably dualistic. Following along Protestant doctrinal lines, from which it basically evolved, Fundamentalism asserts that humanity exists in a fallen, sinful state. This fallen state began in the Garden of Eden when Adam and Eve acted against God's wishes and partook of fruit from the Tree of the Knowledge of Good and Evil. In this fallen state humans are totally separated from God. Their only hope of salvation from sin and assurance of reentry to the Garden is through the forgiveness of sin by faith in Christ. The requirement on the human side of the equation is repentance. That encapsulation is oversimplified but a fair summation of the Fundamentalist perception of the human situation. Essentially, flesh is evil. The soul, which resides in the body, will rise to join the Father . . . return home to Eden on the "last day."

How do Fundamentalists and Gnostics differ in their understanding of human-ity? The answer is difficult because the themes of both interpretations are complex. They do agree that flesh is evil and bad; the spirit is divine and good. Both agree that humankind is fallen and needs to be saved; for the Gnostics from ignorance and the Fundamentalists from sin. For Fundamentalism, the inner spirit is cor-rupt. Both are capable of communing one-on-one with the transcendent Supreme Spirit. For the Gnostics this is made possible by an inner "divine spark" possessed by only a select few. For the Fundamentalists, the Spirit intervenes, creating a channel of communion with the corrupt inner spirit. In almost all forms of Gnos-ticism, and some brands of Fundamentalism, this divine spark or pneumatic spirit is not available to everyone but only in a select few. Some Baptists, particularly Primitive, hold this view.[18] Mormons, Pentecostals, Church of God, and Seventh-day Adventists maintain this belief, in practice if not doctrinally.[19]

SALVATION

The end goal of both Gnosticism and Fundamentalism is salvation for the indi-vidual, not the community. Salvation for Gnostics and Fundamentalists is individ-ual-centered. Knowledge is the common denominator. The similarity of concepts of knowledge and salvation for Early Gnosticism and Christianity created major problems at the Church in Corinth: "Their ecstatic identification with a heavenly Christ led the Corinthian opponents to stress the freedom of the true believer from the restraints of the material world. . . . The individual attains immortality and freedom in knowing the Savior; not through the death of Christ on the cross or some future resurrection of the body."[20]

In Gnosticism, individuals discover their true identity and receive eternal life, by "knowing" the living divine redeemer, not because of his death on a cross. In Fundamentalism, individuals accept and "know" Christ as their personal savior, a kind of "Gnostic knowing of Jesus through divine acquaintance."[21] As previously indicated, the Fundamentalist concept of "knowing Christ" comes very close to Gnostic understanding or comprehension, which places salvation within the con-trol of the "knower" or "believer," as though it was a possession. In other words, one is saved by "knowing" and not by faith or believing. In the Gnostic and Fundamentalist view, movement is from the individual to the redeemer; the indi-vidual knows the redeemer. With orthodoxy and proto-orthodoxy, the emphasis is on the opposite end of the polarity; the Redeemer knows the individual. Bloom strikes at the heart of the issue: "The most aggressive of Protestantism is no Prot-estantism at all but a pure out-flaring again of an ancient Gnosis. The Jesus who is sought is already both principle and particle in the soul that seeks him."[22]

In Gnosticism, "the concentration on self is a natural result of the passion-ate need to escape the world . . . an escape by withdrawal into the self."[23] Lee draws similarities between Gnosticism and Narcissism. The latter is based upon the beautiful boy, Narcissus, who fell in love with his own reflection in a pool. He was unable to break away from what he saw and thus atrophied and perished.

Gnosticism and Fundamentalism have a savior. The difference is that one saves from ignorance and the other from sin. Both save the individual from imprisonment in an alien material world or, as expressed earlier by Churton and Jonas, the machine. Gnostics do not look for salvation from sin but "from unconsciousness and incomprehension."[24] In the Gospel of Thomas, knowledge rather than behavior is the basis of salvation. In Gnosticism, self-knowledge is the guiding principle. In Fundamentalism, knowledge of the Redeemer and self-knowledge are keys to salvation. The latter is a different kind of self-knowledge. The individual reflects inwardly upon guilt. A negative self-knowledge or self-awareness is created by illumination from divine light above, then outwardly upon the Redeemer, who must become known in a spiritual sense. The Gnostic says "I know my true self" and the Fundamentalist acclaims "I know Jesus."[25] But this Jesus was capable of being known through the divine spirit.

Gnosticism is basically a return to salvation under the law. "The Gnostics believed that salvation must be earned. They believed the individual must make a science out of his own redemption."[26] This also sounds very much like Scientology, where one works through a number of spiritual levels to attain the pure spiritual self through a process called "auditing."[27]

In Fundamentalism, one achieves salvation through personal decision.

This is not a divine act of pure grace and acceptance from above. This is conditional grace. One *must* accept, and "know," Christ before salvation is possible. There is no other way. This is one of the results of dualism. Religions advocating their way is not only *the* way, but the *only* way, imply an either–or dualistic split in reality. This is Fundamentalism. It is Gnosticism.

DIVINE REDEEMER

The most significant similarity between the two religions, the keystone of both and the one upon which this book is predicated, is their concept of divine redeemer, the Anointed One, the Christ.[28] On the surface the two Redeemers appear quite different. The Gnostic Redeemer is all divine. The Fundamentalist Christ is divine, but he is also human. This concept is unthinkable to Gnostics. At a doctrinal level Protestant Fundamentalists state that "the Word became flesh." In principle, their doctrine of Incarnation is orthodox, mainstream. But when we leave the airy heights of doctrine and descend into the hands-on domain of reality, particularly scriptural interpretation, does the Incarnation hold?

For proto-Orthodox, Orthodox, and mainstream Christianity, "The Word became flesh." This is *the* fundamental upon which Christianity was founded and based. God became human "and made his dwelling among us" (John 1: 14). This is incarnational theology that destroys all dualism. Everything comes together in the person of Christ; all dissonant elements are united in His Being. This is *the* Incarnation, and any deviation from it was considered unorthodox or heretical. It was the major difference between Christian proto-orthodoxy and Christian

Gnosticism. The Gnostic Christians' redeemer was a phantomlike figure and only "appeared" to be human.

Doctrinally, Fundamentalists give a tacit cognitive (literal) nod to Christ's humanity. At deeper more visceral levels, with their near-obsessive need for inerrancy and purity, it is very difficult for them to conceive of *the Christ* as capable of doubt, fear, despair, sadness, depression, or loneliness, or to see him as human, of being compatible with sin . . . of being sin. They are much more comfortable with Luke's patient, serene, and resigned righteous martyr who, during his crucifixion from the cross, utters, "Father into your hands I commit my spirit" (23:46); as opposed to the hostile, lonely, despairing, and agitated Jesus of Mark who becomes "deeply distressed and troubled" (14:33); whose soul is "overwhelmed with sorrow to the point of death" (14:34); who asks his Father to "take this cup from me" (14:36); and who, eventually, from the cross, cries out "My God, my God, why have you forsaken me" (15:34)?[29] In short, for Fundamentalists, divinity dominates humanity.

This is the key similarity between Gnosticism and Fundamentalism. Their redeemers never achieve humanity; they never become flesh and blood. They never become real but evolve into fantasies and magic that many scholars argue is the Oriental mystical cradle from which Gnosticism came. It is easy to see how this type of one-sided Christology might affect one's approach to the Bible and scriptural interpretation. The Bible truly becomes the *divine*.

Is this overemphasis on the divine one of the reasons most Fundamental dominations have no creed, nothing that anchors their Redeemer, their Christ, in history? In their anti-intellectualism and inward focus on "getting saved" and being "born again," have they discarded history, including the Christ of history? Are they so focused on the inner experience that their interpretation of scripture is based solely on that spiritual connection? The scripture it interprets, predictably, is pure and untainted, a word that never becomes "flesh." Along this line of thinking, Harold Bloom asserts that "without the Real Presence of the body of Christ in a communion service, the Baptist is alone with his Bible."[30]

Mysticism

In most normative Western religious traditions—Roman Catholic, Eastern Orthodox, mainline Protestantism, Islam, Judaism—the key elements are institutional and supported by history and dogma. God is an external, transcendent Being. Some within these traditions bring the deity much closer. They profess an acquaintance or knowledge of a God who is not transcendent, but within. This internal God has been there before time. These are the mystics and visionaries. They are Gnostics. They are also Fundamentalists.

Gnostics and Fundamentalists have no intermediary. True knowledge comes through spiritual immediacy: "Like Baptists, Quakers and many others, the Gnostic is convinced that whoever receives the spirit communicates directly with the divine. One of Valentinus' students, the Gnostic teacher Heracleon (c. 160) says 'that at first, people believe because of the testimony of others . . .' but then 'they come to believe from the truth itself.'"[31] In one Gnostic initiation ritual "after invoking the spirit," the leader "commands the candidate to speak in prophecy, to demonstrate that the person has received direct contact with the divine."[32]

Both of these passages resonate with anyone who has attended a revival, tent meeting, or Quaker service. The spontaneous outpouring of emotion is evidence of a perception that some individuals have connected with the Almighty.[33] Unobstructed by rules of ritual and unimpeded by reason, the spirit moves freely. For Gnostics and Fundamentalists, the spirit truly does move where it will. Or does it?

Gnosticism and Fundamentalism are spirit-dominated religions. Central to both is the spiritual person and their view that humanity is divided between spirit and flesh. Spiritual in this sense does not mean communication with the dead, though elements of that are found in some fringe sects. The intended meaning is focused on the spirit existing within the body (the divine spark, "inner light") and capable of ascending from that temporary residence.[34] This spirit is able to have direct and unfiltered communication with a Supreme Spirit. It is a form of divine communication necessary to the existence of Gnosticism and Fundamentalism. It is mysticism.

Webster's definition of mysticism is "the doctrine that it is possible to achieve communion with God through contemplation and love without the medium of human reason; any doctrine that asserts the possibility of attaining knowledge of spiritual truths through intuition acquired by fixed meditation."[35] A mystic is "one who professes to undergo mystical experiences by which he intuitively comprehends truths beyond human understanding."[36]

The word derives from the Greek *mustikos*, or "initiate," as in initiate of the Eleusinian Mysteries and *musteria*, or "initiation." In ancient mystery religions, from which Gnosticism partly sprang, the goal of the initiate was to achieve communion or conscious awareness with God. This was accomplished through direct experience, intuition, or insight, and included the belief that such experience was a source of knowledge and Wisdom. This achievement of consciousness with God was also one's destiny.[37] Maintaining a relationship with mainstream religions, mystery religions often go into the esoteric beyond mainstream doctrine. Kabbalah is a mystical movement within Judaism, as is Sufism within Islam and Gnosticism within Christianity. Some argue Christianity is a mystic sect that arose from Judaism.

Mysticism has been examined and written about extensively. It is included in this discussion because of its dualistic nature, spiritualistic knowledge, the immediacy that knowledge is received by the "spiritual person," and the weight of authority given the message because of the manner it was received. In mystical knowledge, finding God in yourself is equivalent to finding self-knowledge or achieving self-discovery. In essence, this is a conversion experience—Gnostic or Fundamentalist. One achieves, "Not only a spiritual state, but a state of mind."[38]

Mysticism presupposes dualism, the dichotomy of spirit and matter, severance of the spiritual from the physical.[39] It allows people to claim that special spiritual knowledge separates them from those lacking it. For Gnostics, this self-knowledge is illuminated by the God within and raises one from the imprisonment of ignorance and incomprehension. For the Fundamentalist, it is self-knowledge of guilt and need for repentance illuminated by the God ("divine spark") within. This kind of spiritual knowledge raises one from the bondage of sin but also from the physical bondage of death. The content of the two approaches is different; the dynamics are virtually identical.

Fundamentalists vehemently deny they believe in human possession of a "divine spark." Behaviorally, however, their actions are contradictory. They do believe there is an ignition within the human spirit, an ignition not caused by the human spirit. The process presupposes a point of divine contact. The contact occurs in such manner, and with such spiritual force for them, it is undeniable. This is the mystical element, the spiritual immediacy that makes the receiver of the message or illumination one with the Messenger or Illuminator. This is the drawn line between insiders and outsiders, the relegation of faithful into inner and outer circles. It is clearly dualism. The consequences are divisiveness, separation: "As in the Fourth Gospel, recognition and knowing the true identity of the revealer separate the elect from the rest of humanity. . . . Without the knowledge that leads the believer to a spiritual identification with the revealer, cultic actions have no effect."[40]

The "born again," second birth phenomenon in America (and transported abroad) is an example of the intimation of divinity. It is present in most American Fundamentalism. Mormon Founder, Joseph Smith, ranks in the category with the great visionaries of Christian mystics, Kabbalists, and Islamic Sufi. It is argued by some that when Smith replaced monism with polytheism, every Mormon became a little god. Pentecostals, Assembly of God, and Seventh-day Adventists belong in this tradition. The distance between God and humanity is lessened, in some cases obliterated all together. In the words of Gilbert Keith Chesterton: "That Jones shall worship the god within him turns out ultimately to mean that Jones shall worship Jones."[41] Therefore, the spirit moves where Jones chooses for it to move.

INTERPRETATION OF SCRIPTURE

"When I use a word," Humpty Dumpty said in rather a scornful tone, "it means just what I choose it to mean—nothing more nor less."
—Lewis Carroll, *Alice in Wonderland*

Everything we read must be interpreted. Otherwise, words are just words. A society where one learns that the words in the Bible are infallible, without error, and were not to be challenged eliminates the possibility of interpretation. "To everything there is a season," cites the preacher of Ecclesiastes. In view of the multitude of translations and interpretations, he might well have written "For every word there is an interpretation." Different branches, sects, and denominations of Christianity abound and with them come innumerable interpretations of texts.

How do people come up with their interpretations? One of the boldest, and most succinct, statements regarding how people interpret texts has been recently made by Dr. Bart D. Ehrman. In his book *Misquoting Jesus, The Story Behind Who Changed the Bible and Why*, he writes,

> Reading a text necessarily involves interpreting a text. . . . [T]exts do not speak for themselves. If texts could speak for themselves, then everyone honestly and openly reading a text would agree on what the text says. . . . Texts are interpreted, and they are interpreted (just as they were written) by living, breathing human beings, who can make sense of the texts only by explaining them in light of their other knowledge, explicating their meaning, putting the words of the text "in other words."
> . . . The only way to make sense of a text is to read it, and the only way to read it is by putting it in other words, and the only way to put it in other words is by having other words to put it into, and the only way to have other words to put it into is that you have a life, and the only way that you have a life is by being filled with desires, longings, needs, wants, beliefs, perspectives, worldviews, opinions, likes, dislikes—and all other things that make human beings human. And so to read a text is, necessarily, to change a text.[42]

Ehrman goes on to describe how the scribes of the New Testament literally put the words "in other words."

Mystical knowledge also applies to the interpretation of scripture. Upon reading holy texts and receiving revelations from them, the mystic attributes the source of the revelation to an internal experience.[43] "Beauty is in the eye of the beholder" becomes "the revelation is in the internal experience of the reader."

This mystical methodology leads not only to a highly subjective interpretation of scripture but also, ultimately, to solipsism—a philosophical term meaning that only the individual exists, all else is illusion. Religious viewpoints of this type abound in Gnosticism and Fundamentalism. There is no central authority, no universal guiding principle or set of principles. Interpretation of the Word of God is democratized to a point that some contend interpretational anarchy reigns: "No one can tell the free soul how to interpret the Bible, or how not to interpret it. The doctrine destroys Fundamentalism by sanctioning endless interpretative possibilities so that the weird metaphor of a 'literal' or 'inerrant' reading totally vaporizes."[44] The early Church fathers saw the implications of this logic. Its impact on the young Church could affect attempts to establish authority. Besides the unrealized eschaton (last day), this may be another reason for the more rapid development of organization and hierarchy.

Though the Roman Catholic Church is a broad tent and mystics dwell within its theological drip-line, Catholicism represents the opposite of subjective ideology. Word and tradition are authoritative. Dissenters are quickly brought into line or excommunicated. No atmosphere is allowed for fragmentation of doctrine or scriptural interpretation, deviation from the orthodox, or "correct teaching"[45]: "since the death of the apostles, believers accept the word of the priests and bishops, who have claimed, from the second century, to be their only legitimate heirs."[46]

Fundamentalists, on the other hand, reject this linear succession of spiritual power. In that respect, they are descendants of the Gnostics, where the divine word has meaning only within a personal, subjective context. For Gnostics, and Fundamentalists, true revelation is unavailable to outsiders. Gnostics and Fundamentalists apply this principle to the interpretation of scripture. For Gnostics, comprehending the true Scriptures was very important, but it was not easy. *Gnosis* involved not only comprehending the true Scripture but also the comprehension had to be an understanding of the *hidden* teachings within the scripture. Embedded in the Scripture were secret messages that only "The Knowers" could decipher. These secret messages were accessible to the *pneumatics*, not the more literal-minded *psychics*. This accessibility to hidden, secret messages is mysticism.

Fundamentalists, whether Christian, Islamic, or Hindu, tend to read and interpret texts selectively. Because they are spirit-led, which each of the major religions interpret differently, the text can mean whatever they determine it to mean. Context, which also means history, is crucial to understanding and interpreting any textual passage. But with mystical methodology, it was never part of the interpretive equation.

The Gnostic *pneumatics* operate on a pure spiritual plane with no intermediaries required. A conduit, immediacy of communication, connects them with the deity. Special knowledge was assessable only to the initiated,[47] the saved, who had direct access to God without going through any bishop or priest. This allowed them freedom to interpret scripture as they chose and often through the slippery filter of symbolism, something they accused the apologists of doing. Origen, in particular, was targeted. The Gnostic *psychics*, however, who exist between the spiritual and physical worlds, attain salvation through good conduct, observing the law and a literal interpretation of scriptures. The *hylics*, or earthly ones, are a lost cause. Within the Gnostic camp there were literalists, such as Marcion, and those who interpreted using allegory, such as Valentinus. Because of the underlying subjective process, there was no universal Gnostic method of interpreting scripture. To the early Church fathers, it became imperative they all fall.

On the issue of scriptural interpretation, Fundamentalists are clear and, for the most part, united. Holy Scripture is inerrant and to be interpreted literally. This is their authority: the unerring word. Between Genesis 1:1 and Revelation 22:21 are instructions for righteous living and salvation. One need only read and follow. This works also for authoritarian religions, only the interpretation filters downward from a hierarchical apex. The spirit moves only one way from one source.

But Fundamentalists operate on a democratized, subjective plane of spiritual immediacy, which ultimately results in no authority, that is, anarchy. It is not unusual to find a touch of magic in this concept of spiritual immediacy. Not only can scripture be interpreted by any one who is spirit-filled but also the physical bound Bible itself assumes a seductive aura. After imbuing it with godlike purity, "what is left is the Bible as physical object, limp and leather, a final icon or magical talisman."[48] Individuals with problems need only open the Bible and the first words their eyes encounter will offer guidance, solace, and address the solution. Interpretation becomes based upon the movement of the spirit at any given moment and in any given circumstance.[49]

The implications of a literal interpretation of an inerrant Word of God are far-reaching. They go to the heart of the Incarnation. Gnostics and Fundamentalists uphold spiritual *and* literal interpretations. Spiritual means spiritual immediacy, movement of spirit without reality orientation, without context, as required by objective interpretation. Literal means "following exactly the wording of the original, but also as 'matter-of-fact . . . restricted to the facts.'"[50] When the Fundamentalists state that the Bible is the literal "Word of God," they mean a literalness uncorrupted by reality, one that is spiritually pure. This is a purely Gnostic concept.

Because of this dichotomy of spirit and flesh, the word does not become real in an incarnational, matter-of-fact "crucified, dead, and buried" sense presented by Matthew, Mark, Luke, John, Paul, and the early Church fathers. To the Fundamentalists, the Word is analogous to the pure spiritual Gnostic Christ, Docetic, or Separationist, who takes on the "appearance" of humanness but never becomes flesh and blood. This Christ is perfect in every way. In fact, the Gnostics expunged, or significantly edited, those passages referring to Christ's humanity (in the process violating their own literalism) when using Christian texts for their own purposes.[51] Therefore, by disavowing the human dimension, the Word of Fundamental theology does not, and cannot, become flesh.

Fundamentalism and Gnosticism hold no exclusive claim to an inerrant and infallible word. In 1854 the doctrine of the Immaculate Conception became the first such Roman Catholic proclamation. This was seen by many as a test case for the doctrine of papal infallibility, which followed in 1870. There are currently only three infallible doctrines in Catholicism. The third is the Assumption of Mary proclaimed in 1950. By "infallible" Catholics mean something that is affirmed only in relation to faith and doctrine. The principle is expressed by the Vatican Council in its efforts as guardians of the faith, a right they possess by divine authority. The Pope cannot merely speak and his statement be declared infallible. A doctrine becomes officially infallible only when the Pope makes the declaration ex cathedra, that is, while on the papal throne, in the seat of Peter.

It was no coincidence that Fundamentalist and Catholic doctrines of infallibility emerged within the same time frame. The Industrial Revolution was full throttle and modernity was making its initial assaults on traditional religion: "It remained for modern Catholicism, in erecting the bulwarks against modernity, to articulate the method of harmonizing tradition. The infallibility of the pope provides the church with a living tradition."[52] Roman Catholicism, however, does not hold the written scriptures to be infallible: "The Bible does not claim to be the sole authority of the church. . . . The authority of Scripture is not the authority of a naked book, but the authority of a book in process of being interpreted. Tradition is that by which Scripture is continually being interpreted. Therefore, the Council of Trent puts the authority of tradition on the same level with the authority of Scripture."[53]

VIEW OF THE CHURCH

Dualistic theology conceives dualistic cosmogony, which produces dualistic humanity, which generates dualistic community: outsiders versus insiders. "We might speak of 'exclusionists' and 'inclusionists' because Conservative Christians, unlike liberal Christians, tend to define the word Christian to exclude others—except their fellow conservative Christians."[54] The Gnostics did likewise. The Gnostic community was seen as a "secure zone of the spirit. . . . Its holiness is assured by divine action."[55] In other words, individual elitism becomes communal elitism. An individual who is "saved" belongs only to a like community of "saved" and together they form, as with the Gnostics of old, a "secure zone of the spirit." An individual is set against the unsaved who exist outside the circle: "The strongly docetic cast of Gnostic myth suggests a communal sense of separation from the larger social world."[56]

The elitist feature of Gnosticism may have represented the greatest danger to the early Church. Elitism, characteristic of its inherent dualism, is divisive. Groups and congregations splinter into factions. True believers are saved and belong on a higher spiritual plane, while the others are damned and relegated to a lower level. To combat this type of divisiveness, the early apologists chastised those who bragged of their own knowledge and spirituality, while disparaging that of others. Christian Gnostics often quoted Paul in their appeals: "For God does not show favoritism" (Romans 2:11). "You are all sons of God through faith in Christ Jesus. . . . There is neither Jew nor Greek, slave nor free, male nor female, for you are all one" (Galatians 3:26-28). "If I have the gift of prophesy . . . and all knowledge . . . but have not love, I am nothing" (I Corinthians 13: 1–2).

The turn Calvinism took in the new world created a "spiritual aristocracy" in New England.[57] During the great surge of revivalism those adhering to the "born again" concept were branded as "unconverted." For the elitist Old Lights one conversion, the first, was enough.

In terms of communal structure within the circle of saved, the Gnostics, consistent with their strong emphasis upon the individual, "had no interest in an ecclesiastical system . . . the value lay in the soul experience."[58] Hall agrees: "As is usual with philosophical groups, the Gnostics were individualists and opposed to any intense program of organization."[59] All of this blends with the Gnostic theory of immediate, mystical communication with the divine. Due to its essence—spontaneous, charismatic, open, free-flowing—this theory cannot fit any structure of authority and institutional framework. Gnosticism encourages insubordination to clerical authority.

Fundamentalists resist church hierarchy. Martin Luther had problems with Catholic hierarchy and its theology. It is the nature of spontaneous charisma to be at odds with a structure of authority. Radical democracy and egalitarian politics are more closely associated with Fundamental movements. The American Revolution was fueled by the Great Awakening of the 1730s and 1740s, with its emphasis on individuality, personal emotion, and detachment from ritual and ceremony. It also forged an individual freethinking firebrand named Patrick Henry.[60]

Based upon research available, the earliest Gnostic congregations were loosely organized along the principle of radical equality, the concept "priesthood of all believers" taken to its logical conclusion. The structure of authority was not vertical but horizontal. Individuals drew lots for clerical and priestly functions. There was no acknowledgment of distinctions. Various roles within the congregation rotated. One might read a scripture one service and lead hymns the next. Members participated equally in the government of the congregation or group. Matters at hand were left to casting lots: "They believed that since God directs everything in the universe, the way the lots fell expressed his choice."[61]

Though Fundamental church governments and congregations are not as egalitarian, the same principles apply. Compared to mainstream Christianity, the Fundamentalist mind is suspicious of hierarchy and organization along vertical lines. This characteristic is more evident in Quaker than Southern Baptist churches. Despite their protests against vertical organization, Baptists are more organized in that manner than some mainstream Protestant denominations. Fundamental denominations today are the by-product of the First and Second Great Awakenings. President George W. Bush clearly understands this hereditary linkage. It is arguably the reason for his election and the reason he returned to that segment of the populace in September of 2006 when he called for a Third Great Awakening in the battle against the forces of evil.

In their excessive emphasis on spiritual experience and rejection of materiality, Gnosticism and Fundamentalism have little use for the sacraments. The minimizing of sacraments with Fundamentalism may be related more to logistics than ideology. The sacramental utensils would not easily fit in the saddle bags of circuit riders and the distance between churches precluded frequent use of sacraments. This is one of the reasons Methodists today celebrate Holy Communion once a month, whereas their founder, John Wesley celebrated the sacrament two to three times a week. The emphasis of Gnosticism and Fundamentalism is on the individual experience, not outward participation in sacraments. The most significant event to occur at the altar or altar rail during the two Great Awakenings was not sacramental. It was the emotional experience of being born again: "It is significant that in the doctrinal tests so important to American fundamentalists for distinguishing between authentic Christianity and liberal heresy, the sacraments are never mentioned."[62]

Another commonality was their effects upon the established religions of their time. Gnosticism's impact upon the early Church differs from the impact of Fundamentalism upon mainstream Christianity in the twentieth and twenty-first century. Stanley Hall made this observation: "mysticism, because it is entirely an internal individual experience, worked a serious hardship upon formal religious organizations. If man's search for truth is inward to a spiritual core within himself, then formalized religions with their vast followings become comparatively inconsequential."[63] In short, Gnosticism and Fundamentalism create havoc for organized religion.

VIEW OF TIME AND HISTORY

Gnosticism and Fundamentalism, by their dualistic nature, are apocalyptic. With all apocalyptic theology, the theme is that the best is yet to be and destined to occur at the *eschaton*, or end of time. At that time, the evil powers of this earth will be defeated by the Divine Redeemer; the spiritual heavenly powers and a new eternal age will be ushered in. "Gnostics revolt against time. . . . The Gnostic hope is not that the clock will keep ticking, but that it will be mercifully stopped."[64]

Early American Fundamentalism had a similar philosophy. It was a hard, harsh world and the best was yet to be. Time is bifurcated, compartmentalized into a mythical past and future. Dualism again prevails. Gnostics and Fundamentalists have a problem with the present. The present is viewed as bad news that is getting no better, and it requires dealing with and facing this worldly reality. Gnosticism and Fundamentalism, by default (dualism again), are more otherworldly in their focus.

In its earliest stages, American Christianity was a religion of escapism that denied history. The only time worthy of focus was the eschaton, the last day. This was a day of harsh judgment but one of glory for the elect. One example of this in American homegrown religion is the Jehovah's Witnesses. For this religious group, the end of time came in 1975 at the completion of six thousands years of existence. Due to their extreme elitism, the rapture for Jehovah's Witnesses is not the rapture for everyone else. When the world did not end in 1843–45 according to the Millerite[65] expectation, the Seventh-day Adventists were born. The Mormons, who share similar apocalyptic leanings, fiercely believe Christ will come again and the New Jerusalem will be built on American soil. Little wonder America has been called "the most apocalyptic of nations."[66] All of these homegrown American original religions are Gnostic.

Gnosticism drew heavily from Jewish Apocalypticism. Fundamentalists draw heavily from the New Testament where Jesus is portrayed as a Jewish apocalyptic figure. The earliest doctrinal form of apocalypticism emerged in the 1800s with John Nelson Darby's (1800–1882)[67] doctrine of the Rapture where he combined a variety of passages in the New Testament, including Revelation. But the key scripture was 1 Thessalonians 4:15–18:

> According to the Lord's own word, we tell you that we who are still alive, who are left till the coming of the Lord, will certainly not precede those who have fallen asleep. For the Lord Himself will come down from heaven, with a loud command, with the voice of the archangel and with the trumpet call of God, and the dead in Christ will rise first. After that, we who are still alive and are left will be caught up together with them in the clouds to meet the Lord in the air. And so we will be with the Lord forever. Therefore encourage others with these words.

Cyrus Scofield popularized Darby's Rapture doctrine in his *Scofield Reference Bible* where the theme was promoted as Fundamentalism. From that seed it began to grow. More recently, this theological viewpoint found renewed popularity in the 1970s with Hal Lindsey's *Late Great Planet Earth* and Tim Lahaye's *Left Behind* series. It is ironic that "American Christian Fundamentalism, and the Islamic Shi'ite fundamentalism of Iran are rival heirs of Zoroastrian imaginings of the Last Things."[68]

MORALITY

Individual salvation, a key tenet of Gnosticism and Fundamentalism, tends to exclude a sense of community and communal responsibility. The same is true toward the world of nature and the natural order: "The Gnostic initiate was taught to acknowledge no responsibility. His ethic was to be one of complete freedom from any constraint or any obligation towards society and government regarding which he entertained the most pessimistic opinions. The world was in the iron control of evil powers."[69] Individual salvation shifts focus from Jesus's political ideal of bringing the kingdom into this world to the inner spirit or "divine spark." The welfare of the social order is ignored. Conversion is wholly inward. The experience of "knowing" Jesus is solitary and takes priority over corporate worship or social outreach.

This emphasis translates into an inner circle of believers versus an outer circle of unbelievers and, in turn, translates into a theology of communal elitist salvation versus the rest of the world. These are not underlying attitudes that promote social welfare and reform. Morality becomes an individual matter. Overtly expressed in Fundamentalism and directly associated with Gnosticism, this form of dualism is reflected in escape from the physical, that is, the physical body. Gnostics and Fundamentalists maintained a deep distrust of the body and its functions. This view led Gnostics to a docetic interpretation of Christ. It led the Fundamentalists to one that, if not docetic, is otherworldly and spiritually detached.

New England theologians took dualism and expanded it to its logical limits. Pleasure was wrong. Sex was wrong. "Urination and defecation were daily reminders of the inner corruption of human nature."[70] The emphasis was upon denial of pleasure. To engage in pleasure meant contamination of the spiritual self with the physical body, a mindset and practice followed by the ancient ascetic Gnostics. Sins of the flesh, or sexuality, have held center stage in American revivalism throughout the past century and into the twenty-first century. The dualistic split rears its head once again. Fundamentalists of this generation, and the Gnostics of old, are unable to accept sex as a gift from the Creator. They are unable to bring a theology of incarnation home to the human body.

Gnostic writings emphasize control over individual passions. So do Paul, John, and other New Testament writers. This is a common theme throughout Christianity, particularly in the monastic movements where a similar dualism surfaces. This puritanical theme is present in Hawthorne's *The Scarlet Letter*.

Some conservative denominations, such as the Mennonites and Amish, enforce dress codes in support of purity. Fundamentalist Muslim countries have passed laws requiring a woman to wear a *hijab*, the traditional public headdress for Muslim women. It is illegal for women to wear dresses that show their legs or high heel shoes considered capable of sexual arousal.[71] There are other reasons unrelated to religious preference for these social prohibitions, but they stem from that basic driving principal: dualism where two forces comprise reality and battle relentlessly for its heart and soul.

Asceticism and self-denial are persistent and ongoing subjects in Christianity. Though probably not created by Gnosticism, both Gnosticism and Christianity have absorbed these characteristics from other sources and appropriated them to their own theological ends. Strict asceticism, separation from the material world, leads to knowledge of God. Whether the Essenes belonged to this school is still in question.

With Asceticism, dualism again is the dominant underlying factor. The Gnostics, "who ridiculed the idea of bodily resurrection frequently devalued the body, and considered its actions (sexual acts, for example) unimportant to the spiritual person."[72] "Because nothing is quite so earthy as sexuality, it is not hard to understand why the Gnostics did everything they could to interpret Holy Writ in an anti-sexual way."[73] With their attention on the spiritual world and away from the physical, Gnostics are more interested in living in the hereafter and escaping the entanglements of this world. This is reflected in two different types of Gnosticism: the puritanical and the licentious. The former denies the physical world of pleasure to become associated with the spiritual world; the latter focuses so totally on the afterlife-to-come that the present physical world has an ineffectual, powerless neutral quality, which is impotent. For that reason it can be enjoyed.

The one gospel that approximates Gnosticism, The Gospel According to John, lacks emphasis on ethics. As noted earlier, the command to "love one another" appears only at the last supper (John 13:34–35) "and is clearly directed inward toward those in the cultic community, (community of insiders) not outward toward others. . . . The Fourth Gospel has internalized the 'light' so that it points to the revealer himself, not God's righteousness or a way of life."[74] Perkins continues: "Reinforcing the solidarity of those who hear the word of revelation emerges as the primary ethical functions of discourses of the revealer in both the Gnostic and the Johannine tradition."[75] The sheep parables and images in the Gospel of Truth equate salvation to possessing insight.[76] Some Gnostics did, however, have a proselytizing component and emphasized "the necessity of expanding the call to salvation to those who are not among the elect."[77]

There is evidence in historical documents of Gnostic missionary activity. The Gnostic organization, if it could be called that, was basically a loose and wide expansion of cells, or groups, without central administration. Individual schools fragmented into various branches. One element of cohesiveness detected by scholars was that of traveling laity, missionaries traveling from the centers of learning—Alexandria, Rome, and Jerusalem—fanning out with propaganda about their religion. Similar activity is seen in the Christian Church with the travels of Paul and his coterie.[78] The difference, however, between Paul and Gnostic missionaries was in the message. His possessed a love ethic that focused outward. The Gnostic message focused inward on knowledge of the inner self. Paul's message was one of salvation from sin; the Gnostics, salvation from ignorance, "*mea culpa* having been replaced by *mea ignorantia*" so that "the function of the Gospel becomes solely that of enlightening the soul concerning what has previously been hidden."[79] This is far a field from any social gospel.

The implication of dualism for social ethics is profound. Matter and worldly objects are considered evil or part of the domain of all that is evil. Nature and environmental concerns are abandoned: "For when a person is able to accept the Gnostic vision, all temporal concerns are left behind: unemployment, North-South relations, East-West conflicts, the polluting of the oceans and atmosphere, the possibility of human error creating a man-made hell."[80] This type of extreme individualism and hyperspiritualism is unlikely to join forces to implement gun control, Medicare, nuclear disarmament, and environmental responsibility.[81] Granted, some Fundamentalist denominations have successful mission programs, but missions stop there. Their natural inward-looking conservatism precludes any support for larger social issues, with possibly two exceptions: antiabortion and pro–death penalty movements, the former pro-life, the latter pro-law and order. Pro-life seems to be an issue for doctrinal, not social, reasons. The death penalty, or law and order, seems on the surface a social issue with an underlying concern for self-protection. The key word is "self" as opposed to "others" and "community."

RELIGIONS OF ESCAPISM

Perhaps one word accurately sums up the similarities of these two religious expressions: escape. In the final analysis, both are designed to escape reality. Their dualistic rejection of the world and spiritual inward focus result in withdrawal, not only from the world but also from other human beings. Ultimately, Gnosticism and Fundamentalism are religions of isolation.

The psychological implications of Gnosticism and Fundamentalism will be expanded below in Chapter 11, but a brief precursory comment follows here. When faced with danger, the human body has two instinctive reactions: fight or flight. It has been called by psychologists, the "fight–flight stress response syndrome." Historically, the Church has often chosen to stand and fight. St. Paul is clear on this issue: "But since we belong to the day, let us be self-controlled, putting on faith and love as a breastplate, and the hope of salvation as a helmet" (1 Thessalonians 5:8). Though Pauline authorship of Ephesians is questionable for some, there is a similar call to "put on the full armor of God. . . . Stand firm then, with the belt of truth buckled around your waist, with the breastplate of righteousness in place, and with your feet fitted with the readiness that comes from the gospel of peace. In addition to all this take up the shield of faith . . . the helmet of salvation and the sword of the spirit which is the word of God" (6:11–17). None of this equipage was made for the back. There are other metaphors in the Bible with which the reader is familiar. They abound in the Old Testament.

When the battle becomes a siege that turns into a continuous war, people typically react by fleeing if faced with overwhelming odds that instill despair. This is true of the religions that developed out of sieges or their perception of sieges. Gnostic, dualist elements did not find their way into Jewish theology in the times of power and prosperity but rather in the days of captivity (Babylon) and subjugation (Hellenistic rulers—Antiochus Epiphanes IV).

John Calvin, the fountainhead of most of American Fundamentalism, did not flinch from engagement with the opposition. He encouraged his followers to be active and bold, but his American disciples felt overpowered, beaten. The pioneers of colonial America cried for deliverance much in the way the Hebrews did in captivity: "How long can we sing the songs of the Lord while in a foreign land" (Psalm 137:4)? They did not want to sing the song forever: "Their escape route . . . was mapped by the New England theology . . . and remains today the prevailing way of one strong segment of American Protestantism."[82] The sign along the route pointed the way: "Be Born Again." It was the same for the early Gnostics, a failure of nerve, "a demand for something clear and dogmatic which explained the universe, and for an assured hope in immortality."[83]

SUMMARY

Separated by two millennia, Gnosticism and Fundamentalism emerged from similar matrices of similar underlying sociological, cultural, and psychological makeup. In the Roman Empire as well as the twentieth and twenty-first centuries, individuals felt dehumanized and trapped in a network of imperial machinery, overwhelmed by an influx of migrants from surrounding cultures (primarily Africa and the Orient) and bored with institutionalized religions that previously had brought some semblance of comfort and hope. In their effort to reclaim that optimism amidst the drudgery of their everyday lives, many in their search found it in Gnosticism and Fundamentalism.

Both of these religious expressions are diverse and fragmented, broken into numerous manifestations. Yet in their diversity they incorporate unifying underlying philosophical concepts, which color much of their doctrines. In Gnosticism this unifying principle is seen most clearly in dualism and a radical split between spirit and matter, good and evil, light and dark, God and Satan, the saved and the unsaved, and so on. In Fundamentalism the basic tenets are expressed in the "Five Fundamentals": inerrancy of scripture, the virgin birth, substitutional atonement, bodily resurrection, and historicity of miracles.

The similarities between Gnosticism, particularly Christian Gnosticism, and Fundamentalism spin off from the core dualism of spirit and matter. In this dualistic worldview, everything divided simplistically between the spiritual and physical; the spirit is good, the flesh is evil. The polarity of these forces is present throughout the New Testament, most prominently in the Gospel of John and the letters of Paul. Through the theological eyes of these writers, dualism collapsed into the singular event of the Incarnation of Jesus Christ; the Word became flesh, God became human. Within Gnosticism and Fundamentalism, this incarnational balance of spirit and flesh is obliterated. The humanness of Christ and his Word is eclipsed by an overemphasis upon his spiritual, divine nature.

Though clearly evidenced in Gnosticism, this radical cleavage of reality is not as obvious in Fundamentalism. It is neither stated in the "Five Fundamentals" nor clearly outlined in any early conservative religious writings. But an emphasis on the spirit-filled life and sin-filled flesh implies this dichotomy. The dualistic world-view of the two religious movements yields a dualistic view of humanity. Humans are divided between spirit and flesh. Dualism is implied in the "Five Fundamentals" where Christ never fully becomes human or incorporates flesh. Theoretically, his humanity is verbalized, but in practice he is divine, wholly spirit.

Dualism is evidenced in the similarity between the Gnostic inner "divine spark" and the Fundamental concept of inner spirit of inner light. Both share an immediacy of contact with the Divine and are highly individualistic. This extends into the similar manner Gnosticism and Fundamentalism employ an inerrant, literal interpretation of scripture. Holy writ is interpreted in a subjective mystical manner. Revelation becomes an internal experience of the believer rather than through a channel of ecclesiastical authority. Sensing the impact of this individu-alism upon the existence of the authority of their fledgling religion, the early Church fathers were energized into literary challenge and organizational activism. A literal inerrant interpretation of scripture has far reaching implications and goes to the heart of Christ's Incarnation. A spiritually pure, literal, and inerrant interpretation precludes any aspect of humanity to the Word made flesh. This is a major problem for Fundamentalism today as reflected in their Christology.

Gnosticism and Fundamentalism understand salvation as individual-centered. Knowledge is a key component. Individuals "know" their Redeemer. Though they differ in the type of knowledge implied, the process is similar. Salvation must be earned. Superficially, their respective Redeemers seem different, but in actuality they are similar. Both are heavily overendowed with spirit. The Word never truly becomes flesh.

On an organizational level Gnostic and Fundamental churches are similar. Both embrace elitist "insiders," while the remainder of unsaved humanity exists "outside the flock." Both are democratic, though of varying intensity, and eschew a hierarchical chain of command. Gnostic congregations were more loosely orga-nized than those of current Fundamentalism were, but they operated along simi-lar lines of communal elitism. They were spirit endowed, which distinguished them as carriers and interpreters of a divine message.

Morally and ethically, the individual took precedence over the community. The focus was on individual, not communal, salvation. This translates into an inner circle of faithful versus an excluded group of nonbelievers. Dualism again determined ethical behavior. Denial of pleasure became the central rule. The spiritual self must not become contaminated by the physical world. Despite some early sources charging the Gnostics with licentious behavior, Puritan, Fundamentalist practice was in lockstep with some ascetical forms of Gnosticism. This practice is also seen in the ancient Essenes and early Christian monastic movements. Emphasis upon individual spiritual salvation over the concerns of others and the physical world has significant implications for contemporary Fundamentalism. Nature and the environment, along with other global issues, such as nuclear proliferation and disarmament, war, and peace, are abandoned at the expense of individual salvation.

In their understanding of time, Gnostics and Fundamentalists look to a golden past to which they expect to return when the forces of evil are defeated by the forces of good. They are apocalyptical. Morality was an individual matter with limited emphasis upon a social gospel. Though their means differ, both have a sense of mission: Gnostics strive to eradicate ignorance, while Fundamentalists work to wipe out sin.

Finally, both Fundamentalism and Gnosticism are religions of escape and isolation. This follows logically from their dualistic interpretation of reality and their emphasis upon individual salvation.

CHAPTER 9

THE DIFFERENCES BETWEEN GNOSTICISM AND FUNDAMENTALISM

THE SIMILARITIES BETWEEN CHRISTIAN GNOSTICISM AND FUNDAMENTALISM ARE significant and substantive. But, as with all religious movements and phenomena, there are differences. Not surprisingly, some of these variances occur in the same areas of similarity. They represent nuances and shades of diversity along related themes.

HUMANITY

As emphasized in Chapter 8, the Gnostic and Fundamentalist understanding of humanity is complex. For both, humankind is fallen and in need of salvation. Gnostics salvation is from ignorance and incomprehension; Fundamentalist salvation is from sin. How they achieve their respective understanding of salvation, however, is different.

Gnostics rely upon an inner "divine spark" possessed by only a select few. This "divine spark" enables them to communicate one-on-one with a Redeemer or transcendent supreme Spirit. Fundamentalists deny they possess anything comparable to a "divine spark." They are totally corrupt. Their salvation comes through an intervening spirit. Some Gnostics believe only a select few will achieve salvation. Fundamentalists are not unanimous on this issue. Some believe that all are capable of receiving the divine spirit while others hold to a more predestined formula.

MORALITY

As long as morality is kept on an individual level, Gnosticism and Fundamentalism are very similar. Emphasis falls upon the individual and rejection of the material world and its many vices. Once morality, however, moves onto the social plane, Fundamentalism and Gnosticism part ways. Primitive Christianity, the earliest manifestation of the church, which some Fundamentalist sects attempt to emulate, was one of social outreach. Some church historians credit this as one reason Christianity caught on and Gnosticism faded: "In a word, Christianity directly answered to the human quest for true happiness—by which more is meant than *feeling* happy. . . . The practical application of charity was probably the most potent single cause of Christian success."[1] Charity was manifested in care for the poor, widows, orphans, and prisoners. It was "social action in a time of calamity like famine, earthquake, pestilence, or war."[2] Some Fundamentalist churches today attempt to mirror primitive Christianity with outreach programs. Gnosticism, on the other hand, was simply too abstract for the issues of day-to-day living. In short, its word never became flesh: "Gnosis, as a movement, was self-defeating. Furthermore, its appeal to the 'elect' who by definition must be few, would see it whittle down to a virtual club membership . . . the Gnostics were not interested in 'seeing it all out' until Jesus returned with angels and trumpets sounding. When you had received the 'Light', you were effectively out of history."[3] Some scholars have expressed that the apocalyptic nature of the New Testament tended to deemphasize social outreach. The kingdom was imminent. "'The time has come,' Jesus said, 'the kingdom of God is near. Repent and believe the good news'" (Mark 1:15). With the kingdom of heaven at hand, why engage in programs that meet individual and communal needs. Ultimately, God would provide.

Despite these theories, there are New Testament passages that, literally, leave little room for any interpretation other than social outreach:

> So in everything, do to others what you would have them do to you, for this sums up the Law and the Prophets. (Matthew 7:12; Luke 6:31; Luke 10:27)

> Then the king will say to those on his right, "Come you who are blessed by my father, take your inheritance, the kingdom prepared for you since the creation of the world. For I was hungry and you gave me something to eat, I was thirsty and you gave me something to drink, I was a stranger and you invited me in, I needed clothes and you clothed me, I was sick and you looked after me, I was in prison and you came to visit me . . . I tell you the truth that whatever you did for one of the least of these brothers of mine, you did for me." (Matthew 25:34–40)

> The spirit of the Lord is on me, because he has anointed me to preach good news to the poor. He has sent me to proclaim freedom for the prisoners and recovery of sight for the blind, to release the oppressed, to proclaim the year of the Lord's favor. (Luke 4: 18–19)

According to Luke's gospel, the ministry of Jesus of Nazareth was aimed primarily at the poor. Regarding the end time and the coming kingdom, Luke portrays a different Jesus from the other gospel writers. "In Luke Jesus knows the end is not imminent. . . . More than either of the other Synoptics, Luke emphasizes Jesus' concerns for the social ills of his day."[4] There will be a final calamitous upheaval but not in the lifetime of the disciples (Luke 21:7–32). For Luke the kingdom has already come. Though his emphasis falls upon the poor, the rich are not omitted: "Woe to you who are rich . . . woe to you who are full now . . . woe to you who are laughing now"(Luke 6:24–26).[5]

From the beginning of Jesus's ministry and through Acts, Luke's objective has an international, global scope. The goal of his Jesus is to save the entire world, which included Gentiles. The good news, or gospel, is equated with social outreach and meeting the physical needs of the outcast and downtrodden. The message is clear. Christians are to be shepherds and caretakers. In some Fundamentalist quarters, this message has been taken literally. In the category of social morality, some Fundamentalists do not resemble the abstract Gnostics. Despite this dissimilarity with Christian Gnosticism, Luke was the only Gospel that Marcion chose for his Gnostic Bible.

Contemporary Fundamentalism is criticized for its overemphasis on individual salvation at the expense of a balanced focus on social issues. Much of this depends on one's understanding of the definition of "social issue." If social issues mean capital punishment, abortion, war and peace, the death penalty, and homosexuality, many Fundamentalists line up on the conservative side. But, when social issues are defined as providing for, and meeting, the needs of others, some conservative denominations and churches that fit the Fundamentalist model have strong mission programs. Most of these are geared to humanitarian hunger, health, and illiteracy needs. The Wycliffe Translators, for example, have solid global outreach programs built around translating the Bible into other languages. Paired with that ministry is teaching the recipients of their translated Bibles how to read, how to grow crops, how to breed cattle, and how to protect themselves from diseases. In administering these programs, Fundamentalists are out of sync with Gnosticism. They generally follow New Testament scripture and themes.

As noted in Chapter 2, Gnostics were alleged to be licentious, amoral, and using religion as an excuse to have orgiastic parties. Their complete emphasis upon another spiritual realm, it was charged, left them free to do as they pleased in this earthly realm. Those making these allegations were the early church fathers (Clement of Alexandria, Irenaeus, and Tertullian leading the chorus) who were hardly objective and unbiased sources. Though no document in the Nag Hammadi supports these claims, some would argue "where there's smoke there's fire." If even a fraction of those charges were true, Gnostic personal morality pales in comparison to the more puritanical aspects of Fundamentalism. Their religious enthusiasm and passion to the contrary, Fundamentalists decry what they term wicked and dissolute behavior. This includes use of alcohol, sexuality, dancing, frequenting night clubs, displaying nudity, pornography, that is, anything that is considered un-Godlike. Some research, also previously noted, indicates some Gnostic sects may have been more puritan that the Puritans and their Fundamentalist progeny. They were ascetics, vegetarians, and practiced celibacy, the latter so rigorously they self-destructed. Regardless of the actual facts, Gnostics both past and present are perceived as less strict and less legal-oriented, allowing for a looser interpretation of what constitutes good behavior and the good life.

A caveat is in order. There are times the Fundamentalist passion does not remain within the sanctuary. Harold Bloom is quick to point out that Cane Ridge 1801 was the Woodstock festival of its day.[6] There was as much passion in the surrounding bushes as there was in the pews: "There is no way to disentangle the sexual drive from Pentacostalism any more than we can excise it from the Enthusiastic at Cane Ridge. . . . The drunk sexually aroused Woodstockian descendants participated in a kind of orgiastic individualism, in which all the holy rolling was the outward mark of an inward grace."[7] Perhaps because of their rigid code of behavior, Fundamentalists receive an overabundance of attention and press when they step over the line. But the Elmer Gantrys are out there. And when they sin the entire country hears about it: Jim Baker, Jim Jones, Jimmy Haggert, Marvin Gorman. On more provincial and local levels their behavior is easily spotlighted. But the difference should be noted. As a rule, Fundamentalists are by far more straight-laced and rule-bound than Gnostics.

Before leaving the segment on morality, a final comment is in order on the themes of war and of peace. A significant difference between current Fundamentalists and Gnostics is in the area of foreign policy and the relationship of America with other nations and cultures. Consistent with their philosophy that it is better to *know* than to *believe*, contemporary Gnostic organizations such as The Gnostic Institute, Ecclesiastica Gnostica, and Gnostic Church of St. Mary Magdalene focus on the dissemination of knowledge and the individual's inward spiritual journey. As a rule, they do not pursue political or economic ends and reject intervention in the affairs of other nationalities.

To the contrary, Fundamentalists move in the opposite direction. Consistent with a dualistic worldview, their positions on politics and foreign policy reflect a struggle between the polarities of light and darkness, good and evil, right and wrong. The world is viewed as a conflict between "the good guys" and "the bad guys." The enemy is combated in absolute terms with a call for total destruction or total surrender. There is no middle ground. This mentality states, "you are either for us or you are against us." This type of thinking allows a group to assume the role of God; it becomes the formula for a crusade. Some of the greatest wars in history have been purges or genocides based upon the dualistic view of a moral, social, and political universe. Gnosticism, not incarnational Christine doctrine, is the core concept driving the destructive behavior. In this, as previously noted, Fundamentalists differ from contemporary Gnostics.

CHRIST AND THE INCARNATION

Despite inconsistencies between Fundamentalists' inerrancy dogma and Christology, in the final analysis their Jesus *is* different from the Gnostic Redeemer. Throughout its liturgy and hymns, the Jesus of Fundamentalism does suffer. Songs like "Old Rugged Cross," "Beneath the Cross of Jesus," "Power in the Blood," "Alas, And Did My Savior Bleed?," and many others of similar theme and motif evoke the strong images of a suffering Christ who died for the sins of the world.[8] One may disagree with the theology implied in the words, but the message is unmistakable. The literal and inerrant interpreted Word of Fundamentalism may be Gnostic in its purity of presentation but, nuances of theology aside, the Christ within the word was a human who actually lived, was crucified, and was buried. For Fundamentalists this is a *fait accompli.* Jesus is the unique Son of God, "he remains forever distinct from the rest of humanity whom he came to save."[9] Clearly and simply, this is not Gnosticism.

ATONEMENT

One of the "Five Fundamentals" of Fundamentalism is substitutionary atonement, the belief that Christ experienced God's punishment for the sins of the world. Surprisingly, for a theological position that embraces literalism, there is no proof text for this doctrine. With an infusion of spirituality, mystic understanding, and subjective interpretation, one can be generated. Antonio's ringing line in Shakespeare's *Merchant of Venice* comes to mind: "The devil can cite scripture to suit his purpose."[10]

The differences between Fundamentalism and Gnosticism in this doctrinal area are significant. The key words are knowledge and sin. The Redeemer of the Gnostics comes not as someone to hear repentance or save people from sin but as someone who opens up the self for spiritual understanding, enlightenment, or "insight." The Fundamentalist Jesus of the New Testament comes to hear and forgive sin, to suffer for the sins of the world. Except in the Gospel of John, knowledge does not figure in the Christian scheme(s) of atonement. Fundamentalists, however, do veer close to Gnosticism when they speak of "knowing" Jesus and "believing" in him as though either, or both, are litmus tests for salvation. Grace tends to become lost in the equation. Separating Fundamentalists from Gnostics is the kind and quality of the knowledge. For Fundamentalists, knowing Jesus presupposes that Christ has claimed the believer. Grace is experienced. This kind of grace is not the knowledge of esoteric wisdom but the knowledge of being known by Christ. The knowledge of Christ, and by Christ, is inseparable. To know Christ is to receive grace. The argument has been made previously that the Fundamentalist conversion experience rests upon the decision of the individual. Fundamentalists, however, would argue that the decision presupposes one has received grace, thus enabling them to affirm the doctrine. It is necessary to adhere to right beliefs, which equates to adhering to the truth. This would align Fundamentalists with New Testament themes. There is still a fine line between salvation from "right belief" and salvation by grace. Doctrinally, Fundamentalists aver that the knowledge of Christ and by Christ is inseparable, that to know Christ is to receive grace. Experientially, emphasis in the conversion experience and "being born again," seems to fall upon "right belief" and knowing Christ in which the knowledge moves outward from the believer and not the reverse, which would be the traditional understanding of God's grace at work among humanity.

RESURRECTION

For Fundamentalists, the resurrection of Christ is a physical resurrection. St. Paul is taken seriously. If there had been no resurrection of the body, there would be no Christianity: "If there is no resurrection of the dead, then not even Christ has been raised. And if Christ has not been raised, our preaching is useless and so is your faith" (I Corinthians 15:13). When Paul speaks of the resurrection, it is a physical, bodily resurrection he denotes. In Greek the phrase means "spiritual body." The church fathers were equally strong on this issue. Tertullian stated anyone denying the resurrection of the flesh was not a Christian but a heretic. He added, "It must be believed, because it is absurd."[11]

Christ's resurrection was the proclamation that launched the church. It was the fundamental basis of its existence. The importance of the bodily resurrection of Jesus was underscored recently with the alleged discovery of Jesus's grave and the shock waves the story sent across the Christian world, which means the Fundamental Christian world as well.

The Christian concept of resurrection is far removed from Gnosticism. Gnostics focused on the illumination of knowledge through the "divine spark." They were more aligned with the Platonic and Hellenistic concepts of immortality of the soul. They understand the resurrection of Christ symbolically, not literally. The risen Christ is encountered at a spiritual level, which can occur in a variety of media including trances, dreams, and other spiritualist media. Gnostics even reverse the chronology and begin with Jesus's resurrection and spiritual appearances. Christ is symbolically experienced in the present, that is, a spiritual, not literal, vision. In Gnostic literature—*Gospel of Mary, Apocalypse of Peter*—resurrection experiences of Jesus are portrayed as trances or visions.

Variations on this mystical theme do occur in Fundamentalism as well as in other denominations. Catholicism accepts mysticism as a viable medium of contact with the Divine Power. Aspects of its theology could lend to a symbolic or spiritual interpretation of the resurrection. Yet, it is difficult to dismiss the Apostle's Creed, which is central to mainstream Christianity: "I believe in Jesus Christ . . . who suffered under Pontius Pilate, was crucified dead and buried . . . and I believe in . . . the resurrection of *the body* and the life everlasting."

Admittedly, some scriptures do seem to support the Gnostic position: "I tell you this, brethren: flesh and blood cannot inherit the Kingdom of God, nor does the perishable [that is, the mortal body] inherit the imperishable" (1 Corinthians 15:50); the resurrection is referred to as "a mystery" (I Corinthians 15:51–53); Luke tells of appearances in which the resurrected Jesus eats with his disciples (Acts 2:22–36).[12]

ROLE OF WOMEN

Women in the early primitive church were accorded status and played important roles. They served as deacons, pastors, prophets, teachers, and evangelists. Many of them were wealthy or married to wealthy husbands and offered their homes as places of worship and refuge. It is undisputed that women played a strong role in the ministry of Jesus. We know, for example, that Mary Magdalene was a woman of means with friends that included the wife of a high dignitary in the court of Herod (Luke 8:2–3). Women were included in the coterie of Paul's coworkers. One named Junia is called "foremost among the apostles" by Paul (Romans 16:7). Paul gave women equal spiritual status with men (Galatians 3:27-28) and implied that if equality among the congregation was not observed, the consequences could prove to be unfortunate (1 Corinthians 11: 27–30).

There is a caveat to Paul's understanding of the social order: "Paul's view, however, did not prompt him to urge all Christians to free their slaves or Christian slaves to seek their release. On the contrary, 'the time was short,' everyone was to be content with the roles they were presently in; they were not to try to change them" (1 Corinthians 7: 17–24).[13] In Paul's eyes there were still sexual differences between men and women: "To eradicate that difference, in Paul's view, was unnatural and wrong."[14] Women were still to continue covering their head when they prayed or spoke prophecies (1 Corinthians 1: 3–16). Women did participate with men but within the stereotype of that day. For example, women wore their hair long, men short, and that should not change: "For Paul, therefore, even though men and women were equal in Christ, this equality had not yet become a full social reality. . . . While living in this age, men and women were to continue to accept their 'natural' social roles with women subordinate to men just as men were subordinate to Christ and Christ was subordinate to God" (1 Corinthians 11:3).[15]

The letters of Timothy and Titus surfaced and presented a different view of the role of women in the church.[16] Women were not to teach. They were to be silent in church. Pastors were to appoint married male leaders (1Timothy 3:2–5, 12). In other words, women were to stay home, tend the hearth, and raise children. The reasons for this dramatic attitude reversal are multiple and continue to be debated. One factor often mentioned relates to the waning of apocalyptic passion. As long as the expected Parousia seemed near at hand, the moment when everyone would be on an equal basis and taken up in a mighty cloud of glory, rules of social and sexual distinction became irrelevant. But when the end of time, or *eschaton*, did not come and no longer appeared imminent, the church began to organize along the male line of authority typical of that time.

The demise of women in the early church is attributed, in part, to Gnostic deification of the feminine and the perceived threat this posed to the early church apologists. Gnostics attributed feminine qualities to the deity. In many cases this was a divine androgynous mix of male and female. This would be intolerable to religions that developed from Judaism where the deity was not only *the* only God around but also singular and male. It is therefore understandable that Fundamentalism would follow the Roman Catholic and Protestant traditions regarding the female role.

INTELLECTUALISM

Gnostics were an intellectual and abstract lot. By today's standards they might be dubbed brainy, nerdish, or "artsy." They were a "right-brained" crowd given to aesthetics and mystical experiences. Gnostics were considered more abstract and theoretical.[17] In this respect, the average Gnostic was significantly different from the average early Christian.

Fully aware of this intellectual tendency, the early fathers, heavyweight intellectuals in their on right, encouraged skepticism toward intellectualism. "From its very beginning, Christianity . . . took a position against intellectualism (Gnosticism) with the greatest possible awareness and consistency."[18] They preached a simple faith, a singular path to salvation. In this perspective, the early church might be compared to contemporary Fundamentalists. Many seem threatened by intellectual exploration and view it as an intrusion into the realm of faith. Perkins notes: "The emerging orthodoxy becomes the foreign element that shut down the liberal, individualistic, freethinking Gnostics."[19] By today's standards, they would be labeled "liberal." Manly P. Hall described Gnosticism as "extremely liberal and by constitution, nonmilitant. It suffered from uncertainties natural to extreme liberalism."[20] There is some question, however, that ancient Gnostics were liberal by "today's standard." There were many forms of Gnosticism, some of which would be considered conservative by contemporary norms.

Other differences worth noting include the Gnostic use of secret societies, belief among some sects in reincarnation,[21] and their rejection of the Old Testament. Some questioned the inspiration of the Apostles (Marcion, however, did include the Gospel of Luke in his canon), denied the infallibility of the clergy, and chose only St. Paul as a reliable authentic authority. Gnostics also had their own secret tradition of apostolic succession and most of those—including Paul, Mary Magdalene, and James—stand outside the orthodox tradition of the original twelve.

SUMMARY

Despite their similarities, Gnosticism and Fundamentalism do have differences. Gnosticism saves one from ignorance and incomprehension. Fundamentalism saves one from sin. The Gnostic approach is most vividly detailed in their Docetic and Separatist Christologies: Christ was all spirit. He manifested only the "appearance" of flesh.

They also diverge when it comes to morality. Despite Fundamentalism's emphasis upon individual salvation, it does have social outreach programs that sharply contrast with Gnosticism. The Fundamentalist Christ of scripture did reach out to humanity and many Fundamentalist denominations emulate this behavior. The scriptural messages to this effect are clear.

In some ways, the spiritual Christ of Fundamentalism resembles the spiritual Gnostic Redeemer. But, unlike the Gnostic Christ, the Fundamental Jesus suffers. He does shed blood for the forgiveness of sins. The Fundamentalist concept of the substitutionary atonement of Christ, unsupported by scripture, is also absent in Gnostic Redeemer theories. The bodily resurrection, one of the "Five Fundamentals," does not resonate with Gnostic belief in the spiritual resurrection, which they interpreted as symbolic rather than real.

One of the most distinctive differences between these two religious movements is their perception and understanding of the role of women. Gnostics incorporated the feminine into their deity. Women had important functional roles within the congregations. This is far removed from the all-male religion of Fundamentalism and most of Christianity. Initially, women in the early church were afforded roles of importance. As the early church fathers became embroiled in their battle with the Gnostics, the role of the female was sacrificed.

CHAPTER 10

THE CASE AGAINST INERRANCY

INERRANCY IS THE KEYSTONE FOR THE FUNDAMENTALIST CREED. Its central position in Fundamentalism plus its lack of incarnational meaning are the linchpins of this chapter. The intent is not to argue points. The purpose is to draw alternative perspectives, offer varying viewpoints, and provide information to those struggling in the development and formation of their own personal faith system.

The word "system" is used because we incorporate in our thinking a scheme or arrangement of faith principles that comprises our creeds. The integral parts must connect, relate, and be cohesive, thus creating a system. For many, this creed changes over time. It is shaped by continuing new experiences and knowledge. If an idea makes sense, we incorporate it; if not, we discard it. Within that spirit this book was written. Within that spirit of openness the following information is provided.

Within all theological circles, Fundamental or otherwise, scholars generally agree the *Holy Bible* was not, as Teabling sarcastically quips in Brown's *The Da Vinci Code*, a fax from God. Nor was it something lowered from heaven "like the modern sanitary products that boast they are 'untouched by human hands.'"[1] New Testament authority Arthur G. Patzia offers this description of one Fundamentalist perception of the process:

> Some students of the New Testament approach the text with preconceived ideas of how it came into being. Certain theories of inspiration, dictation and inerrancy have led individuals to believe that the New Testament was lowered down from heaven on a golden string . . . It is not uncommon to meet Christians who think that God told Luke, for example, to take a pen and some papyrus, find a desk then sit down and write at the dictation of some heavenly voice. It just did not happen that way.[2]

Bart Ehrman, who alludes to his "born again" Fundamental origins in several of his books, frames the issue from a different perspective:

> When I was a student just beginning to think about those fifteen centuries of copying and the vicissitudes of the text, I kept reverting to the fact that whatever else we

may say about the Christian scribes—whether of the early centuries or the Middle Ages—we have to admit that in addition to copying scripture, they were changing scripture. Sometimes they didn't mean to—they were simply tired, or inattentive, or, on occasion, inept. At other times though they did mean to make changes . . . as when they wanted the text to emphasize precisely what they themselves believed, for example, about the nature of Christ, or about the role of women in the church, or about the wicked character of their Jewish opponents. . . . I began seeing the New Testament as a very human book. The New Testament as we actually have it, I knew, was the product of human hands, the hands of the scribes who transmitted it. Then I began to see that not just the scribal text but the original text itself was a very human book.[3]

Again, quoting Patzia: "What God did do, however, was subject his written Word to the same historical process as he did his incarnate Word, Jesus. The Bible is both a divine and human entity: divine in its inspiration and preservation, human in the sense of God's subjecting it to the historical process and entrusting it to the church."[4] In other words, "The Word became flesh" (John 1:14); it became incarnated in the person of Christ. This was an incarnation in the oral *and* written words of his ministry, message, and the movement he inspired.

Human beings wrote the Bible . . . "human beings with needs, beliefs, world-views, opinions, loves, hates, longings, desires, situations, problems—and surely all these affected what they wrote."[5] With the crude writing implements of their time, on papyrus or parchment or vellum, they scratched out the general texts that became the *Holy Bible*.[6] Those original documents, called autographs (literally from the Greek, self-writing or the writings themselves), were written at various times and places by various authors. There was no single filter, no one clearing house in Alexandria, Ephesus, or Rome to which the manuscripts were sent for collection, and no publishing house to which they were then transferred for collation, assemblage, printing, and binding (or scrolling). Like most ancient writings, their entry into the world was often dictated by the religious, cultural, and political pressures of the time. There was no organizational body behind their emergence onto the world scene. The systematic collection of these Hebrew and Greek texts came later.

Those who take the inerrancy position believe the original writings, the autographs, were pure, undefiled, and error free; not just syntactically and grammatically but also theologically and ethically. Muslims hold a similar view about the Koran. It was dictated to Muhammad by Allah, and Muhammad in turn memorized the words and flawlessly dictated them to others who put them in writing.

The Fundamentalist position on inerrancy presents several problems. First, we do not possess the original autographs. They simply do not exist. As Ehrman points out, "even if God inspired the original words, we don't have the original words."[7] We not only have no copies of the autographs, we do not have a copy of a copy of a copy of the autographs. In time, perhaps more archeological discoveries will be forthcoming and we will move closer to the originals. Or miraculously, one will surface. For now, we must be content with the copies we have, which are generations removed from the originals.

To counter this point Fundamentalists rely on absolute faith. Most Fundamentalist scholars admit the autographs are human productions. But these human productions were divinely inspired. These divinely inspired words were kept pure and untainted by any copying process. In other words, what we have *is* the original. The *King James Bible* is the same directly inspired word of God that came to the first divinely inspired writers. The Fundamentalist reader accepts this on faith. God simply would not transmit His word, or cause His word to be transmitted, in error or with contradictions and flaws. There are variations on this theme within Fundamentalism, but this is the thrust of their defense. One accepts the literal words on faith. They are *the* true and undefiled Word of God.

Secondly, and of equal significance, the concept of inerrancy of Holy Scripture has not been around forever: "we know of no theologians before the nineteenth century who made claims for the autographs that they did not also make for the texts and translations of the Bible which they had in their possession."[8] There was a premillennialist (the doctrine that the Second Coming of Christ will occur before the millennium) drive in the 1870s, which carried a sense of new dispensationalism (a type of millennialism, cf. Appendix A, "Glossary of Key Terms") and it was those dispensationalists who first circulated the term "inerrancy." Humphreys and Wise note the refining of this position since the nineteenth century. Specifically, they reference an interdenominational committee of scholars who, in 1978, produced The Chicago Statement on Biblical Inerrancy.[9]

Traditionally, the Church has considered Scripture to be its written authority, the inspired written Word of God. Though some Gnostics, Marcion in particular, championed a literal interpretation of scriptural texts, apologists of the early Church never espoused this position. It was not an issue until introduced by the Fundamentalists. Loader encourages readers to go straight to the gospel writers themselves: "Even Q and Matthew and Luke, who in various ways stress the immutability of scripture, and its authority, are far from espousing literalism, or an approach that would portray God as more interested in laws than in people."[10]

Thirdly, perfection raises a high window of expectation. When the standard is not met and an error appears, an unfortunate dilemma for believers occurs. If Moses wrote the Pentateuch, the first five books of the Old Testament, how could he write about his own death? If the resurrection scenes in the four Gospels differ, which they do—different sets of characters, different numbers of characters, different sequence of events—which one is right? If Mark portrays Jesus as angry and hostile as he approaches and endures his crucifixion and Luke portrays him as calm and forgiving, which one is right? Which Jesus was crucified? How can these discrepancies be rectified or harmonized?

There are other examples. Jesus's temptation sequences in Matthew and Luke differ. In Matthew, Jesus is tempted to throw himself from the Temple pinnacle before the temptation to worship Satan. Luke reverses the sequence. The sequence of the Last Supper and Trial in John and Mark occur at different times.

These inconsistencies and many others cause pause. Why are the gospel writers not in sync? Were they mistaken? Was one right and the other wrong? If that is the case, that high window of expectation suddenly slams shut. The Bible is no longer the inerrant, unerring Word of God. This "all or none" thinking, referred to by psychologists as "irrational" thinking, or "cognitive traps," creates significant discrepancies s in the very source sought by believers to solve their own problems. Ironically, the same "all or nothing" thinking probably created those problems. ("Cognitive traps," will be explored more fully in Chapter 11, "Psychological Issues and Implications.")

This form of perfectionism stemming from the mystical belief in pure and unimpeded communication, that is, spiritual immediacy with God, veers close to Gnostic spiritualism and individuality. Ehrman, Metzger, and others point out how interpretation via spiritual immediacy, or straightforward word without interpretation, obliterates context. There is no concern for the historical meaning without critical examination of context. And context, as we have seen, is everything with regard to textual interpretation:

> The concern to understand the socio-historical context within which an occasional writing was produced is rooted in a theoretical view of language shared by many scholars, that knowing a documents historical context is absolutely vital for its interpretation. According to this view, words convey meaning only within a context; thus when you change the context of words, you change what they mean. This is because, as we have seen, words and phrases do not have any inherent meaning but mean what they do only in relationship to other words and phrases, so that words and phrases can be made to mean a wide variety of things (practically anything according to some theorists). . . . if we are to understand a person's words, we have to understand the context in which they are spoken.[11]

To understand the case against inerrancy, we must understand the historical context. To achieve this, our efforts might best be served by beginning at the end of the process that brought us the current Bible and New Testament and working backward.[12]

HISTORY OF NEW TESTAMENT TRANSLATIONS

There were times in the pastorate following a worship service that a parishioner would ask, usually indignantly, why I used the Revised Standard Version and not the "true" *King James*. "That's the original," once an elderly lady said, "that's the Bible Jesus used." Those comments seem antiquated. But they are as prevalent now as they were then. Arguably, the King James Version, of all the translations of the Holy Bible, continues to be the most revered. It is the version quoted most by Fundamentalists, essayists, and novelists. It is an appropriate point of departure for the case against inerrancy.

The King James Version was commissioned by King James I of England (James Stuart VI of Scotland) and completed in 1611. What many do not know are the primary sources used in the translation process. This requires a step back in history, to a couple of prominent names: Johann Gutenberg (1400–1468) and Disiderius Erasmus (1466–1536).

Prior to Gutenberg's invention of the printing press, manuscripts were copied and recopied by hand, a laborious process fraught with errors. The moveable type printing press, however, created a dramatic transformation in the production of books. Since pages could be reproduced exactly, the frequency of errors dropped significantly. Gutenberg's first major production was the Latin Bible.[13] Since its production in the fourth century, this had been the Bible of the Church. There had been no translations from Greek. Greek was associated with the apostate Greek Orthodox Church and considered foreign and heretical.

Greek was the language most closely related to the language of Jesus. The demand for Greek texts, especially the New Testament, grew and translations began to appear in print. In 1516, the first published version was produced by the Dutch humanist intellectual Disiderius Erasmus.[14] Erasmus actually produced five translations "all based on the first rather hastily assembled one."[15] It was thrown together so quickly that New Testament scholar F. H. A. Scrivner declared it to be "the most faulty book I know."[16]

What were Erasmus' sources? Did he have access to original autographs? Libraries were few and their texts and documents limited. A complete copy of the Greek New Testament was not available. He used fragments of existing translations in a piecemeal fashion to create a whole literary fabric. The result was an approximation of the whole. He located two twelfth-century Greek New Testament texts of inferior quality in a monastic library in Basle, Switzerland that included the Gospels, Acts, and Epistles. He borrowed a text of The Book of Revelation, also of twelfth-century vintage, from a friend named Reuchlin. (These texts actually came from what is now known among scholars as the "Byzantine" text generated around the eighth century CE and considered to be of poor quality.) This Revelation text was missing the final leaf or last six verses of the book. For these and other missing or eligible fragments, he used Jerome's Latin Vulgate, translating it into Greek.[17] Metzger, responsible for much of this background, expresses "here and there in Erasmus' self-made Greek text are readings which have never been found in any known Greek manuscript—but which are still perpetuated today in printings of the so-called Textus Receptus of the Greek New Testament."[18]

Some examples of these discrepancies are noteworthy. Based upon the oldest New Testament manuscripts available, it is considered established fact that the story of the adulterous woman in John and the final twelve verses of the Gospel of Mark probably did not originally appear in the autographs of those respective Gospels. Yet the primary manuscript Erasmus used for the Gospels contained both.[19] Erasmus's manuscript also omitted another key passage, now referred to by scholars as the Johannine Comma (1 John 5:7–8). This is the only passage in the Bible that implies the doctrine of the Trinity, that is, that there are three in the godhead and all three comprise one God. Otherwise the doctrine must be knitted together from a handful of passages reflecting Christ as God, or the Spirit as the Father, the Spirit as Christ, the Father and the son, and so on. The passage as it is found in the Latin Vulgate is worth quoting: "*There are three that bear witness in heaven: the Father the Word, and the Spirit, and these three are one; and there are three that bear witness on earth, the Spirit, the water, and the blood, and these three are one.*"[20] The Trinity is clearly stated, not just implied. Erasmus's translation of this passage, however, reads differently: "*There are three that bear witness: the Spirit, water, and the blood, and these three are one.*" There is nothing about the Father, the Word, or the Spirit. They were missing in his Greek manuscripts. Theologians were incensed at this omission, and under extraordinary ecclesiastical pressure Erasmus retained the Johannine Comma in his next edition.

What is the point? The King James Version was based on a Greek translation of the Bible that was derived from faulty Latin and Greek translations that came from other flawed translations. Ehrman summarizes, "And so, familiar passages to readers of the English Bible—from the King James in 1611 onward, up until modern editions of the twentieth century—include the woman taken in adultery, the last twelve verses of Mark, and the Johannine Comma, even though *none* of these passages can be found in the oldest and superior manuscripts of the Greek New Testament."[21] Prior to Erasmus's publication and editions of his Greek Bible, the most prominent text was the Latin Bible, or Vulgate (common) provided by Sophronius Eusebius Hieronymus, known today as St. Jerome (347–420).[22] While performing the task requested by Pope Damasus around 382 CE, Jerome noted the numerous versions, as many as there were manuscripts, and complained of copyists who "write down not what they find but what they think is the meaning; and while they attempt to rectify the errors of others, they merely expose their own."[23] Copied many times over, this was the Bible used by the Western Church and into the modern era.[24]

During the first three centuries of Christianity prior to the Vulgate, there was a flurry of textual copying, editing, and publishing. Most of the individuals copying the variety of scriptural texts floating around in the early centuries were not professionally trained but consisted of the few literates comprising the early congregations who volunteered for the job. Patzia notes: "At first it is likely that some manuscripts were copied by individual Christians for personal and devotional reasons. However, with the spread of Christianity through the Roman Empire, the ability to mass produce texts was needed."[25] During this time of prolific literary production, errors abounded and the frequency of variance was higher.[26] Metzger observes that "the speed of production sometimes outran accuracy of execution."[27] Later, during and after the reign of Constantine, a more professional class of paid scribes evolved and maintained tighter control on copying practices.[28]

Scholars agree that the transmission of the New Testament occurred as follows. First, there was the oral tradition where individuals spread the news of Christ's resurrection and ministry by word of mouth. Then, for a variety of reasons, the spoken word was recorded in written form. Paul was writing letters to various congregations to help them resolve internal problems. Another possible reason for committing the oral gospel ("good news") to writing was the failed occurrence of the Parousia, the return of Christ and the final resurrection. This hoped for event of salvation was delayed. The message needed to be preserved. Regardless of the reasons, around the turn of the first century, a flurry of copying commenced. Patzia, with graphic tables and flow charts, provides a good overall view of what happened:

> Soon after the autographs were written they began their long and exciting journey of transmission. At first, a second copy—or perhaps several copies—was made from the original manuscript. Shortly after, copies were made from the copies, and so on, so that in a very short time there were many copies in circulation. By the second century a similar process developed in the church, with the creation of lectionaries for public and private worship and the use of the New Testament texts by the church fathers in preaching and writing.[29]

Around 200 C E Latin began replacing Greek in the Roman Empire. The widespread shift in language necessitated a good Latin translation and resulted in Pope Damasus's request to Jerome and, eventually, *The Vulgate*. Previously, the early congregations were limited to possessions of the Hebrew Scriptures and copies of the Greek Old Testament or Septuagint (LXX).[30]

With its many editions and translations, the New Testament has had a long, tortuous, and convoluted history. One of the best descriptions of this early publishing process comes from Kurt and Barbara Aland:

> As copies multiplied their circulation became steadily wider and wider, like the ripples from a pebble cast in a pond. This means that from the writing of a document to its use in all the churches of a single diocese or throughout the whole Church, a certain amount of time must have elapsed. Meanwhile, every copy made from another copy repeated the same pattern of expansion, like another pebble cast into the pond making a new series of ripples. These rippling circles would intersect. Two manuscripts in a single place (each with its own range of textual peculiarities, depending on its distance from the original text) would influence each other, producing a textual mixture and starting a new pattern of ripples—a process which would be repeated continually. Finally, to continue the metaphor, the pool becomes so filled with overlapping circles that it is practically impossible to distinguish their sources and their mutual relationships. This is precisely the situation the textual critic finds when attempting to analyze the history of the New Testament text.[31]

One could stop here and rest a strong case against inerrancy. Facts prove there was too much going on; too many hands were involved in too many varying transmissions. But, as indicated above by the Alands, the task would not be complete without a discussion of textual criticism.

TEXTUAL CRITICISM:
WHAT IS IT?

Defined by *The Oxford Classical Dictionary*, textual criticism is "the technique and art of restoring a text to its original state, as far as possible, in the editing of Greek and Latin authors."[32]

Fundamentalists see no need for textual criticism. Why criticize something that is perfect? In the opinion of those who share that viewpoint, textual criticism is perceived as a violent intruder, a wrecking ball within the halls of holy writ.

Textual criticism is precisely the opposite: "Textual criticism is not a pejorative term or an evil enterprise. *Criticize* (Greek *krino*) means 'to judge,' 'decide,' 'determine' or 'consider.' By definition, textual criticism is a study that seeks to reconstruct the original text from existing texts because the autographs are not available. The fact is that very few autographs survive for any ancient work."[33] Patzia then adds this historical perspective: "The works of Plato (d. 347 B.C.) survive mostly in Byzantine manuscripts of the Middle Ages, the earliest of which dates to A.D. 895, more than twelve hundred years after his death. The same is true of such ancient authors as Livy, Tacitus, Herodotus and Thucydides, where only small portions of their works survive in late manuscripts."[34] Noted New Testament authority Philip Comfort agrees: "The purpose of textual criticism, classically defined, is to recover the original wording of an ancient written text, no longer extant in its original form by means of examining the extant manuscript copies and then applying the canons of the discipline for determining the wording most likely original. . . . Textual critics must sort through these manuscripts and the variant readings therein in an effort to reconstruct the original meaning of the Greek New Testament."[35] Textual criticism highlights the human process involved in the production of the Bible, the human variants, and inconsistencies of the end product. The divine factor in the evolution of holy writ is not obliterated. The overemphasis on that dimension is merely corrected and balanced, that the word can become flesh. With the inerrancy position, if anything has been obliterated, the human dimension has been sacrificed at the expense of the divine. This is a Gnostic position and orientation. The approach presented in this book is intended to help return balance to the interpretation, a restoration of the Incarnational Word.

MODERN METHODS OF TEXTUAL CRITICISM

Textual criticism begins with questions about texts. When were they written? Who wrote them? Are there other texts supporting them, attesting to them? If so, what are they? Are they reliable? If they are reliable, what data and texts support their reliability? If not, what supports their unreliability? Biblical textual criticism dates back to the early Church fathers. It has a long and interesting, at times colorful, history. Over the centuries, various techniques have become more refined. The end result has brought us closer to origins, to the wording of the earliest manuscripts.

According to Metzger, modern methods of textual criticism involve two main processes. One is *recension* or "the selection, after examination of all available material, of the most trustworthy evidence on which to base a text."[36] The other is *emendation*: the attempt to eliminate the errors that are found in the best manuscripts.[37] Ehrman, Metzger's pupil and protégé, breaks the process down to examination of "external" and "internal" evidences. A technical review of the process falls beyond the scope of this presentation, but some aspects of each component are worth noting.

External evidence basically involves the outward appearance of texts, what they say, their variations, and which ones agree and do not agree. The manuscript best representing the original form of the text may not be the manuscript with the *most* witnesses or most supporting copies. This is more than counting numbers. For example, if eight texts say the same thing, the content might be quickly classified as original. However, what if they date from the eighth century CE and you have another similar text, with a different slant or wording, dating from the fifth century CE?

The age of the manuscript is an important factor. It is possible that manuscripts dated from one century may have been copied from a much earlier century, for example the eighth century may have been copied from a fourth century manuscript. If the copy is good, the eighth century text would be the oldest, thus closer to the original. Also, manuscripts copied before the time of Constantine were copied by "volunteer" nonprofessional scribes, thus are susceptible to more errors. Geographical range is another consideration. Different texts were generated in different geographical areas. If a text is associated with the geographical area designated Rome, this means there is good evidence it was generated within that locale. Any error within that text would likely be reproduced in other manuscripts from that same locale, which is what scholars have learned happened.[38]

Besides the locality factor, manuscripts also tended to belong to certain genealogical or "textual families."[39] Metzger points out that textual witnesses were "weighed rather than counted."[40] Texts coming from what has been called the Alexandrian School are superior in quality to the Byzantine (the source of the King James Version). For a reading to be considered original, it should be found in manuscripts of the highest quality and associated with those geographical areas or "textual families" noted for high quality.[41]

There are two types of internal evidence: intrinsic probabilities and transcriptional probabilities. The former is based on what we know about the author, his writing style, vocabulary, syntax, and theology. To this list Metzger adds "immediate context, harmony of the usage of the author elsewhere, the Aramaic background of the teaching of Jesus, priority of the Gospel according to Mark, and the influence of the Christian community upon the formulation and transmission of the passage in question."[42]

In short, determining the original text is neither simple nor straightforward! It requires a lot of thought and careful sifting of the evidence, and different scholars invariably come to different conclusions—not only about minor matters that have no bearing on the meaning of the passage (such as the spelling of a word or change of word order in Greek that cannot even be replicated in English translation) but also about matters of major importance, that is, matters that affect the interpretation of an entire book of the New Testament.[43]

CAUSES OF ERROR IN THE SCRIPTURES

Dedicated textual critics affirm the texts they study and analyze represent the divinely inspired Word of God. They also recognize that those same texts were written and copied by human hands, which meant one part of the age-old adage applied: "To err is human." Often, footnotes in Bibles explain changes in the text. For example, the *New International Version* footnote in reference to Matthew 6:13 in the Lord's Prayer explains: "*Or from evil: some late manuscripts add 'for yours is the kingdom and the power and the glory forever. Amen.'*" Some other examples include Matthew 6:25; Luke 8:43; Acts 8:36; and 1 John 5:7–8.[44] Those understanding *koine* Greek (the language in which the early texts of the New Testament were written) will see, in reading one of the compilations of Greek New Testaments (Nestlé-Aland, for example) what the typical reader will not see: literally, thousands of other variants. The reason again: the Bible is a human production, that is, "The Word became flesh."

UNINTENTIONAL ERRORS

Approximately 95 percent of the errors in the New Testament are unintentional.[45] What types of errors might those be? What types of errors might you make when copying something, anything, such as, arecipe, a term paper, an address, or a phone numbers? Below is a list of unintentional errors:[46]

- Errors arising from faulty vision.
- Errors arising from faulty hearing: Scribes often made copies from dictation and confusion would sometimes result in words having the same pronunciation but different in spelling, for example, "there" and "their" and confusion among similar Greek letters ѡ and o.
- Errors of memory: These occur with all of us when, in the process of holding the memory of the written passage in our mind, we begin writing and something is lost in the glance from one page to the other.[47]
- Errors of writing: A good example of this type of error is seen in Luke 2:14 where the King James Version reads "Glory to God in the highest and on earth peace, good will toward men" and the New Revised Standard Version is translated to read "Glory to God in the highest heaven, and on earth peace among those whom he favors." Patzia points out the difference in translations relates to the addition, or omission, of a single Greek letter, ς.[48]
- Errors of judgment: Whether a Neanderthal chiseling in stone, a Sumerian copying cuneiform script, or a Middle Age scribe duplicating Biblical text, errors occurred through faulty judgment.[49]

Most New Testament scholars agree that the extent of unintentional errors is minimal and insignificant and creates no major changes in meaning or interpretation. Most of these types of errors are flagrant and traceable and have been corrected. The same cannot be said, however, for intentional, or what Ehrman has termed "theological" errors in which the meaning of an entire passage was often changed.

INTENTIONAL CHANGES

Intentional changes were just that, conscious and deliberate attempts of a scribe to alter a text in order to right a wrong. An intentional change replaced an unorthodox word or phraseology with one considered to be correct. Some of these were probably innocently motivated. Metzger again: "Many of the alterations that may be classified as intentional were no doubt introduced in good faith by copyists who believed that they were correcting an error in the sacred text that needed to be rectified."[50] Many scholars agree on the following catalogue of intentional changes:

- Revisions of grammar and spelling: An example of this would be a scribe from one geographical area correcting something unfamiliar to them from another.[51]
- Harmonization of similar passages: One well-known example of this is the shorter form of the Lord's Prayer in Luke 11:2–4, which was intentionally edited to resemble the longer passage in Matthew 6:9–13.[52]
- Elimination of discrepancies and difficulties: A classical example is seen in Mark 1:2–3, which reads, "it is written in the prophet Isaiah." The following quote actually comes from Malachi 3:1. To cover the error, some copyists dropped the reference to Isaiah and others wrote "in the prophets."[53]
- Rounding off of phrases: Often scribes could not resist the temptation to embroider when they came to the name "Jesus." Many of the early texts do not include the additions of "Christ" or "Lord" as the name was lengthened to "Lord Jesus Christ."[54]
- Conflation of texts: Another temptation on the part of copyists was to avoid making a decision. Upon encountering two texts of similar reading, rather than choose one over the other, they would simply combine them, a stylistic tact often associated with the Byzantine textual "family." Metzger offers this example from the closing of Luke. Some early manuscripts read that the "disciples were continually in the temple blessing God" and others read "the disciples were continually in the temple praising God." The resulting conflation by later copyists became "the disciples were continually in the temple praising and blessing God."
- Miscellaneous details: Metzger illustrates how several ancient codices tamper with Matthew's genealogy of Jesus by adding names.[55] Also, in some texts, Jesus's words to Peter in Luke 6:4 and Matthew 20:28 have been expanded.[56]

- Theologically motivated changes: Entire volumes have consumed this issue.[57] During the second through the fourth centuries, in their scramble to combat Marcion and other Gnostic heretics, the early Church fathers made, or caused to be made, alterations in scripture due to doctrinal considerations. Ehrman goes to great lengths in his book *The Orthodox Corruption of Scripture*, and to a lesser degree in *Misquoting Jesus*, to demonstrate the alterations in scripture that were made in combating the three major heresies: Early Christian Adoptionism, Docetism, and Separatism.[58]

CONCLUSION

Learning of errors and alterations in what has been taught to be the infallible Word of God is a disconcerting experience. When the issue is reframed and presented as the Word of Christ in comparison to the person of Christ (compare the message with the person), it all makes sense: "The Word became flesh."

For sake of argument, if someone could prove there were no errors in the Bible, would that be a word one could trust? Would it be a word that could save? Accordingly, if the evidence proved that Christ was pure and flawless, that he was not flesh but perfect spirit, could He save?

In order to save humanity, the Word had to become flesh.

By recovering its humanity, the Word was made more complete. Paul echoes the same in the well-known passage in Philippians where Christ "who being in very nature God, did not consider equality with God something to be grasped, but made himself nothing" (Phil. 2:6–7a).

Most scholars began their studies of scripture as part of a spiritual quest, not a mission of scriptural destruction. They would agree that biblical discoveries, research, and enlightenment have not destroyed the divine nature of the Word. The illumination of its human side has enhanced its power to provide hope, comfort, forgiveness, and salvation. Bruce Metzger, after making several examples of scribal faithfulness to the text, makes the following reinforcing statement: "examples of dogged fidelity on the part of the scribes could be multiplied, and serve to counterbalance, to some extent, the impression which this chapter may otherwise make upon the beginner in New Testament textual criticism."[59]

Should any of this research affect one's belief in the Bible as God's inspired and authoritative word? Yes. There is an element of the miraculous. Words of spiritual inspiration written long ago that have been corrupted or expunged, can be recovered: "Moreover, even if scholars have by and large succeeded in reconstructing the New Testament, this, in itself, has no bearing on the truthfulness of its message. It simply means that we can be reasonably certain of what the New Testament authors actually said, just as we can be reasonably certain what Plato and Euripides and Josephus and Seutonius all said."[60] We are indebted to those scholars[61] for helping further refine what we believe.

SUMMARY

Reality testing, intellectual honesty, and scholars agree: the Bible, though divinely inspired, is a human product. Unless one wishes to entertain delusions of fantasy, it is difficult to get around this fact. What happened when the "Word became flesh" also occurred with the message itself: the divine and human came together.

Some individuals and bodies of belief, such as Fundamentalists and Muslims, continue to believe in the purity of the message, the inerrancy of scripture, and its literal interpretation. Problems with this position include the nonexistence of the autographs, or original texts, the lack of advocacy historically of this position and its recent adoption, the high window of expectation it raises for the reader or believer, and the multitude of inconsistencies and errors within the texts.

The humanity of the Bible is also emphasized in its production, editing, redacting, and translations over time. From the early monastery manuscripts to contemporary versions, biblical scholars have tried to interpret the word anew for each age. In the process, holy writ has undergone detrimental changes. An example is the King James Version of the Bible based on Erasmus' translation that was compiled from significantly flawed Byzantine twelfth-century texts.

Textual criticism is the art of restoring texts to their original state. Scholars who are text critics have been able to reconstruct, with reasonable accuracy, the basic form and message of the earliest manuscripts. Modern methods of textual criticism entail two key processes: *recension*, or selection of the most trustworthy evidence; and *emendation*, elimination of errors found in the most trusted manuscripts that incorporates the careful scrutiny of external and internal evidence. External evidence pertains to the outer appearance of the text whereas internal evidence focuses on intrinsic and transcriptional probabilities. Intrinsic probabilities relate to author, writing style, theology, and the context of the passage.

Errors in the biblical text fall into different categories: unintentional—faulty vision and hearing, poor memory and judgment, flawed writing and deliberate alteration for theological and doctrinal purposes. The latter includes revisions of grammar and spelling, harmonization of similar passages, elimination of discrepancies and difficulties, rounding off of phrases, conflation of texts, miscellaneous details, and theologically motivated changes.

In conclusion, overwhelming evidence portrays the Bible as a human product that has survived centuries of human tampering. Despite this earthly and flawed process, scripture has not lost its meaning for the twenty-first century. Conversely, its meaning and spiritual basis have been enhanced much in the way the Godhead became human in the person of Jesus of Nazareth; much in the way the "Word became flesh." What was true for incarnational Christology is also true for an incarnational hermeneutic: interpretation of the divinely inspired word.

Chapter 11

Psychological Issues
and Implications

Psychology is the study of human and animal behavior and thinking. Religion, according to *Webster*, is "the belief in and worship of God or gods."[1] For many years the position in both quarters allowed for little or no dialogue. But in recent years there has been a rapprochement.[2] The study of a religion necessitates the study of its psychology, the make up of the mental and emotional processes fueling its beliefs and behaviors, and vice versa. Both disciplines are attempting to understand human existence and answer many of the same questions: Who am I? Where did I come from? What does my existence mean? Where am I going? What will my death mean?

More often than not, one's behavior says more about the person than pedigree or resume. This is as true for groups as individuals. On paper Catholic and Baptist beliefs and practices are poles apart. Yet, psychologically and behaviorally they have many common traits. Striking similarities also surface in psychological profiles of Gnosticism and Fundamentalism.

Again, dualism is our starting point. Dualism in religion has already been addressed. Dualism in psychology descended from the French philosopher René Descartes (1596–1650) who described mind and body as two distinct entities which interact to create a person.[3] This belief in separation between the physical body and the immaterial mind (or soul) permeates Gnosticism and Fundamentalism. It has pervaded most of Christian theology from the early Church to the present.[4]

Gnosticism and Fundamentalism operate from a pronounced cut-and-dried dualism (the mystical element or divine spark within the human body). Mainstream Christianity is based upon incarnational theology. Dualistic thinking has a higher need for clarity and clearly drawn lines. Incarnational thinking has a higher tolerance for ambiguity. The fact that one has a greater need for absolute certainty and the other can tolerate paradoxes says something about their psychological makeup and how it does, or does not, interface with faith.

Dualistic theology has a low tolerance for ambiguity. Everything must be clearly resolved, neatly wrapped with no loose ends. Reality, with all its gray and cloudy issues, is packaged in black or white, no middle ground. So, the question is raised: Why, from a psychological perspective, would a theology or worldview need to be dualistic? Why would there have to be a good God and an evil God? Why would everything need to be so clearly defined, black or white, no in-between, no allowance for ambiguity? To reframe the question, why do some people gravitate toward religions and denominations with clearly established doctrines, laws, and regulations, elaborate rituals, and organizational hierarchy, the road to salvation clearly spelled out? Why do others prefer religious organizations that offer more freedom of choice in their doctrines and beliefs and allow more room for the venture of faith? Are the former more emotionally and intellectually insecure, perhaps less disciplined, and therefore need more structure or higher clarity? Are there some who need to feel a direct pipeline to the Almighty (mysticism), while others are comfortable, more trusting, with a less direct form of spiritual communication? Why do some need to feel more sense of control, while others are willing to let God be God?

Basically, these questions go to the issue of belief, or faith. What is faith? *Webster* defines faith as "unquestioning belief, specifically in God, a religion . . . complete trust or confidence."[5] The New Testament defines faith as "being sure of what we hope for and certain of what we do not see" (Hebrews 11:1). (The most quoted translation is the King James Version: "Now faith is the substance of things hoped for, the evidence of things not seen.") Regardless of one's preference, the interpretation indicates we must believe in what we do not know in the human, empirical, and scientific sense of knowing. Perhaps the poet Tennyson said it best: "We have but faith: we cannot know; For knowledge is of things we see."[6] Faith, by definition, is complete trust and confidence. But there is a difference between trust and confidence, and empirical scientific certainty. The famous Danish theologian Søren Kierkegaard drives the point home: a faith in need of defense is not faith.[7]

This understanding of faith flies in the face of any theology based upon knowledge; or mysticism, which communicates with the deity through the senses and implies spiritual certainty. Gnosticism, through its "divine spark" and Fundamentalism, through its "knowing" of Jesus and "once saved, always saved," bear psychological resemblance. They are not alone. Roman Catholicism and Orthodox Judaism are both heavily structured and legalistic. Hand-in-hand with certainty is inflexible and rigid dogma. Through observation of human behavior, it appears that individuals who are inclined to be more secure in their beliefs and opinions also tend to be less threatened and thus more tolerant of the beliefs of others. They tend to be more open to alternative interpretations, have less need for elaborate structure, tight dogma, and the apparatuses of "sound" doctrine.

In Chapter 7, "The Basic Tenets of Fundamentalism," reference is made to Martin and Appleby's classic study and the nine factors of generic fundamentalism. Several of these do not apply to Gnosticism: militancy, authoritarian male leaders, and totalitarian impulse. The characteristics that are common to Fundamentalism and Gnosticism are religious origin, selective use of tradition, reaction against aspects of a modern world, siege mentality, apocalyptic view of history, and definite boundaries. This latter, "definite boundaries," continually draws our attention.

Dualism creates theoretical and ideological boundaries. Those boundaries translate into social boundaries of knowers and nonknowers, insiders and outsiders, believers and nonbelievers, saved and nonsaved (or damned). These boundaries are mutually exclusive; they do not overlap. Any overlapping indicates either contamination with ignorance or evil; thus overlapping is intolerable. Purism, the ultimate offspring of dualism, reigns.

Dualism, with its distinctive lines and neat compartmentalization of reality also has a tendency to simplify, that is, to present a picture of "the way things are" in a manner that requires little critical examination. Everything is clear-cut. This is "the way things are" and nothing can change it. Psychologically, this is known as a "cognitive trap." Those familiar with cognitive psychology, the study of human thinking and thought processes, are familiar with this term. It is a form of illusional thinking caused by individuals who are overconfident and anchored in their own knowledge. "All or none" thinking, a psychological symptom of Gnosticism and Fundamentalism, is a cognitive trap. One mistake tarnishes a brilliant career. A single flaw shatters an entire work of art. Other manifestations are observed in people who, if they cannot get it right the first time, refuse to try again. Or, if they think they cannot get it right the first time, they do not try. A less than perfect performance in an endeavor is considered futile and thus trashed. Psychologists call this faulty, or "stinking thinking," and engage their clientele in a form of therapy called "cognitive restructuring."

Cognitive trap applied to the domain of religion is a product of dualism, which leads to "knowing" versus "believing." It was the Pharisees' version of Judaism that made them *certain* Jesus was a heretic. In their eyes, they were right and he was wrong. This dichotomous thinking led to his crucifixion. Dualism crucifies. Every religion is vulnerable to an arrogance of certainty that the deity, or God, is on their side, and that this "faithfulness" (a full-of-themselves faithfulness) portrays all others as enemies who must be destroyed. Despite numerous biblical sayings to the contrary—"Blessed are the poor in spirit" (Matthew 5:3); "Do not judge or you, too, will be judged" (Matthew 7:1); "Knowledge puffs up, but love builds up" (I Corinthians 8:1)—this type of certainty indeed "puffs up."[8]

The same message comes from the writer of 1 John. This Johannine author might be responding to a heretical movement within the Church when he writes, "if we claim to be without sin, we deceive ourselves, and the truth is not in us. . . . We know that we have come to know (*ginoskomen*) him, if we obey his commands. The man who says, 'I know (*egnoka*) him, but does not do what he commands is a liar and the truth is not in him'" (1 John 1:8; 2:3–4). Dualism leads to crusades and jihads, to Armageddon's and eschatological cataclysms. Dualism results in ethnic cleansings and massacres, annihilation of one people over another. It promotes chauvinism and jingoism; boastful devotion to ones race, sex, or religion and foreign policies based upon inflated patriotism and xenophobia. Dualism leads to absolutes, and absolutes mask deep and profound insecurities.

Dualism raises psychological questions about personality. Is it the low self-esteem of a bully that causes him (or her) to overcompensate with brute force against a much weaker opponent? Is it fear of personal inadequacies that cause a dictator to rule with an iron fist and subject his people to ruthless tyranny? Does the guilt-induced fear of rejection and punishment turn religion into an impossible network of laws and regulations guaranteeing salvation?

Those who play out a dualistic philosophy, whether in thought or deed, become what they fear. They exploit buffers against the unknown—against fear, anxiety, evil, death, the terror of the gods—and magnify their voltage. The result, instead of reducing insecurity and anxiety, is the opposite; fear becomes a contagion that nourishes itself. It becomes "Us" against "Them."

As Fisher Humphreys and Philip Wise point out, the attitudes generated by this type of thinking include suspicion, anger, fear, and separatism.[9] Suspicion is manifested in response to the mindset that liberals are intentionally attempting to undermine the Church. Frequently this degenerates into a state of paranoia, a downward spiral based on the dualistic "all or nothing" concept, a type of domino theory that if one idea falls, they all fall. Conversely, if an individual holds one liberal idea, he or she is "totally" infected with liberalism. This creates a mindset among Fundamentalists (shared by Gnostics) of hypervigilance vis-à-vis the beliefs of others. When this type of "all or nothing" thinking exists within liberal minds, the dualistic psychology supporting it is easily identified.

Fear, a natural psychological emotion, can be rational or irrational. It was an irrational fear that drove the Gnostics into their esoteric enclaves. It is an irrational fear that spurs Fundamentalists today into a heightened awareness of evil lurking in the secular world surrounding them.

Anger can be a response to a real threat or one imagined. It can be justified or unjustified. Because so many of their publications were destroyed, little is known of Gnostic expressions of anger. They obviously felt their backs to the wall, which could only fuel their fears and paranoia. By normal psychological standards this would lead to anger. The threats to the early Gnostics were very real, not imagined as with contemporary Fundamentalists. Their anger may be more justified.

With Fundamentalism, however, "anger is understood as an appropriate motivator, and so it is cultivated."[10] In his book, *Falwell, An Autobiography*, Jerry Falwell tends to confirm this conclusion: "A fundamentalist is an evangelical who is mad about something."[11] Liberalism poses as a threat to their values and beliefs. If you have a desire to experience this anger first hand, listen to a Fundamentalist preacher.

Separatism is well founded in the Gnostic documents available. Fundamentalists manifest this behaviorally when they condemn other Fundamentalists, because they quote from a non-Fundamental book or share a dais with a non-Fundamentalist. Liberals do the same when they criticize one of their own for an action, such as appearing on a conservative talk show. More explicitly, separatism is manifested by Fundamentalists when they evacuate from mainstream protestant churches and flee to churches collectively organized to fit their own beliefs and agendas. It is not unusual to see these churches split basically because of purges, a recurring prominent feature of purism and dictatorships. One group believes the other is not pure enough. This constant process of subdivision happens frequently among Fundamentalist branches. It is the history of the Christian Church. It is the history of every religion. It is human behavior. It is dualism: "You are either with us or against us."

To this point in our study, several buzz words have been used to characterize Gnosticism and Fundamentalism: dualism, *gnosis*, inerrancy, literalism, separatism, and so on. One word, however, that best captures the psychological essence of both religious phenomena, escapism, surfaced in Philip Lee's *Against the Protestant Gnostics*: "Modern Escape—from the Home of the Brave?" (See chapter 9: "Religions of Escapism".)[12]

Fundamentally innate to human behavior for millions of years is a psychological mechanism popularly labeled the "fight–flight" response: "when we are faced with situations that require adjustment of our behavior, an involuntary response increases our blood pressure, heart rate, breathing, blood flow to the muscles, and metabolism, preparing us for conflict or escape."[13] Proto-orthodox, Orthodox, and Reformed theologians chose to fight. The Gnostics and frontier Calvinists of the new world chose to flee—not physically, but theologically. For the former this was symptomatic of their disappearance from the scene, their flight into the desert and hills of what today comprises parts of eastern Turkey, Iraq, and Iran. For the latter it is more expressive in their theology.

The Gnostic accomplishes an escape into the self: "knowledge of God involves the knower, not in a further or more profound relationship with the world—nature and other persons—but rather in a disengagement from the world and a concentration on the self and the self's concern."[14] This escape is psychologically motivated. The object of illumination in the Gnostic journey is the self. Unlike the prodigal son when he saw the light, the Gnostic returns to himself and not another. The narcissistic overtones are profound. In seeing God, Gnostics see themselves. This is a far cry from the prophet from Nazareth who said, "whatever you did for one of the least of these brothers of mine, you did for me" (Matthew 25: 40). "If we find God only through self-awareness, how can the God we find be anything more or less than a reflection of ourselves?"[15] Gilbert Keith Chesterton's quip is more poignant than ever: "that Jones shall worship the god within him turns out ultimately to mean that Jones shall worship Jones."

The escape route for pioneer and Fundamentalist theology is rebirth, the born-again conversion experience. On a more visible public level, this escape route blatantly flares when one has committed a crime or social error then "sees the light." They become "born-again." The concept is based on a single passage of scripture (John 3: 1–8) in which Jesus tells the Pharisee Nicodemus "no one can see the kingdom of God unless he is born again" (John 1:3). It became then in Protestant revivalism, and remains today, the trumpet call to salvation; "it was a call, almost totally lacking in content, to accept Christ, to surrender, to be saved. The same lack of content even today (from the evidence of radio and television) characterizes much of what might seem to be the predominant Christianity of modern America."[16]

One rarely escapes *to* something but rather *from* something. Gnostics and Fundamentalists, with their common dualistic bond, had a profound need to escape the evil world. This is neither biblical nor orthodox. The world is not inherently evil: "In the beginning God created the heavens and the earth. . . . And God saw that it was good" (Genesis 1:1, 10b).Yet the Puritan mind was uncomfortable with any relationship between the realms of spiritual humanity and the material, natural world.[17] Consistent with their need to escape nature, Gnostics and early conservative Protestants felt impelled to escape time. Except within the camps of African American Protestantism, this stance has resulted in an unfortunate avoidance of involvement in social issues.

Dualism leads to overbalanced focus on self, a narcissistic tendency to focus inward and separate self from all else. As a religion, Gnosticism, designed to rescue one from depression, paradoxically encourages depression. In his classic book *Depression*, Karl Menninger states that ultimately all depression (except chemically induced and certain mood disorders) is self-centered and self-oriented. We live in an age of preoccupation with self, "a narcissistic fascination with one's own spiritual being,"[18] an age of self-analysis, self-actualization, self-realization, and self-help.

Is it possible that this drive for self-realization is the source of original sin, a form of narcissism first evidenced beneath an apple tree in the Garden of Eden? Is it possible the narcissism of the believer is transferred to the evangelist regarding number of souls saved? Is it plausible that the focus creates and adds to the neurosis, incongruence, and psychological split? Do the four Gospels not frequently revisit the theme that "whoever finds his life will lose it, and whoever loses his life for my sake will find it" (Matthew 10:39). In comparable fashion, Karl Menninger's treatment for depression offered a similar paradoxical cure. He encouraged his patients to close the doors of their homes, cross the tracks, and help a fellow human in need. This type of outreach is precluded by a thoroughgoing dualistic Gnosticism. As noted, this is one of the differences between American Fundamentalism and Gnosticism. Some Fundamentalists do have mission outreach programs.

One significant psychological difference between Gnosticism and Fundamentalism is their attitude toward intelligence. Gnostics were considered intellectuals in their day, which drew the suspicion of the early Church fathers.[19] Like those early apologists, Fundamentalists fear intellectuals and intellectualism. Sociologically, this is evidenced in their choice of schools and colleges with minimal or no exposure to differing theological or cultural models, and curriculums that match the Fundamental mindset. Because these institutions are private and privately funded, their admissions policies are selective and often are discriminatory. One private interdenominational Christian secondary school accepts only students who profess a salvation experience and who come from homes where at least one parent has "been saved" or "reborn." The teachers must meet the same criteria.

Barred from attending are nonbelievers, Jews, agnostics, and homosexuals. Besides meeting Martin Marty and Scott Applebee's definite boundaries criteria, this situation also illustrates the factors of siege mentality and fear of modernity.

On the same side of that psychological coin, those of Far Left, liberal persuasion engage in similar discriminatory behavior. They tend to avoid institutions considered right-wing, conservative television channels, and conservative literature. In short, the two mutually exclude each other. In this respect, contemporary Gnosticism is similar to the intellectual Gnostics of old. They exclude conservative Christian theology for the same reason they did centuries ago: dualism.

One's attitude toward intelligence also influences decision-making orientation, whether choices are made on a cognitive or emotional, basis. The two are different. Cognition is the mental process that includes reasoning, memory, thinking, and learning. Emotion has to do with the feeling component of our personality and behavior. Both cognition and emotion influence each other and play roles in our decision making. Cognitive processes can lead to rational and sound decisions that are reality-oriented. Cognitive biases, or mental distortions of reality, cause individuals to make flawed decisions. By the same token, when emotions take over in decision making, emotional biases play a role and affect cognitive biases. When this occurs, there is cognitive dissonance. Cognitive dissonance is a mental process by which individuals reject new facts because they are contrary to their existing beliefs—or knowledge, prejudices, habits, commitments—and thus make them *feel* uncomfortable. More often than not, they reject this new knowledge and continue to look only for knowledge that fits their belief system. This is played out in daily routines and pastimes. They watch only particular television channels, read only certain authors, view only certain movies, and so on. Their friends include only those who watch the same channels, read the same authors, and so on. Their process of decision making narrows, which in turn produces narrow results and a narrow and restricted existence, because they do not want to become contaminated by anything that is considered evil or bad. This is dualism.

How Gnostics made decisions is unknown, but they did aggressively read proto-orthodox literature. Massive amounts of it. They were self-exiled or driven from proto-orthodox congregations. At some point they retreated unto themselves and eventually became confined to desert and mountain fringe areas. Psychologically, this would be called "withdrawal." We are able to observe how Fundamentalists make decisions. The underlying basis is a dualistic split between emotion and cognition. Emotions also tend to influence their worship services, revivals, and rituals. Individuals are saved if they "know" Jesus, but this "knowing" is basically rooted in feeling, a process characteristic of mysticism.

To counter these insecurities and fears over time, individuals, groups, and societies develop belief systems. Many of these belief systems are rational, meaning they align with reality and the real world. They make sense. Within that context they are helpful and adaptive. Some of these belief systems, however, are irrational. They are based on cognitive and emotional biases, handed down and positively reinforced over the centuries.

Psychology plays a role in the success and failure of individuals. When they make faulty decisions based on faulty biases, their lives, families, and destinies are affected. Similar results of irrational thinking also afflict organizations and groups.

Mainstream Christianity has been a continuous, sustained force in world history. Gnosticism has not. With both, different psychological forces have fueled their thinking and decision making. Orthodox mainstream Christian thought processes have been based on a unified reality, a unified redeemer, "a Word made flesh." Gnostic thought processes have been based upon dualism. Is this bifurcated view of reality a key reason Gnosticism comes and goes on the world scene? Others include its tight boundaries and exclusiveness; its narrow secret knowledge, and focus on individual salvation. Its message is based upon a dualistic understanding of reality; it never becomes flesh. Is this truncated worldview why some current religious phenomena with similar dualistic interpretations of reality and salvation come and go? They are theological flashes that flare and fade but never die. They preach an alluring and seductive message: if individuals believe the *absolute* word of God and bend their lives in harmony with that word, they can be certain of God's favor and assured of their salvation. Dualism offers a seemingly easy solution to the problem of evil. The key word is "seems." The Christ of the Gnostics was never real. He only "seemed" real.

SUMMARY

Religion and psychology overlap and ask similar questions in their application to human concerns. For this reason, a study of religion would be incomplete without addressing its psychological implications.

Gnosticism and Fundamentalism as religious models share similar psychological traits. Their dualistic basis is a key to understanding their similarities. Dualism creates a psychological attitudinal split in the way one views the world: everything is either black or white. This simplistic interpretation of reality also creates a low tolerance for ambiguity. One's worldview must be unmistakable and clear-cut. Psychologically, this can be interpreted as representing an underlying basic insecurity that reflects one's concept of faith or lack of faith. Faith implies belief, not certainty. It can possess a certain confidence that knows in part, not in full. Gnosticism and Fundamentalism cross the line from confidence to certainty. The vehicle for that passage is mysticism.

Dualism is also the underlying basis for mysticism in which the receiver of a divine message becomes one with the message and the sender of the message. Gnostics believe certain individuals were predestined to possess the "divine spark," thus they were preordained and preinvested with the equipage for salvation. Of the remainder, some were left to earn their salvation while others were doomed. Forms of Fundamentalism with an obsessive component embrace this position.

Obsessive thinking is a by-product of dualism where one deals in absolutes, the pure versus the impure. In turn, this leads to spiritual purity that often converts to psychological arrogance and condescension. The psychological and sociological result of this process is exclusion versus inclusion. Gnosticism and Fundamentalism both create boundaries that divide the insiders from the outsiders.

Another result of dualism is "all or nothing" thinking that creates a cognitive trap for the individual. A cognitive trap occurs when an individual allows one negative thought to obliterate all positive thoughts. Another variation on that theme is judging a person or group of people as evil based on one negative aspect of their behavior or thinking. Such polarized reasoning launches crusades and ethnic cleansings and breeds suspicion, fear, anger, and separatism.

A significant difference in Gnosticism and Fundamentalism is their perception of intellectuals. Today, as in the first centuries CE, Gnostics seek to enlist intellectuals. On the other hand, Fundamentalists are highly suspicious of intellectuals and tend to exclude them. They commonly attend educational institutions that teach their brand of religion. Conversely, some Gnostics and intellectuals tend to speak condescendingly of "right wing" fundamental schools and colleges and choose to attend other educational institutions.

CHAPTER 12

AN ALTERNATIVE
TO DUALISM

INCARNATION—THE WORD
MADE FLESH

HISTORICALLY, RELIGIONS WITH DUALISTIC ELEMENTS HAVE DOMINATED THE world. How did that happen? Where and how did it all begin?: "Its birth lies far back in the days when man first consciously looked at the world and saw that it was bad; and he wondered how such evil should be, and why God, if there be a God, could permit it."[1] Job raised the question in the Old Testament: "When a land falls into the hands of the wicked, he blindfolds its judges. If it is not He then who is it" (Job 9:24)? The question of evil and suffering faces every religion. It might be ignored for a while, but for a religion to survive, the question of suffering cannot be evaded.

The solution for many ancient thinkers—Greek Philosophers, Hellenistic Jews, Egyptian Hermetics, Zoroastrians—continues to be appealing. It takes a good God off the hook. The Demiurge or devil, or some other power or aeon created the world which relieved God, the Supreme Principle, from responsibility for sin and suffering. The spirit, which came from God, was good. All else was evil. Matter was condemned, spirit uplifted. This explained the misery of the world in terms common folk could understand. Gnostics restated the theme and refashioned it to fit their agenda.

This simplistic solution to the problem of suffering and evil is one of the reasons dualism, in the guise of Gnosticism, spread in successive centuries. It began in the east and swept westward (Bogomils, Paternes, and Cathars) from the Black Sea to Biscay, keeping the Church constantly on guard. Without the complexities of ancestry or incarnation or Trinitarian beliefs, the creed of dualism fits easily into one's thinking.[2] Another factor contributing to its success is its focus on the individual, the appeal to the psychological gravity of ego. Dualism's hush-hush seductive air of covertness was also alluring.

Little wonder proto-orthodoxy, and later Orthodoxy, became alarmed. Gnostics made up a large part of the early Christian communities. They saw themselves as "pure" Christians, not as heretics. For Orthodoxy, any religion that denied God as creator and humanity as fallen was intolerable. Like the hydra-headed monster of myth, no sooner had the Church extinguished one dualistic Gnostic heresy than another would pop up.

Dualism and Gnosticism do not solve the problem of evil and suffering. Their theories fall short. They do not explain the presence of *good*. If Satan created the world, how did God allow the element of good to be present? In the absence of good there is no religion. To skirt this problem, the dualists "had to invent innumerable stories to explain the presence of good in the world. But all of them involved a definite restriction of the sovereignty of God."[3] God was not truly omnipotent; Satan had clipped his wings. Ultimately, this position did not explain why there is a mix of good and evil in a physical body. But the problem dualism creates for Fundamentalism and Gnosticism is resolved in Orthodoxy. The uniqueness of the Incarnation brings closure. "The heresy of one age becomes the orthodoxy of the next." It would seem the aphorism that opened this study has been validated. One might despairingly admit defeat and declare Gnosticism is everywhere: "There is none that is without Gnosticism." But there is another option.

IMPLICATIONS OF INCARNATIONAL THEOLOGY

By definition incarnation means "endowed with a human body (in + *caro*, flesh); personified; incarnated; to give bodily form to . . . to be the embodiment of."[4] Christianity is not the only religion whose centerpiece is the embodiment of the deity. Savior figures who take on the appearance of divinity are numerous throughout religious history. In none of those cases, however, does the divine, in reality, *become* flesh, blood, and bone.

The absence of true incarnation in other religions has to do with its implications for dualism. When the word becomes "flesh," it can no longer be wholly spirit. Dualism is shattered, vanquished. With Incarnation the two, spirit and flesh, are united. Good and evil, white and black, light and dark, saints and sinners, are thrown together but not merged. The dialectical nuance is important. The divine does not get dissolved into the human or the human into the divine. They are consubstantial, fully God, fully human; "all have sinned" (Romans 3:23). When St. Paul wrote those words, he was putting every one on equal footing, leveling the playing field of salvation. In other words, he was proclaiming the Incarnation. Perhaps no clearer statement of this concept can be found than in this poetic expression in Paul's Letter to the Philippians, where pride is emptied, purity abolished: "Your attitude should be the same as that of Christ Jesus who, being in very nature God, did not consider equality with God something to be grasped but made himself nothing, taking the very nature of a servant, being made in human likeness, and being found in appearance as a man he humbled himself and became obedient to death—even death on a cross" (Philippians 2:5–8).

When the Word becomes flesh, He who was on high is brought low. Humility becomes a deterrent to arrogance and condescending theology; "He has brought down rulers from their thrones but has lifted up the humble" (Luke 1:52). With the Incarnation, God becomes one with humankind. In Christ there is no longer a gulf between the divine and the human. Nothing is bridged; distance simply collapses. The divine *becomes* human. This is the genius and distinguishing mark of Christianity: in its infancy, during its formative centuries of Orthodoxy, through the Middle Ages of Reform and Reformation, and into the present century of ultramodernity.

What Christian theology means by Incarnation, by "the Word became flesh," is more than just the embodiment of the deity. It is more than the divine invasion of humanity, more than a doctrine hammered out in committees to mean more than its words convey on paper. Incarnation means not just the reduction of distance between polarities but also their abolition. It is the destruction of law and legalism. The simplicity of achieving one's salvation the old-fashioned way, by earning it, is replaced with the simplicity of salvation to all by grace. His resolution "to know nothing . . . except Jesus Christ and him crucified" (1 Corinthians 2:2) is Paul's shorthand for Incarnation.

This simple faith is not the oversimplicity of dualism. Pauline faith demands more from one than the mental act of knowing. It demands faith, not certitude. It requires a higher level for tolerating ambiguity. Incarnation is a dialectic that interfaces with what Kierkegaard called "the dialectic of faith, the finest and most remarkable of all" from which, in the same breath, he proclaims, "I am able to make from the springboard the great leap whereby I pass into infinity."[5] With belief, something is at stake; one takes a risk. Gnosticism is cut-and-dried; Incarnation carries peril and jeopardy. It is the paradox that defies, and continually frustrates, absolutism and certainty.

Faith in the Incarnation implies a dialectical element, a truth that cannot be nailed down; God, by definition, cannot be nailed down. Once defined, God is no longer the infinite, indefinable One. God tells Moses he will put him in a cleft of the rock. He will pass by and Moses will see his back but, "no man may see me and live" (Exodus 33:20).

The mythological tale of Rumpelstiltskin comes to mind. As long as no one could pronounce his name, the legendary gnome had magical powers. But once his name was uttered, those powers vanished. The Israelites were not allowed to speak the Lord's name. The privilege to speak the name Yahweh belonged only to the High Priest who could pronounce it only one day of the year and in one place, that is, the holy of holies, innermost sanctum of the tabernacle. Does the analogy transfer to the current time and the seeming powerlessness of the name of God and His Word? The mystery, the *mysterium tremendum* or "Wholly Other," which Rudolph Otto expressed in his classic, *The Idea of the Holy*, has vanished. It has become *known*.[6]

"Heresy implies a lack of dialectical tension."[7] Dualism, or heresy, destroys tension. In that sense it is unrealistic and given to fantasy. Dualism reflects an oversimplification of reality. It speaks of good without speaking of evil, of the divine without speaking of the human, of the soul without the body, of spirit without matter or flesh. Incarnation means, and maintains, dialectical tension. Incarnation dispels fantasy, sentimentalism, superficiality, and wishful thinking. Accepting the Incarnation means no longer being able to view the world as we wish but rather viewing the world as it is. It means being able to hold and balance (or weigh) good and evil, the spirit and the flesh, light and dark, soul and body. With Incarnation, one can speak of the normal polarities of life because they are part of the whole. The ultimate demand of this unity of polarities, the ultimate challenge of faith, is the God-man, Jesus the Christ. Because dualism is built on knowledge and the absence of dialectical tension, it does not require a leap of faith. Incarnation requires—demands—that leap. With Incarnation there are no longer clear answers. This is the demand and challenge of Incarnation, of faith. It is a risky adventure, a pilgrimage through the world with nothing guaranteed except Emmanuel, God with us. It is involvement in the world, not a phantasmal escape from the world.

By Incarnation Christian theology does not mean the abolishing of all distinctions, which would mean the loss of distinction between humanity and divinity. It does not mean a shifting or reordering of boundaries, rather the destruction of those boundaries so that what was divided and fragmented becomes united. There are no longer special religious interests nor privately owned conduits to the Almighty. The "outside" is eradicated. Everyone is inside. Exclusiveness is replaced with inclusiveness; "from early days American evangelical experience has required an elitist-self-understanding."[8] A theology of grace through Incarnation erases boundaries and replaces exclusiveness with inclusiveness.

Mysticism is no longer viable. With mysticism, a spark of the deity is already within the individual. The individual connects with that divine spark within, a form of self-identity that allows for the immediate conduit to Godhead. The *Gospel of Thomas* "contains several allusions to self-knowledge as a means to and as identical to the knowledge of God."[9]

Incarnation destroys the spark within because it is no longer needed. The emphasis of salvation falls not upon whom you know but who knows you: "you do not seek Him, He seeks you; you do not find Him, He finds you; your faith comes from Him, not from you; everything that faith works in you comes from Him."[10] As close as Luther veered at times toward Gnosticism, the Incarnation for him was always the corrective, that is, the force pulling him back from the dualistic mysticism, that was so tempting. With Incarnation, "faith is the opposite of finding ourselves; it is being found by God."[11] With Fundamentalism, as with Gnosticism, one effected salvation through their own knowledge of the divine. With their emphasis upon the word, *sola scriptura*, the Protestant Reformers (Luther, Calvin, Zwingli, and others) came very close to a form of knowledge (*gnosis*) that saves. This saving knowledge had to be accepted and the acceptance on the part of believers caused their salvation.

The repercussions of Incarnation are felt in the sacrament of Holy Communion and baptism. As a deterrent to any form of elitist self-aggrandizement, any puffed up sense of self-importance or narcissistic rhapsodizing, the leaders of the Reformation insisted upon infant baptism. Individuals cannot take credit for their salvation. Calvin and other reformers saw the dangers and emphasized the congregational nature of the sacerdotal blessing; "for Calvin, a reformed church's view of infant baptism differentiated a church from a sect."[12] God's love is not restricted to our knowledge, understanding, and appreciation of it. The Reformers were thoroughly anti-Gnostic.

As a repudiation of Gnosticism, the Apostles' Creed emerged near the beginning of the early Church. It was required of candidates at their baptism to insure they did not belong to Gnostic sects within the congregation. The recitation of the Creed marked the separation of the true believer from the false believer, or Gnostic, who did not believe in "God the Father Almighty, Maker of heaven and earth" or "Jesus Christ, born of the Virgin Mary, suffered under Pontius Pilate, was crucified and buried."[13]

The importance of baptism also emphasized the communal nature of Christianity in opposition to the Gnostic emphasis on individual salvation. Biblical scholar Joachim Jeremias provides this summary: "The whole people of God were baptized when they passed through the Red Sea (1 Cor. 10:1f.), the whole family of Noah was saved in the ark (1 Peter 3:20f.), the promise of the Spirit is referred to the 'houses,' 'to you and your children' (Acts 2:39). They are seen as one unit in the sight of God . . . the universal character of Christ's grace reveals itself in that it is the "houses" which are summoned to believe and are baptized."[14]

Within that same context, Irenaeus wrote of the Incarnation: "Christ did not despise or evade any condition of humanity but sanctified every age. . . . He therefore passes through every age, becoming an infant, thus sanctifying infants, a child for children, thus sanctifying those who are at this age . . . a youth for youths . . . and . . . because he was an old man for old people . . . sanctifying at the same time the aged also . . . then, at last, he came onto death itself."[15] The Incarnation is the union of mind, body, and soul and their convergence into a unified whole. It is the resurrection of a spiritual body, as Paul states (1 Corinthians 15:44). When Paul says we will rise with a spiritual body (*pneuma somatika*), he is drawing on the logical consequences of incarnational theology. When the Incarnation eliminated a divided Christ, it also expunged the compartmentalization of personality.

Under incarnational theology, ethics and morality based upon the narrow tunnel of subjective and private sins are replaced with corporate morality. All sins are revealed and fall under ethical scrutiny. Because all have sinned and fallen short, all must be served and saved. Ethics becomes a social phenomenon. Individuals must no longer look only to saving themselves, whether from ignorance or sin and turn toward saving society and humankind. Incarnation is, therefore, the priesthood of all believers. Each person is not a priest unto themselves but a priest for others: "everyman his neighbor's priest, one the Christ of the other . . .

the incarnate, resurrected, and ascended Christ has no real presence in the world apart from the fellowship-creating relationship."[16]

A rigorous and radical theology of incarnation does not escape from, cover up, or duck the horrible atrocities of this world: the Dachau's and Buchenwald's, mass graves in Iraq and Bosnia, Iraqi prisons. It does not escape the real issues that affect humankind—nuclear disarmament, ecological responsibility, gun control, war and peace, depressed third world countries, capital punishment. A theology of incarnation exports openness and acceptance of others regardless of sex, race, creed, or socioeconomic status. Salvation is through the world, not from the world. Whereas the spirit-tilted Gnostics and Fundamentalists would escape from this world and its many problems, the believer in the Incarnation makes a pilgrimage through the world.

Incarnation embraces intellectual honesty. The Holy Scriptures are as sacred in their humanness as in their divineness. They manifest more meaning in their inspired corruption than in their uninspired incorruption. Just as God spoke through Jesus of Nazareth in spite of his humanity, He does the same through "a fallible but ordained Word whose content is defined by and shaped in terms of a flawed . . . text."[17] The Word is allowed to breathe rather than strain against the constraints of imposed literalism. The written word is freed for scholarly divine interpretation, that is, to "make sense" within the context in which it was written. As Ehrman is earlier quoted: "texts are interpreted (just as they were written) by living breathing human beings, who can make sense of the texts only by explaining them in the light of their other knowledge, explicating their meaning, putting the words of their texts 'in other words.'"[18]

The Bible possesses spiritual power precisely because it is a human production arising from real life situations, from men and women grappling with real life issues, such as emotions, fears, torments, disappointments, hopes, and dreams. If the Word became flesh in the person of Jesus of Nazareth, the same applies to his message and the messages of those before and after him, The Old and New Testaments. As the late conservative Protestant theologian Emil Brunner expressed, to treat the Bible any differently not only breaks the first commandment but also makes a claim for the Scriptures the Scriptures do not make for themselves.[19]

Incarnation represents the living, not the dead. If tradition is not revitalized, reinterpreted for each new age it enters, it dies. It becomes traditionalism, rather than a living tradition. The same occurs with other words of tradition. Whether it is Plato's *The Republic*, The U.S. Constitution, *The Merchant of Venice*, *Alice in Wonderland*, or any text of any age, if they are simply read and not reinterpreted to interface meaningfully with the era in which they are read, they lose meaning and vibrancy. They no longer resonate and will eventually die. Is this why the Bible is no longer relevant in much of the world?

Incarnation changes one's concept of time. Time no longer functions on a two-dimensional linear, horizontal and vertical, continuum, neatly bifurcated into a glorious past and glorious final future to come. It becomes holographic. This Incarnation is once-and-for-all, eternal, available in every time. There is no reincarnation, which is the belief one's soul is reborn in another body. Reincarnation is a belief that can thrive only under dualism.

Incarnation changes the way we see ourselves. We can accept our bodies and sexuality as gifts from God, not another evil among evils. Though at a different level, sexuality becomes a subtle form of incarnation. In sexuality creation continues. Therefore, abstinence from sex is the ultimate denial of humanness, the death of humanity. One Gnostic sect embracing this concept simply died out.

SUMMARY

At the time of Christ, dualist theology, with its is convenient solution to the problem of suffering by posing two gods, dominated the Mediterranean world. Gnostics infiltrated early Christian congregations with dualism. To counter this heresy, the early fathers forged what would become the central principle of Christianity: "The Word became flesh" or the Incarnation of Christ.

The implications of incarnational theology for dualism are radical and extraordinarily far-reaching. Dualism no longer becomes a viable concept. Not only is there one God but also God is one with, yet apart from, humankind; a paradox that maintains a tension faith must reject or accept. This is different from the simple structure of dualism. In dualism, reality is negated. But with Incarnation, reality is affirmed and becomes the guiding principle of the faith journey.

Dualism allows for the compartmentalization of individuals into "the knowers" versus "the unknowers," the saved versus the unsaved. The Incarnation of Christ abolishes all boundaries of separation. It eradicates the concept of divinity within humans, or mysticism. There is no special conduit or access to the Almighty. In a theology of Incarnation, God is available to all. The spiritual playing field is leveled.

The effects of the Incarnation can be seen in the sacraments. In Holy Communion Christ comes to us; we do not go to him. The Reformers embraced infant baptism because it emphasized the Christ who knows the believer, not the reverse. One cannot effect his or her own salvation. The Apostles' Creed, used by most mainline orthodox denominations, marks the Incarnation in history. It proclaims that Christ (God) becomes a physical reality who suffered, was crucified, buried, and resurrected.

Incarnation takes religion out of the individual sphere of spiritual activity and places it firmly in a social context. We are placed upon this earth to care for others. We are not to turn our backs on an evil material world, but, as stewards and caretakers, we are to turn toward the world. This means taking action on issues important to all humankind, including the environment, global warming, starvation, poverty, and wars. Morality becomes a corporate matter rather than an issue of individual concern. Salvation is open to everyone, not just a select few. Along this same line, our physical bodies are not evil; sex is not "of the devil." We are called to experience our sexuality in productive and meaningful ways, to lift up humankind, not to degrade or destroy it.

Most importantly, and germane to this study, Incarnation changes the way we interpret the Bible. Scripture becomes divine in its humanness, a spiritual guide because of its flaws. The words of that old spiritual song resonate on this theme: "Nobody knows the troubles I've seen, nobody knows but Jesus." He has walked the same earth humans walk and can save the people from their sins. The same applies to the written word and the hands that wrote it. The Bible's human dimension makes it *holy*, a word in its original Greek that meant whole, complete.

CHAPTER 13

GNOSTICISM, FUNDAMENTALISM, AND ORTHODOXY

WHERE DO WE GO FROM HERE?

DESPITE MASSIVE EFFORTS BY ORTHODOX CHRISTIANITY TWO MILLENNIA AGO TO wipe it from the face of the earth, Gnosticism not only survives, it thrives. For verification and bountiful references visit the Web, scan the Yellow Pages, explore a bookstore, or read popular sci-fi books by Philip K. Dick or Philip Pullman's trilogy, *His Dark Materials*. The effects of Gnosticism can be seen in movies like *Dark City, The Matrix, The Truman Show, Twelve Monkeys,* or *Toy Story.* Gnosticism abounds in worship services of the many Fundamentalist churches and the latest pop-religion books: *The Purpose-Driven Life, The Celestine Prophesy, Shaking the World for Jesus, With God on Our Side, Your Best Life Now.* In conservative talk radio programs, on television with televangelists, and in unlimited numbers on the internet, Gnosticism is alive. Its effects are far-reaching in today's society.

The core hypothesis of this book proposes that elements of Gnosticism permeate Fundamentalist theology. Fundamentalism is, therefore, another form of the first heresy that challenged early Christianity, as it does mainstream denominations today. Harold Bloom states that, "Most Americans . . . are closer to ancient Gnostics than to early Christians."[1]

An analysis of Gnosticism and Fundamentalism revealed similar basic tenets:

- Dualistic understanding of reality and humanity (accentuation of the spiritual, denial of the physical)
- Mysticism (spiritual immediacy with the divine)
- Scriptural inerrancy and literalism
- Mutually exclusive spheres of believers versus nonbelievers
- A Christology that is all-divine, or more divine than human
- Salvation as an individual process

- Apocalyptic view of time and history
- Escapist orientation

Gnosticism has been in existence longer than orthodox Christianity. Classical Gnosticism erupted over two millennia ago. It remained a viable force for three hundred years then faded into the wilderness of the Near East and Orient. Generic fundamentalism predates both schools. Christian Fundamentalism, as we know it today, has a much shorter history. At the time of the publication of this book, it has been around approximately a century.

Regardless of their beginnings, over the centuries Gnosticism and Fundamentalism have found and embraced each other. They were not known by the names they are known today. The words "Gnosticism" and "Fundamentalism" originated in the eighteenth and nineteenth centuries respectively, but their core beliefs have been around at least two millennia.

It has been said that past behavior is a good predictor of future behavior. Does this apply also in religious movements? Will history repeat itself? Are these current flares of Gnosticism flashes in the pan, populist religious fads of chimerical fly-by-night fantasy that will die out? Or will Gnostic churches continue to increase and their congregations grow? Will their message expand in this rapidly advancing world of technology?

Will Fundamentalism, like its progenitors, rise and fall or wax and wane? Is this Third Great Awakening, like the First and Second, in such a state of disharmony that it cannot find its rhythm? Or will Fundamentalism continue to influence the sociopolitical scene? Will the charismatic spiritualists continue to dominate television and radio media?

THE FUTURE OF GNOSTICISM

Some argue that these Gnostic bursts throughout history are moods reflecting social conditions and emotive needs of particular cultures at particular times. In order to escape a vile and hopeless material world, humanity is always seeking to become as spiritual as possible. Often this spirituality is not found in the more stilted channels of Orthodoxy or any form of organized religion.

In its various manifestations, Gnosticism has appeared at times to almost eclipse all other religions. Within a century of Mani's death in 276 CE, it seemed his followers, the Manichees, might take over the world. At a time when Gnosticism was peaking, Valentinus was almost elected Bishop of Rome (Pope). Key Church leaders (Ambrose and Augustine) formerly belonged to the Marcionites and Manichees respectively. At times Gnosticism had the leadership and organization to entrench itself as a world religion.

But few Gnostic faith systems have ever caught on. A truncated and morphed form of Marcionism is detected in the dwindling Mandean religion, arguably the oldest existing Gnostic religion (approximately sixty thousand remaining), in southern Iraq and southeastern Iran. Manichaeism was "the only universal religion to emerge from the great spiritual turmoil in third century Mesopotamia."[2]

Gnostic-Manichaean doctrines were prominent from late antiquity through the Middle Ages before they were extinguished. Current manifestations of Gnosticism are a collage of syncretism, a potpourri of the old and the new, but basically the same old system garbed in New Age vernacular and nomenclature.

Relying upon typology models advanced by Max Weber[3] and Ernst Troeltsch,[4] Philip Lee identifies several Gnostic types connecting ancient and current Gnosticism:[5]

- Mood of despair—appealing to those with little or no hope
- Sense of alienation—the physical world, from the beginning, was one colossal cosmic error
- Escape—the logical consequence of a world-denying faith
- Escape from the things of the world, except self: salvation comes from redemptive insight, inner wisdom
- Intellectual elitism
- Syncretism—borrowing from other sources, employing whatever is available

Lee builds a strong case: "Gnostics, whether of the second century or the twentieth century, will not be constrained in the use of material. They will employ whatever is available, in whatever way they choose, to answer the needs of Gnostic faith, which is to say, the spiritual needs of the self."[6] Gnosticism is a perfect prescription for this current age whose sociopsychological dynamics vary little from those of second- and third-century Empire. With international terrorism (much of it, ironically, from Muslim sects with strong Gnostic strains), global warming, worldwide immigration (racial fusion and confusion), nuclear armament by rogue states, economic instability—the atmosphere is ripe for Gnostic activity.

Historically with Orthodoxy and Gnosticism, when one was rising, the other was declining. Current demographics suggest no change to that cyclical seesaw relationship. Conditions that nourish Gnosticism are not waning but waxing. Organized Christianity is not sounding a clear, comforting, or convincing message.[7] According to recent statistics, membership within mainstream Protestant churches is on a decline while percentages within Fundamentalist churches have sharply increased.[8] The prognosis of a "pro-gnostic" climate is good. The prognosis for a long-term presence of Gnosticism is good, but for how long? How permanent?

Theories abound why Gnostic systems—unlike Judaism, Christianity, and Islam—lack continuity. Scholars still question why the Gnostic movement of the first centuries vanished. We may never know all the reasons. Some blame sociopolitical circumstances. Once Christianity gained legitimate status under Constantine and became the religion of the Empire in 391 CE under Theodosius (347–395), heretics became imperial outlaws. As the Church gained in strength and wealth during the Middle Ages, orthodoxy was in control. Islam dominated Gnostics in the Near East. Gnostics either converted or were killed.

With its emphasis on elitism and individualism, some argue Gnosticism would have died without an orthodox attack. Poor reality testing and syncretistic nature might be another reason. Gnosticism would eventually morph itself into something completely different from its origins. Prohibitions against marriage did not encourage regeneration. Some cults practiced sexual abstinence. One school of thought believes that regardless of Constantine or the Muslims Gnosticism would have faded. It is a religious expression simply not designed for longevity. The symbol for The Gnostic Institute, a serpent eating his tail, may reflect more than just a little irony.[9] Unlike the world's dominant religions, Gnosticism has always had an identity problem. Three interrelated factors contribute to this: syncretism, individualism, and unrealism.

The world's major religions—Islam, Judaism, Hinduism, Buddhism, Christianity—have all borrowed from each other and from others. The syncretism of Christianity was more accidental than intentional and maintained one direction, the Incarnation. Gnosticism, by nature, cannot focus on one direction. The syncretism of Gnosticism excelled in religious plagiarism. It extrapolated and compounded deities, myths, doctrines, and practices from other cults.[10] Hans Jonas insists this amalgam is not a haphazard process, but intentional and "not a directionless eclecticism."[11] Justifiably, Gnosticism has been tagged with plagiarism, which leads to identity issues. Trying to view Gnosticism is like looking through a rotating kaleidoscope; the fragmentary mosaic is constantly changing.

As with adolescents and adults without consistent role models, syncretism leads to loss of identity by borrowing from multiple others. The end result is a hodgepodge of personalities, "a directionless eclecticism."[12] Gnostic focus on the self intensifies escapism from the real world, poor reality testing, elitism, and fatalism, as well as the belief that everything is predestined and preordained.

People who want identity and control over their lives look to religions that give them a choice. Choice, or making decisions, is the crucible of identity, and identity is inwardly what the human personality craves. Ironically, Gnosticism subverts this same inward process.

Consistent with its rejection of materiality, Gnosticism also rejects rituals and anything dependent upon nature. This includes the sacraments, church and liturgical calendars, lectionary preaching, and other rituals. Rituals keep us on track. Without rituals individuals and animals become directionless. Orthodoxy and other stabilized dominant world religions, offer accouterments of worship that are anchored in their world to help them lead their daily lives, get from one point to the next, and get from one day to the next. These rituals give them a hope that is grounded in meaningful routine.

If modern-day "new-age" Gnosticism succeeds in setting roots, it may be they have learned from the opposition. Gnostics are antitradition, yet they cling to a tradition as old as the orthodox tradition they oppose. They are skeptical of organized religion yet, ironically, are becoming as organized. They question the reliability of orthodox scripture yet rely on scriptures from their own Gnostic sources, that is, the recent adoration of the Nag Hammadi documents. They reject the orthodox use of the term "spirit," yet they consider themselves spiritual travelers who follow their own "spiritual path." They reject the "truth" of orthodoxy, but truth is very important to them. Traditionally, Gnostics have rejected liturgies and rituals yet "neo-Gnostics" include them now in their worship services.

In other parts of the world Gnosticism flourishes. The extreme Shi'ite sect of Ismailism carries Gnostic elements. Elements of Mani's theology thread the Koran. Though not in classical form, Gnostics have succeeded in becoming a permanent part of the religious landscape in North America.

The world has an insatiable need to "solve" the origin of evil and suffering. Over the centuries, much of the world's population has registered dissatisfaction with an incarnational explanation. It seems probable that Orthodoxy will continue, periodically, "to encounter and resume its battle against the theologically dying and rising 'other god.'"[13]

THE FUTURE OF FUNDAMENTALISM: A FOURTH GREAT AWAKENING?

President George W. Bush evoked the concept as though it were a *fait accompli*. In September 2006, he stated that he sensed a "'Third Awakening' of religious devotion in the United States that has coincided with the nation's struggle against international terrorism, a war he depicted as 'a confrontation between good and evil.'"[14] He may be unaware the Third Great Awakening has already come and gone. It was a period of religious activism in America between 1850 to the 1900s.[15] Regardless of the name assigned by President Bush, his description is consistent with Fundamental millennialism. Dualistic ingredients of Gnosticism are there: satanic powers, forces of good and evil, light and darkness, epic struggles, and crusades.[16]

President Bush is not the only one who senses a resurgence of salvation *via* focus on self. Nobel laureate (1993, Economics) Robert William Fogel, an authority on U.S. religious history says we are in the midst of a Fourth Great Awakening, one that began around 1960:

The new religious revival is fueled by a revulsion with what believers see as a corruption of contemporary society. Believers in the new religious revival are against . . . forms of self-indulgence that titillate the senses and destroy the soul. The leaders of the revival advocate piety and an ethic that extols individual responsibility, hard work, a simple life, and dedication to the family. They emphasize that in order to resist the corruptions promoted by Satan . . . individuals must dedicate themselves to God by embracing an unrelenting struggle for self-purification. They call on their adherents to strive for mystical experience that will cleanse them of sin and lead to spiritual rebirth.[17]

Those words are tailor-made for Gnosticism. The passage could be lifted and inserted, without alteration, into any Gnostic text, about any Gnostic sect from any era—Zoroastrians (1500 BCE) to Fundamental twenty-first century—and it would apply.

Journalist and essayist Tom Wolfe, in an article entitled "The Me Decade and the Third Great Awakening," portrays individualism in America as a Gnostic epidemic.[18] Whether or not he is aware of a prior "Third Great Awakening" is immaterial. He states that this current "Awakening" parallels the First led by Jonathan Edwards in the 1740s and the Second (1825–50). It revives an ancient precept "first propounded by the Gnostic Christians some eighteen hundred years ago: namely, that at the apex of every human soul there exists a spark of the light of God."[19] Salvation comes only by realizing the spark within the human self and "entails the willingness to separate self from all binding earthly ties . . . and, according to Wolfe 'has the mightiest, holiest roll of all, the beat that goes . . . Me . . . Me . . . Me . . . Me.'"[20]

Demographic statistics indicate that membership of Fundamental denominations are rising at a rapid rate. Unlike the revival during the Jacksonian era, Fogel notes the recent political crisis of the 1990s has occurred simultaneously with a religious upsurge. Galvanized by Ronald Reagan, the religious right began to flex its political muscles. The result: a significant fourteen-point shift from religious conservatives, once Democrats, to the Republican Party.[21]

Will Fundamentalism go the way of its Gnostic cousins or will it survive? Will it disappear for a while then surface again in another guise? Based on the previously mentioned reports, Fundamentalism is gaining momentum and will survive. Perhaps the appropriate question is will Orthodoxy survive?

Gnosticism and Fundamentalism share similar beliefs and concepts, but Fundamentalism is not classical Gnosticism. Fundamentalism has accommodated and adjusted to the American scene, to its economy and mood, its rugged individualistic mold. Fundamentalism has done so well, in fact, that change will be difficult: "It will not be easy for North American Protestantism to move away from its individualistic moorings. To renounce a born-againism that centers the faith in the individual's emotional achievements will bring down the wrath of the religious right and the charge that the Churches are abandoning 'historic Christianity.'"[22]

Humphrey and Wise sound a similar note: "It seems likely to us that Fundamentalism will remain an important part of American life for the foreseeable future. We know of no convincing reason to suppose that it is going to disappear. It is a vigorous movement with a network of effective institutional support and a history of achievement in areas such as Christian missions, and its message clearly appeals to many people today."[23] Foreseeable means how far one can see into time and down the tunnel of years to come. Whether Fundamentalism will be "among us until the end of time or the end of republic," as Bloom suggests,[24] is debatable. With the fading of apocalyptic reality, Gnostics of the first centuries CE may have been objective about their longevity. Marcion's successes gave them reason for such optimism. He created a vigorous movement and an institutional network with a history of achievement in Christian missions. Marcion's message clearly appealed to many people. At its height the Marcion Christian Gnostic Church dwarfed anything proto-orthodoxy could assemble. Proto-orthodoxy eventually succeeded and surpassed Marcion, but historians will always question the outcome of orthodoxy had the victor at the Milvian Bridge on October 28, in 312 C E been Maxentius and not Constantine.[25] Where would orthodoxy be? Where would Marcionism be? Would we be Marcionites and use his truncated New Testament for our Bible? Would we be Manichees (Mani built his theology on Marcion's dualism)? We can only speculate on the answers.

One of the reasons Orthodoxy is still around is its ability, over time, to accommodate to culture without being devoured by it, by finding that balance between extremes. Ronald Knox reminds us that "traditional Christianity is a balance of doctrines, and not merely of doctrines but of emphases. You must not exaggerate in either direction, or the balance is disturbed."[26] For that reason, Orthodoxy is called "mainstream." It has been able to navigate through sociopolitical and cultural polarities without losing its balance or identity while maintaining its cutting edge, its healing, and its prophetic voice. This sense of balance may be one of the reasons Orthodoxy is still the majority faith among Christians. Its theology is more realistic, "honest," open, and flexible. It accommodates without sacrificing principle. Its word becomes flesh.

Is the Fundamentalist Christ on paper the same as the Fundamentalist emotional suffering and risen Christ in the pew? In theory the Fundamentalist Christ "sounds" incarnate. In reality, however, the Fundamentalist Christ seems comparable to an emotional mystical (Gnostic) Christ. Fundamental literal interpretation of the Holy Bible and spiritual mysticism to the contrary, the Word of long ago did become flesh. The challenge for Fundamentalism today is transporting *that* incarnate Word and *that* incarnate Christ into the twenty-first century in a manner that the message resonates with the real world; not as some romantically, far away "sweet by and by," mystical, phantasmal, Gnostic escape. In other words, the Jesus of Fundamentalism may *feel* real; he may *seem* real (echoes of the docetic Christ). But does this Christ ever *become* real in the doctrinal sense the Word became flesh? Does he ever really "take hold?" One wonders why Fundamentalism, with its literal interpretation of Holy Writ, cannot be as literal *behaviorally* as it is scripturally with its understanding of the Incarnation. What keeps Fundamentalists from allowing the Word to become flesh? What keeps them from abandoning an unrealistic inerrant interpretation of scripture?

The contradiction between pronounced and enacted Incarnation raises serious questions about the future of Fundamentalism. Will Fundamentalism maintain the same rigid status quo or make changes? Will it continue to believe in a Word that "became flesh" while it protects the embodiment of that Word within the prophylactic sheath of spiritual perfection of inerrancy? Will it gain integrity by allowing the written word to become incarnate and move forward into the twenty-first century? Or will the Word remain a relic of the Gnostic past?

There are strong movements among moderates within Fundamentalism on the issues of scriptural inerrancy and literalism. This may be the reason moderate Baptist denominations are sharply declining. Born in 1854, the Southern Baptist Convention has split several times and is threatening to fracture once more. At the center of these fissures is the conflict between their Fundamentalist majority and a strong Moderate minority. According to Bloom, "the moderate minority descend from mystics of the Inner Light, who read the Bible in radically individualist ways, while the conservatives of the Convention insist that the Bible reads itself (as it were), requires no interpretation, declares its literal and unerring truth in every verse."[27] But will the majority Fundamentalist wing of the Southern Baptist Convention, the largest Protestant denomination, continue to thrive while the moderates lose ground?

Based upon extreme comments by some of their leaders, the continued acceleration of the conservative wing is questionable: "now if the Bible is the Word of God, and if God inspired it, then it cannot contain any scientific mistakes because God knew every truth and fact of science from the beginning."[28] Common sense would suggest that this and similar statements by Wallie Amos Criswell, retired pastor of First Baptist Church in Dallas and leader of the conservative branch, would drive people toward the more moderate base. This type of statement is "not so much Christian as Muslim, since it applies more to the Koran than to the Bible. The Koran gives us one voice, the voice of God himself."[29] In other words, "Southern Baptist Fundamentalism is similar to Islamic Fundamentalism. 'Inerrancy' for both movements is an unconscious metaphor for the repression of individuality."[30] Based on this association and the fact the Muslim religion is the fastest growing religion today in the world, we might expect a continued surge among those who herald the inerrant and literal Word. The moderates have accepted the challenge and appear to be holding their own. Perhaps they understand the body of Christ must die before it can rise and live again; that the sacrifice must continue.

There are some within the so-called liberal camp—Metzger, Ehrman, Trobish, and others—who accept the results of scholarship as revelatory of a moving and vibrant word of God, a "treasure in jars of clay [earthen vessels] to show that this all-surpassing power is from God and not from us" (2 Corinthians 4:7). They go to great lengths to defend the Scriptures. The composition time of New Testament books is relatively brief when compared with classical authors, where there are lapses of thousands of years. Metzger notes, "The works of several ancient authors are preserved to us by the thinnest thread of transmission."[31] A history of Rome by Velleius Paterculus has survived to modern times. This single manuscript is incomplete and based upon a copy lost in the seventeenth century. Also available are the *Annals* of Tacitus, a single manuscript that dates to the ninth century. Most work we have from ancient writers dates back only to the Middle to Late Middle Ages. Metzger and other scholars reveal that the papyrus manuscripts we possess are within a century or so of the Christ event.[32]

The thrill of reading my *Egermeier Bible Story Book* at a time when those words were considered inviolate and uncorrupted has been replaced by the thrill of knowing the words have endured through ages of copying and editing and manipulation and corruption and yet, despite all that, thanks to dedicated scholars, they are words that have virtually remained unchanged. They are the words made flesh, about *the* Word made flesh. And in that sense, they are the Incarnate Word of God.

FUNDAMENTALISM AND ORTHODOXY:
A BASIS FOR RAPPROCHEMENT

The contact point for Fundamentalism and Orthodoxy, the one issue on which they can arguably come closer to agreement than any other, is the Incarnation of Jesus Christ. Though not stated explicitly in its "Five Fundamentals," the Incarnation is implied; it is a core belief. The difference between Fundamentalists and mainstream orthodox Christians on the Incarnation is one of practice, not of doctrine.

Doctrinally, Fundamentalists advocate the Incarnation. How it is reflected in practice, however, is the key issue. The Apostles' Creed emphasizes the Incarnation—Jesus "crucified under Pontius Pilate, dead and buried." Candidates for baptism in the early Church were required to recite this credo. In most Fundamental churches it is all but forgotten. Lee points out that "in the doctrinal tests so important to American fundamentalists for distinguishing between authentic Christianity and liberal heresy, sacraments are never mentioned."[33] Sacramental theology, vitally important to the Incarnation is a nonfactor in the Fundamentalist plan of salvation. The symbolism attached to the Lord's Supper has been diluted to the point grape juice substitutes for wine. Baptism is central to some Fundamentalist denominations and sects. The focus is not on the community of faith or the Body of Christ but on the individual conversion experience previously compared with the Gnostic revelation of Inner Light.

Fundamentalists believe in one God who created a world that was good. But all else is of Satan, putting into play a Monarchial dualism: one good God with an evil creator, a fallen angel secondary and inferior to the one true God. The focus of much Fundamentalist preaching is Satan and his power to lead one to hell, which is dualism. The emphasis is upon the conversion experience, the cognitive act of accepting Christ as savior. The Word Fundamentalists preach is pure and untainted, without error. They are guided, it seems, solely by the Spirit. Information from scholarly texts is considered not only unnecessary but also corrupted by human influence. These practices are more in line with Docetic theology, or pure spiritualism, than Incarnation.

Orthodox, mainstream Christians have fewer problems with Fundamentalists than the converse. Most mainstream Christians have minimal difficulty with four of the "Five Fundamentals." Most accept the virgin birth of Jesus. Most would not quibble or waste time and energy arguing over the nature of Christ's Atonement, whether it was substitutionary or otherwise. All would agree; it was atoning. The bodily resurrection of Christ is also not a hot button. Some Conservatives and mainstream Christians alike recite the Apostles Creed each Sunday in which they affirm the resurrection of the body, a phrase the early Church fathers implanted to combat Gnosticism. The historicity of miracles is not a major point of disagreement. Some believe in them and some do not. But no major battles erupt over this issue. The inerrancy of scripture is the point of contention. Ironically, the concept is based upon the Incarnation, "the word became flesh," the one key doctrine on which Fundamentalists and orthodox Christians agree.

For reasons related more to attitude than theology, the problem lies in the inability of both groups to follow incarnational logic to its ultimate conclusion and respond appropriately, both psychologically and behaviorally. The word became flesh. It became human. It did not become partially human. At Nicaea and Chalcedon, the doctrine of Christology was not partitioned, half-God and half-man. Christ, the Word, was fully God, fully human. And that Word dwelt among us. The Greek word literally means "tented." It did not hover. It did not float beyond in some ethereal stratum of purity "far from the madding crowd." It was staked into the ground and tethered to the earth. The writer of the Gospel of John clearly portrayed the images required to be consistent with the Incarnation.

When Wise and Humphreys state that "attitudes are important in any religious movement,"[34] they point to Aiden Wilson Tozer, a leading inspirational Fundamentalist writer who died in 1963. Tozer recognized the attitudinal inadequacies of Fundamentalism, primarily its rigid inability to remain open to the ideas of others and to alternative interpretations.[35]

Rigid and defensive behavior stems from fear. Fear is overcome with trust, acceptance, and love. This is the heart of the message of Jesus Christ and it is the full meaning of the Incarnation: "The Word became flesh." God humbled himself and expects the same from believers. To affirm faith in the Incarnation, the crucifixion of God, and his resurrection is to affirm people of all faiths. This includes other Christians who believe differently. When Fundamentalists condemn other Christians because they do not believe in, and practice, an inerrant and literal interpretation of scripture, they practice separatism and manifest a behavior condemned by the unified Christ and God they worship. Likewise, when "liberal" Christians (usually identified in the form-criticism school of biblical interpretation) and mainstream Christians cast aspersions upon Fundamentalists for their "narrow" restricted literal interpretation of scripture, they exhibit the same legalistic and self-righteous behavior they reject and participate in a theology of separation, rather than union.

In either case, Christ is divided; Christology is fractured. We are back to a theology of partition, as opposed to merger; to "insiders" versus "outsiders;" to knowers versus unknowers; to saved versus unsaved. We are back to Gnosticism, the religion of a distant and fragmented deity.

The anger of Jesus of Nazareth, God incarnate, was reserved for the legalistic, condescending, self-righteous, and hypocritical. It was unleashed only on the pure (not the pure in heart or spirit, but pure from sin). Nowhere in scripture does Jesus castigate the humble. Nowhere does he condemn anyone for self-humiliation or become angry with repentant sinners. These are the ones who will enter the kingdom ahead of their accusers. Error was the norm; error was forgiven. Purity was not the norm, yet even purity was capable of being forgiven;

if one recognized their puritanical attitude, repented, and requested forgiveness. In his memorable book, *The New Being*, Paul Tillich comments, "There is no condition for forgiveness. . . . Forgiveness is unconditional or it is not forgiveness at all . . . sinners were forgiven because they humiliated themselves and confessed that they were unacceptable. . . . Forgiveness creates repentance . . . The woman in Simon's house comes to Jesus, because she *was* forgiven."[36] When Christ forgave the woman who was dragged into his presence to be stoned, he only pronounced a forgiveness already effected by grace. This forgiveness is the opposite of separatist dualism. It is the core of united incarnational theology.

For a rapprochement to occur between Fundamentalism and mainstream Orthodox Christianity, several things must happen. First, both must seek and find balance, which means return to a rigorous and radical incarnational theology. For Fundamentalists, this will require a significant alteration or rejection of inerrancy of scriptures. It will mean accepting that there are inconsistencies and flaws in the Bible. As there was strength in His humanity in the Incarnation, the humanity in His Word is equally a sign of power, not absence of power. That kind of change will indicate accepting the Bible as "a sign that God is not nearly so embarrassed by the humanity and human imperfections evidence in preachers and in the Bible as we are ourselves."[37]

For mainstream and liberal theologians, returning to a radical incarnational theology means shifting from a piecemeal, selective use of the Bible toward acceptance of the book as the sacred Word of God. This does not mean God no longer reveals Himself or that His word stopped centuries ago at the Carthage Synod of 419 when the New Testament canon was closed. If there is to be a basis or common ground for discussion, *The Holy Bible* must be accepted by all parties as *the* canon. This means all groups must be as rigorous in their critical assessment of the big picture as they tend to be with selective proof texts. Liberals must accept the fact that the "scientific method" is not understood by all, which means accepting the fact that persons of intellect and integrity can be Fundamentalists.

CONCLUSION

The heresy of one age becomes the orthodoxy of the next.

—Helen Keller

We have come a long way from Athanasius' Festal Letter and the burial of ancient texts at Nag Hammadi; the beginning of the end of the Gnostic heresy of that era. Gnosticism is still with us.

Early in the development of Christianity, heresy was defined as the "wrong choice." Any form of Gnosticism was classified as the "wrong choice," thus labeled as heretical; "the *Shepherd of Hermas* described the contrast between orthodoxy and heresy as 'men seated on a couch, and another man seated on a chair.'"[38] The comment implied orthodoxy was communal. Its creeds and beliefs were developed among groups. Heresy, on the other hand, was solo. It was dictated by individuals. Over time, Gnosticism and heresy became synonymous.

I began writing this book with the presupposition that Fundamentalism was Gnosticism and therefore it was heresy. The long hours and extensive research began to confirm its proof. But along the way, other pieces of information began to confound the theory. I was not prepared for revelations that Gnosticism exists in all varieties of Christianity. This posed another disturbing question. If true, does it mean all Christians, in one way or another, are heretics? Is orthodoxy the most successful heresy? On that point, Philip Lee comments, "For almost two millennia, Christians have been assailing one another in court and out, with words or weapons, over the issue of who is correct in doctrine and praxis. Is it not self-contradictory for Christians to be judgmental toward one another about anything? Certainly, heresy talk does not seem kind or liberal-minded and is not conducive to the popular notion of what is ecumenical. In fact, within the Church, has heresy not become a heretical word?"[39] The writer of the Gospel of Matthew summarizes the preceding statement: "do not judge or you too will be judged" (7:1). Based on this sobering and leveling logic, when one points and accuses another as a heretic, the finger turns on the accused.

To make good decisions, one must refrain from assuming a self-righteous, condescending, and judgmental attitude about the choices. In orthodoxy, decisions are made by a group sitting on a couch; in heresy, they are made by one person sitting in an elevated chair.

Gnosticism, Fundamentalism, and Orthodoxy reflect different aspects of the human experience. On some points they overlap, on others they are light-years apart. They appeal to the myriad differences within us all. Gnostics and Fundamentalists focus intensely on a private and personal experience. The focus of Orthodoxy is more on relationships with others. Elaine Pagels notes, "the orthodox interpreted evil primarily in terms of violence against others."[40] That same evil, orthodoxy contends, was created by humans. It came from human self-corruption. The Gnostics, in a more subtle manner, invented another god to account for evil. Fundamentalists did the same: "the devil made me do it." Operating along these lines of belief, it is understandable how the teachings of Jesus, the words of Scripture, could be manipulated to fit different themes. Jesus was on point: "you have a fine way of setting aside the commands of God in order to observe your own tradition" (Mark 7:9). An alternative interpretation is, "how well you manipulate the word of God in order to protect your own tradition." This has happened over the centuries and doubtless will continue.

Readers must assimilate the information within these pages and appropriate it within their own personal belief systems. Is Fundamentalism a form of Gnosticism and therefore heresy? If so, what does that mean? Gnosticism, or dualism, permeates world religions. Gnostic influence is found in most Protestant denominations, in Catholicism, in Islam, and in Judaism. Dualism seems axiomatic, a constant in reality with which generations and cultures must contend. Like Original Sin, dualism's lure of convenience and simplicity may be "built-in." And like Original Sin, Gnosticism seems here to stay. In view of its permanence, it is important to become familiar with its myriad features and tenets and the ways they might affect our own personal belief structure. With the revelation of the unearthed texts of Nag Hammadi, "only now are we beginning to consider the questions with which they confront us"[41] and ponder the heresies among us.

SUMMARY

Despite attempts over the centuries to expunge Gnosticism from the human scene, it is pervasive in world religions. One can easily locate it by name (Gnostic temples, organizations, churches, etc.) or witness its phenomenon in the many manifestations of Fundamentalism. In some form, Gnosticism and Fundamentalism are traceable throughout the existence of humanity itself. Their continuation in the twenty-first century is undeterminable. Though both contain self-destructive elements, paradoxically those self-destructive components appeal to people searching for hope in a time of despair. Following that logic, they will breach the twenty-second century and, like a theme of the French existentialist Camus, continue returning.

Inherent in mainstream and Fundamental belief systems is a basis for rapprochement: the Incarnation. The sticking point is the inerrancy of scripture. A resolution of this issue by Fundamentalists could promote an ecumenical union and harmony of gigantic proportion. The resolution rests with these religious conservatives taking seriously the concept of Incarnation and applying it as rigorously to scriptural interpretation as they do to other aspects of their religious expression. This means jettisoning the lynchpin of their theology. But there are strong reality-oriented forces within Fundamentalism that could move in that direction and, in a piecemeal fashion, create a movement of rapprochement.

In conclusion, heresy remains an ambiguous pharisaical term. Perhaps its best definition reflects back to its initial use: a choice. There is probably an element of Gnosticism, or heresy, in us all. Gnosticism, Fundamentalism, and Orthodoxy are reflections of the human experience and elements of each can be found in all people. They appeal to the inborn desire for uniformity and to our personal insecurities. Gnosticism and Fundamentalism are oriented toward the individual experience whereas Orthodoxy has a more communal orientation. Regardless of the personal choice, there is no avoiding the many heresies among us.

Glossary of Key Terms

Adoptionists: Theologians who sought to ensure monotheism by describing Jesus as a gifted man with divine powers who was adopted by God. Paul of Samosata and his followers, called Paulianists by the first Council of Nicea, are styled Adoptionists. Some early adoptionists believed Jesus was adopted at his baptism; others stated his election occurred at his resurrection.

Alexandrian: School of theologians centered in Alexandria, Egypt.

anti-Adoptionists: Church fathers and theologians of the second and third centuries who aggressively opposed any form of Adoptionism. Often they modified biblical texts in order to expunge them of any adoptionist interpretation.

Antiochenes: School of theologians centered in Antioch in Syria whose tendency was the historical interpretation of Scripture and insistence on the full humanity of Christ

antiseparatists: In early Christianity, heresiologists who fought the notion that Christ's spirit could be separated from his humanity.

apocalypticism: A form of belief held by many ancient Jews and Christians that real time was controlled by evil forces that would be destroyed at the *eschaton* or last day. At that time God would intervene and set up his heavenly kingdom on earth. Apocalypticists believed this event was imminent.

Apocrypha/Aprocryphal: From a Greek word that means "hidden," it is a group of books "set aside" or not included in the Old Testament canon. The Apocrypha is found in early Christian versions of the Old Testament. It was not included in Jerome's translation *The Vulgate* and is not included in the Protestant canon of Scripture.

Apologists: Early Church fathers of the first four centuries CE who defended early proto-Christian orthodoxy and vigorously attacked opposing views within the Church they labeled heretical. They also became known as heresiologists or "heresy hunters."

Arians: Faction led by Arius of Alexandria who proposed that the Son of God was created by the Father from nothing as an instrument for the creation and salvation of the universe; not God by nature, this highest of creatures received the title Son of God on account of his foreseen righteousness.

Arminianism: A branch of Protestant thought advanced by Jacobus Arminius in which Calvin's concept of God's sovereignty was revived, allowing freedom of will as opposed to predestination.

autograph: The original manuscript of an author's work. Without original manuscripts, scholars must work from later copies.

Buddhism: East Asian religion that teaches that through right thinking and self-denial one achieves a state of perfect blessedness of nirvana. Aspects of Buddhism probably infiltrated the Mediterranean world via commerce and trade and into some Gnostic systems.

Carpocratians: A second century CE sect founded by Carpocrates. They were attacked by early Church fathers Clement of Alexandria, Irenaeus of Lyon, and Hippolytus of Rome for engaging in wild licentious activities in their liturgical services, reputed to be sexual orgies. Allegedly, they practiced a simple form of communal living in which all property was shared, which extended to spouses.

Christology: A teaching or understanding regarding the nature of Christ.

codex: An ancient manuscript, either of papyrus or vellum, arranged in book form as opposed to the more common scroll. The codex was more versatile. One could turn pages rather than unspool a large scroll. Passages could be located quicker. Both sides of a page could be used. For the early Christians, it also afforded a break with the Jewish custom of using the scroll.

Darwinism: Belief and adherence to Charles Darwin's theory of evolution.

Demiurge: Literally, the word means "maker." Plato used the term in his famous work *Timaeus*. It was adopted by Gnostics and used in their texts to depict a deity that created the world.

dispensationalism/dispensationalists: A form of premillennialism that teaches that biblical history was a number of successive economies or administrations, called dispensations, each of which constitutes continuity with the Old Testament covenants made by God with his chosen people through Abraham, Moses, and King David.

Docetism: A form of dualism and early Christian heresy which denied the humanness of Jesus at the expense of his divinity.

dualism: The philosophic concept that two fundamental opposing entities comprise reality: matter and spirit; a doctrine that the universe is composed of two opposite forces, good and evil, which constantly challenge each other for supremacy.

Ebionites: Jewish Christian Adoptionists of the second century traced their lineage back to apostolic times and strived to maintain their Jewish practices, rituals, and forms of worship. Epiphanius was considered by the heresiologists as the progenitor of the Ebionites.

enthusiasm/enthusiasts: The word *enthusiasm* stems from a Greek word, *entheos*, which means possessed by a god. Originally associated with supernatural inspiration and prophetic ecstasy, it morphed into meaning eager interest, zeal, and fervor. A Syrian sect of the fourth century was known as Enthusiasts. Their beliefs were basically Gnostic: prayer, ascetic practices (the world is evil), contemplation, inspiration by the Holy Spirit over against a ruling evil spirit. Some Protestant sects of the sixteenth and secenteenth centuries were called enthusiasts. In the eighteenth century, John Wesley and George Whitefield were accused of blind enthusiasm, or fanaticism.

eschaton/eschatology: Greek word that means the end of time or "last day." Eschatology is the study of the end of time or final day.

Evangelicalism: A form of conservative Fundamentalism that emerged in the 1940s. It was less rigid and more open to intellectual discussion. Billy Graham was a key proponent.

exegesis: From the Greek word *exegeomai*, "to draw out," it is the study of the meaning of biblical texts and the meaning intended by the author.

form criticism: A study of the oral material of Gospel and New Testament tradition before it was put in writing.

Gnosticism: A complicated religious movement that claimed a secret knowledge (*gnosis*) revealed to the Apostles that was capable of freeing the spiritual element in humans from the evil of the body in which it was trapped by a primal mischance among the higher beings emanating from the Father and of restoring it to its original heavenly home.

Hellenism: Initiated by Alexander the Great and carried out by his successors, the adaptation and assimilation of Greek ideas, language, culture, and religion.

heresy: Literally means "choice"; for Christian orthodoxy, any teaching that deviates from the accepted teachings and doctrine of the Church; a willful and chosen misrepresentation of "the truth."

hereisiologist: An early Christian Church father or apologist who attacked Christian heresy, primarily Gnosticism.

hermeneutics: From the Greek Hermes, messenger of the gods, the science and study of interpreting textual material. Exegesis explains a text according to formal rules; hermeneutics is the science upon which exegetical practices are devised.

Hermeticism: An ancient Egyptian cult that spread throughout the Mediterranean world. Centuries later it would give rise to alchemy in Medieval Europe.

homoosians: Those supporting the term *homoousios*, of one substance, used by Nicaea I to express the relation of the Son to the Father. The term was suspect because of its ambiguity and its use by Gnostics and Paul of Samosata.

hyletics: One of the three types of Gnostic humanity, which meant "earthly," "fleshy." These individuals were earthbound and unsavable.

Inerrancy: The belief the Bible is without error.

Ismailism: A Fundamental Shi'ite sect of Islam, the second largest denomination of the Islamic religion. It emerged around 850 CE, has Gnostic traits, and has been called by some scholars Islamic Gnosticism.

Johannine: Relating to authorship of New Testament books attributed to John, or bearing his name.

Kaballist: A Jewish mystical sect with Gnostic features.

Manichaeism: A religion founded in the third century by the prophet and teacher Mani. It combined Zoroastric, Gnostic, Christian, and pagan elements.

One belief was that God and Satan were separate entities. It was based upon the dualistic concept of two contending principles of good and evil.

Marcionism: Marcionites or followers of the Christian Gnostic Marcion.

Monarchian: Theologians whose primary goal was protecting monotheism by conceptualizing Father, Son, and Holy Spirit as a succession of modes of the single Godhead. The principle proponent of this theory was Sabellius from whom we get the word Sabellianists. They were also called Patripassians because of their belief that the Father suffered with the Son.

Montanism: Heretical form of Christianity of the later second century; major elements included a return to primitive Christianity, distrust of intellect, and sole reliance on inspiration. Their most noted adherent was Tertullian.

Montanists: Apocalyptic followers of Montanus of Phrygia of Asia Minor who preached the imminent coming of the Holy Spirit already manifested in the sect's own prophets and prophetesses. The African Tertullian was attracted to the sect because of its penitential element.

mystery religion(s): Ancient cults who practiced secret mystic rituals and elaborate initiation and purification rites. They were known for using sacred objects, accepting occult knowledge, and participating in sacred drama.

mysticism: The theory or doctrine that one can achieve communion with God through contemplation and love without going through the medium of reason; spiritual truth is ascertainable through intuition.

neoplatonism: School of philosophy founded in Alexandria, Egypt in third century CE; key elements include combination of Plato's doctrines with Hellenistic and ethical concepts common to Judaism and Christianity.

Nestorians: Followers of Nestorius of Constantinople who insisted Mary should not properly be called Mother of God or Theotokos but rather Christokos or Mother of Christ, the prosopon of union.

New Lights: Supporters of the First Great Awakening or revivalists.

Old Lights: During the First Great Awakening they were supporters of institutional, established religion and denounced the "New Lights" as apostates.

oral tradition: Traditions passed on by word of mouth before they were committed to writing. In New Testament understanding it represents that time frame between Jesus's exaltation and the written production of the first Gospel, approximately 33 to 70 CE.

Orphism: Esoteric mystery cult whose key concept was potential divinity of the narcissistic (elitist) self.

Orthodox: In Greek, literally "straight" or "right opinion"; Orthodox Christianity represented the core of beliefs advocated and taught by Jesus and his apostles then later given creedal and doctrinal status by the Church. Any deviation from this doctrine represented heresy.

papyrus: A plant which grows in the Nile delta of Egypt. From the fourth century BCE until the second century CE it was widely used as material for writing.

parchment: Also called velum, it was basically the skins of cattle and other animals, which were treated and used as writing material. As early as the second century CE it began replacing parchment.

Parousia: From the Greek *parousia*, it is a term in the New Testament used to denote the coming of Christ at the end of time.

pastoral epistles: In the New Testament, a designation for the two letters of Timothy and the letter to Titus. The content of both relates to the organization of the Christian ministry, care for the congregations, and the importance of countering false doctrine.

Patripassianism: *See* Monarchian.

Pelagianism: Grace and salvation based upon the will of man in cooperation with God. The doctrine of original sin was absurd, unjust, and contradictory: If sin is natural, it is not voluntary. The sin of Adam injured only him, not the human race; grace as freely given undermines responsibility and teaches cheap grace.

platonism: The philosophical teachings of Plato (427–347 BCE), pupil of Socrates and the teacher of Aristotle. Plato emphasized the ideal over physical, empirical reality and stressed the use of the mind.

pneumatics: The Gnostic spiritual type of humanity who were the spiritually elect and automatically guaranteed salvation.

polytheism: The worship of more than one god.

predestinarianism: The doctrine of predestination, the belief that God predestines certain souls to salvation and others to damnation.

premillennialism: The belief in the doctrine of the Second Coming of Christ and that the event will occur before the millennium.

proto-orthodox: Literally "forerunners of orthodoxy," or the group that would come to represent the established creed and doctrine of the Church. The term is used only in retrospect, since those early "proto-orthodox" Christians were unaware they were, in fact, the "forerunners" of what would become established doctrine. The teachings of the Church during their time were in a state of flux.

pseudepigrapha: Writings attributed someone other than the actual author, done usually to magnify the importance of the text. Some of the Jewish writings not incorporated into the Septuagint versio of the Old Testament are considered to be pseudepigrapha.

psychics: One of the three types of Gnostic humanity, they existed in a state of emotional and mental being. They were savable but had to work out their salvation.

pythagorians: One who follows the teachings and philosophy of Pythagoras, which included transmigration of souls and belief in numbers as the ultimate element of the universe.

Q Source: From the German *Quelle*, meaning source, it refers to textual material not found in Mark but common to Matthew and Luke.

Sabaism: An ancient religion whose main element was worship of the stars.

Sabellianism: *See* Monarchian.

separatism: A view advanced by Gnostic Christians that the spirit could enter and leave the body of Christ, which meant ultimately that he did not suffer. An example would be the theory that the divine spirit entered his body at baptism and separated from his body prior to his death.

Sethians: A classical Gnostic movement whose adherents believed the world was created by a lesser divinity than the One true God who was the object of their worship and adoration.

spiritualism: The philosophic doctrine that all matter is spirit, which means the dead survive as spirits.

Sufiism: A form of mysticism that originated in Persia and contains elements strongly suggestive of Gnosticism.

synoptic(s): From the Greek, "a seeing together." Because of their similar style and content and easy comparison with each other, synoptic became associated with the Gospels of Matthew, Mark, and Luke.

textual criticism: A discipline applied to textual examination in order to discover its original wording.

theosophical: Pertains to a body of doctrine–thought relating to deity, cosmos, and individual (self) with a focus on direct intuition by which initiates could empower nature and thus guide their own destinies.

GLOSSARY OF KEY NAMES

Albigensian Crusade (1209–1229): Twenty-year campaign launched by Pope Innocent III and Philippe II of France to eliminate the Albigensian–Catharism heresy.

Albigensians (1020–1250): Also known as Cathars, a religious sect with Gnostic elements that began in Southern France and spread rapidly throughout parts of Europe.

Antiochus IV Ephiphanes: Seleucid ruler of Palestine from 175 until 164 BCE. Notorious for his persecution of the Jews until overthrown by the Maccabean Revolt of 164.

Appollonius of Tyana: Pythagorian teacher of the first century CE whose life strongly parallels that of his contemporary Jesus of Nazareth.

Arius (ca. 250–336): Greek theologian of Alexandria who founded Arianism or the belief that Jesus was not of the same substance as God, but merely the best creature among all creatures.

Athanasius: *See* Appendix C.

Bardesenes: A Christian teacher of the second century.

Basilides: Second-century Gnostic Christian teacher, influenced by Zoroastrianism. His dualistic teachings drew fire from early Church apologists Clement of Alexandrian, Irenaeus, and Hippolytus. Allegedly, his teacher was an interpreter for St. Peter.

Calvin, John: Protestant reformer responsible for the theological position known as Calvinism, which heavily influenced Protestant theology of colonial America.

Cane Ridge Revival: Took place in Kentucky in 1801; credited with beginning the Second Great Awakening.

Carthage, synods 397 and 419 CE: The canon of the New Testament is established and closed at twenty-seven books, the same listed in Athanasius' thirty-ninth Festal Letter of 367 CE.

Cathars: Medieval heretical group, also known as Albigensians; they were vegetarians, denied the divinity of Christ, believed in pantheism and transmigration of souls. *See also* Albigensian Crusade.

Christian Science: Founded in 1866 by Mary Baker Eddy, a religion and system of healing based upon scriptural interpretation that physical and mental disorders are caused by faulty thinking and can be healed through spiritual means without medical assistance or medication.

Clement of Alexandria: *See* Appendix C.

Constantine: Roman general who became the first Christian emperor of the Roman Empire. His Edict of Milan in 313 established religious freedom throughout the empire. He also called for the first ecumenical Christian council, later known as the Council of Nicaea, 325 CE.

Council of Carthage, 397 CE: The Third Council of Carthage, which officially endorsed the twenty-seven books that now comprise the New Testament.

Council of Chalcedon, 451 CE: Attended by over five hundred bishops of the Christian Church, it accepted the Creed of Constantinople, 381 CE and affirmed the Nicene Creed.

Council of Ephesus, 431 CE: Ecumenical Church council that witnessed the conflict over the title, Mary theotokos, or Mary, Mother of God. The forces of Cyril of Alexandria aligned against those of Nestorius who opposed the title. Nestorius lost but Nestorianism continues to flourish in India, the Middle East and South America.

Council of Nicaea, 325 CE: The first true ecumenical council in which the Trinitarian and Christological doctrines of the Church were established. The Council of Nicaea paved the way for the development of future Church dogma.

Cybele: The goddess of earth and nature in ancient Phrygian mythology. The Greeks identified her with Rhea, wife of Cronos and mother of Zesus or Jupiter. She also became known as Magna Mater or Great Mother, the Mother of the Gods. She became associated with some of the many mystery cults in the Roman Empire during the time of early Christianity.

Darby, John Nelson (1800–82): British preacher and father of Dispensationalism, he propounded themes and tenets that became Christian Fundamentalism.

Dead Sea Scrolls: Manuscripts of Jewish literature, including parts of the Old Testament, dating from approximately 250 BCE to 68 CE, discovered in caves near the Dead Sea in 1947.

Demeter: In Greek and Roman (Ceres) mythology, the goddess of agriculture and fertility. The myth of Demeter is the core or the Eleusinian Mysteries, one of the more important of the ancient mystery religions

Descartes, René(1596–1650): French Philosopher, Rationalist, and metaphysical dualist, often regarded as the founder of modern philosophy. His description of mind and body as two separate entities that interact to create a person fueled the separation between body and soul, which permeated Fundamentalism and Gnosticism.

Deutero-Pauline: Written by a "second" or "another" Paul. The term refers to letters and epistles allegedly written by Paul but written by someone using his name.

Diocletian (245–313 CE): Roman emperor 284–305 CE. With Caesar Galerius, he ruled the Roman Empire east of the Adriatic Sea while Constantius (father of Constantine) and Maximian ruled the West. In 303 Diocletian launched a systematic attack on Christian churches, literature, and clergy. Christian worship was forbidden.

Dionysius: Greek god of vegetation and wine and often associated with ancient mystery religions.

Ebionite: Early Jewish Christian sect that focused on the observance of Mosaic Law and emphasized the humanity of Jesus.

Edwards, Jonathan (1703–58): American colonial theologian and preacher best remembered for his sermon "Sinners in the Hands of an Angry God." A defender of Calvinism, deterministic theology and Puritanism, he is often credited with igniting the First Great Awakening.

Eleusis: The home of the goddess Demeter and sanctuary where the Eleusinian Mysteries were performed. *Eleusis* means "arrival" and combined with *mysterion* meant arrival of the mysteries.

Epiphanius of Salamis (310–403): One of the early Church apologists and here-isologists who became active following the Council of Nicaea.

Erasmus, Disiderius (1466–1536): Dutch humanist, theologian, and humorist noted for his translation of the Greek New Testament in 1516, which became the basis later for the King James Version.

Essenes: Jewish sect of ascetics who flourished in Palestine from the second century BCE until the first century CE. They held messianic and eschatological beliefs and are considered the source for the Dead Sea Scrolls. They are associated with the Qumran community near the Dead Sea which has been reconstructed by archaeologists

Eucharist: From the Greek *eucharisteo*, which means to give thanks, the term became synonymous with the Lord's Supper or Holy Communion.

Eusebius of Caesarea: *See* Appendix C.

Heracleon (ca. 125 CE): A prominent Gnostic and follower of Valentinian. He is alleged to have written the first commentary on the Gospel of John.

Hermes: Son of Zesus and herald of the Greek Olympian gods. He was also the messenger of the gods from which we get the word "hermeneutics."

Hippolytus: *See* Appendix C.

Hippo Regius, Synod 393: Athanasius's list of twenty-seven books were voted upon and accepted as canon.

Ignatius of Antioch: *See* Appendix C.

Irenaeus: *See* Appendix C.

Isis: Sister and wife of Osiris, she was the Egyptian goddess of fertility. Her worship originated in ancient Egypt but expanded throughout the Roman Empire. The combination of Isis, Osiris, and their son Horus was resistant to Christian influence. Her mysteries were still being performed as late as the sixth century.

Jamnia: A town northwest of Jerusalem known to be an important Rabbinic center and mentioned by some sources as the site where the Old Testament was canonized in 90 CE.

Jehovah Witness: A Christian sect founded by Charles T. Russell (1852–1916) following the Millerite fiasco of 1843–45. In 1916 leadership passed to Joseph F.

Rutherford. Key beliefs include opposition to war and governmental authority in matters of religious conscience and expectation of an imminent end of time.

Jerome (347–420 CE): Church scholar and monk responsible for translating the Bible into Latin around 382 CE.

Justin Martyr: *See* Appendix C.

Kabbala: A collection of writings related to Jewish esoteric thought and practices; held authoritative by most Orthodox Jews.

Kierkegaard, Søren (1813–55): Danish theologian philosopher often heralded as the fountainhead of existentialism.

Luther, Martin (1483–1546): German theologian Reformer who launched the Reformation by nailing his "95 Theses" to the Wittenberg Church door on October 31, 1517.

Maccabeans: Members of the Hasmonean family of Jewish leaders that ruled Judea from 166 BCE to 37 BCE. They were responsible for the defeat of Antiochus IV Epiphanes and the Syrians and rededication of the temple in 164 BCE.

Mandaean: Member of an ancient Gnostic sect that still exists in southern Iraq. They revered John the Baptist and rejected Jesus of Nazareth as a false prophet.

Mani (216–276): Third-century prophet believed to be a Mandaean who considered himself a follower of Jesus and founded the Manichees.

Manichees: Followers of the prophet Mani. The teachings of Mani were a form of Gnostic dualism.

Marcion (ca. 110–160 CE): Leading second-century theologian who developed his own canon and well-organized Church that challenged proto-orthodox theologians to establish their own canon and tighten organizational lines

Masoretic Text: A common text introduced between the seventh and tenth centuries CE by Jewish grammarians known as Masoretes.

Messalians (or Massalians): Called by the Greeks the Euchites, or praying ones, they were Gnostic in origin, evangelical, and less interested in intellectual speculation and more emotional in their religious habits than mainstream Gnostics.

Mithra(s): Ancient Persian god of light and truth who opposed the god of dark and evil; became the principle Roman deity of a mystery religion that flourished in the second and third centuries.

Moody, Dwight (1837–99): American evangelist and leading proponent of Fundamentalism; established The Moody Bible Institute.

Mormon: A member of the Church of Jesus Christ of Latter Day Saints, founded 1830 by Joseph Smith. Its bible is The Book of Mormon, allegedly written by a fourth-century prophet named Mormon.

Nag Hammadi: Egyptian village three hundred miles south of Cairo, location of the famous discovery of ancient Gnostic texts translated by James Robertson.

Nestorius (381–451): Patriarch of Constantinople most noted by his rejection of the term Theotokos or Mary, Mother of God, which negated the Virgin Birth and caused a major schism at the Council of Ephesus in 431 CE.

Nicene Creed: Christian confession of faith adopted by the Council of Nicaea 325 CE. It was later expanded by the Council of Constantinople (381 CE) and accepted by the Council of Chalcedon (481 CE).

Origin of Alexandria: *See* Appendix C.

Paterenes: A name, probably of Italian origin, used to label heretic Bogomils of Bosnia.

Paulicans: A heretical sect that developed in the area of Bulgaria during the sixth and seventh century. The Paulicans were distinguished by their use of military force that was rejected by other heretical sects.

Persephone: In Greek mythology, daughter of Zesus and Demeter. A central figure in some mystery cults.

Petrobusians: Medieval heretical sect that forbade worshipping of Christ and infant baptism and denied sacraments.

Ptolemy (90–168 CE): Second-century Christian Gnostic teacher of Alexandria and noted mathematician, astronomer, and geographer.

Pythagoras: Sixth century BCE Greek philosopher and mathematician; main tenets of his philosophy included the transmigration of souls, numbers as the basic elements of the universe, and the universality of law. Pythagoras saw balance and harmony in everything and declared that to be the soul of the universe. Centuries later some Neo-Pythagorians adapted his theories to Gnosticism.

Rosicrucians: Individuals of the seventeenth and eighteenth centuries who professed to be members of a secret society with esoteric doctrines and practices often linked to Gnosticism. Two examples are The Rosicrucian Order and the Ancient Mistic Order Rosae Crucis.

St. Augustine of Hippo: *See* Appendix C.

Saturninus of Antioch: second-century Gnostic teacher, alleged to have been a disciple of Simon Magus.

Septuagint: A Greek translation of the Hebrew Old Testament. It was transcribed in stages and developed in stages but first appeared in Alexandria, Egypt around 285 BCE.

Serapion: Second-century proto-orthodox bishop of Antioch, largely responsible for the exclusion of the Gnostic Gospel of Peter from the New Testament canon.

Seventh-day Adventists: Religious sect bounded by Ellen Harmon White (1827–1915). They share many mainstream Protestant beliefs but uphold Ellen White's writings as scriptural, waver on justification of faith alone, believe in Investigative Judgment in which Christ tallies good and bad deeds and give the Mark of the Beast to those who do not keep the Sabbath holy.

Shakers: Religious sect that began in western New York State and is credited with starting the millennial movement in American. It was founded by Ann Lee who, after a vision of Adam and Eve, decided that human sexuality was sinful. They were called the Shakers because of a dance that became part of their ritual. There are no Shakers today.

Simon Magus: A Samaritan magician and first recorded Gnostic working within a Christian Church (Acts 8:9–24).

Sinaiticus: Fourth-century manuscript that contains most of the New Testament. It was discovered by von Tischendorf at St. Catherine's monastery at the foot of Mount Sinai.

Sophia: For Gnostics she is the source of Divine Wisdom and the "divine spark" believed to inhabit certain individuals chosen for salvation.

Sufi: A Muslim who practices a form of mysticism with origins in Gnosticism.

Tertullian: *See* Appendix C.

Textus Receptus: A Latin phrase that means "received text" and became the name given to Erasmus's Greek translation of the Bible upon which the King James Version is based.

Thecla: An alleged female disciple of Paul, probably legendary, whose stories are documented in fictional narrative style in *The Acts of Paul and Thecla*. The work is attributed to a second-century author.

Theodotos: Second- and third-century adoptionist heretic who asserted that Jesus was mere man with no divinity. He, along with others, was accused by Eusebius of tampering with scriptures in order to advance their theological position.

Theotokos (Mary): The term means "Mother of God." It was proposed at the Council of Ephesus 431 CE to refer to Mary, mother of Jesus. Nestorius and his followers strongly objected creating a split in the Church. Nestorius was eventually excommunicated.

Valentinus of Alexandria (100–175 CE): A Gnostic of the second century who taught baptism was resurrection and resurrection was not something that takes place after death. The early Church fathers viewed his threat second only to Marcion.

Vaticanus: An early fourth century New Testament manuscript that contains the four Gospels, Acts, and letters of Paul.

Vulgate: Latin version of the Bible produced by St. Jerome in the fourth century CE. It was ratified by the Council of Trent in 1546 as the official Scripture of the Roman Catholic Church.

Wesley, John (1703–1791): British Anglican clergyman; founder of Methodism along with his brother, Charles.

Westminster Confession: A Reformed confession of faith drawn up at the 1646 Westminster Assembly. It remains the doctrine of the Church of Scotland and used universally by Presbyterian churches. It has been altered and adapted by some Baptists and Congregationalists.

Zoroaster/Zoroastrian (628–551 BCE): Ancient Persian religious teacher and prophet and founder of Zoroastrianism; some sources establish his life and teachers as early as 1500 BCE. His religious views describe life as an endless war between good and evil. Zoroaster's distinctive contribution was the belief in one god, Ahura Mazda and his fiendish counterpart, Ahriman, who morphed into the Jewish and Christian devil.

THE EARLY CHRISTIAN FATHERS AND APOLOGISTS

CLEMENT OF ROME (CA. 96 CE)

Called *Clemens Romanus*, Clement I of Rome is listed Pope, fourth after Peter, Linus, and Anacletus. That order is disputed and some consider him to follow the Apostle Peter, the undisputed first pope. The dates of his papacy also vary. Some place his reign from 88 to 98 CE and others from 90 to 100 CE. Vatican sources indicate the dates of his papacy as 92–100.

Tradition acknowledges him as author of the famous Letter from the Church of Rome to the Corinthians. Though other individuals named Clement have been considered, the majority of evidence points to Clement of Rome. The letter, probably written from the Church of Rome to the Church at Corinth 94 CE, provides a picture of the Roman Church at the close of the first century. Its primary concern was a split in the Church similar to ones Paul had to deal with during his ministry. The writer of the letter was concerned about the organization of the Christian community, its ministry, and its liturgy. Clement was considered to be a moralist, relied upon Stoicism, and accepted the monotheism associated with the Jewish faith.

Some sources state he was martyred and others attest to a natural death.

IGNATIUS, BISHOP OF ANTIOCH (D. CA. 109–115 CE)

Apart from his letters, we know little about Ignatius, Bishop of Antioch. He may have suffered martyrdom. Allegedly, he was condemned to death in his own city and taken to Rome. This would suggest he was not a Roman citizen, since Roman citizenship disallowed this form of punishment.

Along the route of his journey to Rome, Ignatius was taken through numerous cities with Christian churches. He wrote letters to these various churches, which

---

The source for most of the information in this segment is Henry Bettenson's *The Early Christian Fathers*.

included Ephesus, Smyrna, and Philadelphia, one notably to Polycarp, Bishop of Smyrna. In these epistles he warned against Docetists who denied the humanity of Christ and encouraged unity emphasizing the authority of the bishop. Without the bishop there is no church, baptism, or eucharist. Unity was essential to Christianity. Ignatius affirmed the physical nature of Christ and his sufferings with equal emphasis upon his divine nature. Christ is described as the *Logos* who reveals the Father.

JUSTIN MARTYR (100–165 CE)

Bettenson places the birth of Justin of Caesarea at the end of the first century CE in Samaria at a place now called Nablus. Early in his life Justin was attracted to philosophy and not theology. As a student he was heavily influenced by Plato then as a young adult converted to Christianity and moved to Rome and became a teacher.

Though more philosopher than theologian, Justin claimed Christianity was the ultimate goal and fulfillment of the philosophic quest. His most famous work, *Dialogue with Trypho*, is about an argument Justin had with a Jew he met in Ephesus. Justin, newly converted, presents the evidence for Jewish Christianity and points out how the Old Testament presages the New Testament. His primary goal was justice for Christians and defense of their doctrines. Justin was one of the first to reconcile Christianity with Hellenism. Though the Church possesses complete truth, there are truths of philosophy that belong to the same *Logos* revealed by the incarnate Christ in his life and teachings. Justin's most original contribution to Christian thought was his concept of "Spermatic Logos," or seeds of Divine Reason spread throughout humankind before Christ's advent. With His coming the Logos was made whole and real. This liberal and controversial position allowed for the presence of *Logos* in pagan thought.

Scholars consider Justin a prolific writer, yet only two works have come down to us. *The Dialogue with Trypho,* and *Apology* addressed to emperor Antoninus Pius. Bettenson describes Justin as "no profound thinker, and no stylist; his works are rambling and diffuse; wooly as well in texture of language as of thought"[1] Tradition holds he died a martyr's death in Rome between 162 and 168, under the city prefect Rusticus when Marcus Aurelius was Emperor. His alleged relics can be reviewed in Sacrofano, a few miles north of Rome.

POLYCARP OF SMYRNA (69–155 CE)

Like his friend Ignatius, Polycarp was an early martyr at age eighty-six, well into the second century CE. He was a pacifist model, avowing he would do nothing to provoke the authorities but quietly wait until they came for him. Following a failed attempt to burn him at the stake, he was stabbed. He holds the distinction of attaining sainthood in both the Roman Catholic and Eastern Orthodox churches. He was the Christian bishop of Smyrna, now the Turkish city of Izmir.

Some traditions associate him with the Apostle John. Polycarp taught Irenaeus, which was probably his greatest contribution to Christian thought.

IRENAUS (CA.130–)

Irenaeus was born and grew up in Asia Minor but little else is known of his biography. Tradition holds that, as a youth, he heard and saw Polycarp of Smyrna then later came to Gaul. In 177 CE Irenaeus was installed a presbyter and succeeded Pothinus as the Bishop of Lyons. Irenaeus died early in the third century, possibly martyred.

Irenaeus has been called the first biblical theologian. The Bible was not considered a proof-text, as it was for many of his fellow Apologists, but a recording of God's continuous self-disclosure to humankind, culminating in the work and teachings of Jesus Christ. As Bettenson notes he was "not a systematic thinker. But the chief points are clear"[2]:

- Christ as *Logos* is the total revelation of God.
- The *Logos* is coexistent with the Father.
- Christ is the second Adam, restoring humankind to its capability of perfection and immortality before the Fall.
- His incarnationist theory of atonement is that of ransom and sacrifice.
- There is one church and one true faith.

Irenaeus' greatest work, generally known as *Adversus Haeresus*, also goes by the title *The Refutation of False Gnosis*. Against Gnostic claims to possessing secret knowledge and tradition, he affirmed apostolic tradition, the Church's "Rule of Faith," and scriptural revelation. The Rule of Faith guarantees the teaching of the great sees, whose succession can be traced back to the founding Apostles. Iranaeus was a key proponent in establishing succession of bishops. With Irenaeus, the New Testament for the first time is quoted as scripture; the gospel canon is closed.

TERTULLIAN (LATE SECOND, EARLY THIRD CENTURY)

Tertullian was the other great antignostic champion of Christianity. Born in Carthage around the middle of the second century, he was the son of a pagan Roman centurion. Tertullian was educated in law and became well-established as a case pleader. After witnessing the torture and death of Christians in denial of their rights in 193 CE he converted to Christianity. History does not record Tertullian was ever ordained. In 203 he departed the Church body and joined the Montanists, a group of enthusiasts with rigorous moral standards who believed the New Era had begun.

By some standards, Tertullian might be considered an anti-intellectual. He had little to do with Greek thought or philosophy and once asked the question,

"What has Athens to do with Jerusalem?" He was in harmony with Irenaeus by insisting the Church's teaching should be based upon scripture. Scripture should be interpreted by the Church according to apostolic tradition and the succession of bishops. In opposition to Gnostics he emphasized the humanity of Christ and reality of His suffering. His most famous passage is often misquoted: "The Son of God died; it must needs be believed because it is absurd. He was buried and rose again; it is certain because it was impossible."

Irenaeus was rigorously opposed to Marcion and his teachings, which denied compatibility between New and Old Testaments, the reality of Christ's humanity, and rejected the entire Old Testament. Tertullian wrote five books refuting Marcion's teachings and combating Monarchism. The latter were champions of monotheism (thus the term Monarch) and upheld the unity of God by declaring Christ to be a man upon whom the Holy Spirit descended. Monarchists did not believe in the eternal existence of the Son. In response to these concepts Tertullian laid down the lines, using the same terms of "substance" and "person" from which the Trinitarian Doctrine would later emerge.

CLEMENT OF ALEXANDRIA (CA. 150–211/216 CE)

Alexandria was the center of the Hellenistic world and Jewish theology and in the mid-second century it produced the first distinguished member of the Christian Church. Known as Titus Flavius Clemens, Clement was bishop of Alexandria 190–203 when he retired from Alexandria. According to tradition he was martyred and venerated as a saint but never canonized.

One of Clement's objectives was to rescue Christian thought from Gnostic contamination. Toward this purpose he developed the idea of a "true Gnosis" dependent upon an oral tradition. He called this tradition "The Ecclesiastical Rule," which was similar to the Rule of Faith of Irenaeus and Tertullian. He developed the theme of *Logos* (like Justin): *Logos* was the source of all spiritual and intellectual enlightenment. Clement distinguished between faith and knowledge. Faith was the foundation of Christian belief. Knowledge builds on faith and perfect knowledge is the contemplation of God.

Like Polycarp of Smyrna, Clement's greatness was surpassed by his student: Origin.

ORIGIN

In 203 CE Origin's father was martyred and he was saved by his mother. At age eighteen he became the head teacher of Clement's catechetical school in Alexandria. In order to study the Old Testament, Origin learned Hebrew. On of his most prominent works, which took a quarter of a century to complete, was the *Hexapla*, the Bible in six columns of parallel languages.

A wealthy converted heretic named Ambrose set up an efficient printing shop for Origin. This book-producing organization with seven shorthand-writers, seven copyists, and expert calligraphers encouraged Origin to write and to publish. His theological output, which included the *Hexapla* and *On First Principles*, was massive. The first great scholar of the Church, Origin also became its chief exemplar of allegorical exegesis. Origin's other firsts of the early Church included first devotional writer, first great commentator, and first great dogmatist.

CHRISTIAN GNOSTIC LEADERS

SIMON MAGUS

The first Christian Gnostic is reported in the Book of Acts.(Acts 8:9–13). There seems to be a general agreement among New Testament and church history scholars that Simon Magus, also known as the Magician, is the first recorded Gnostic operating within a Christian congregation. Some three hundred years later in his *Ecclesiastical History*, Eusebius depicted Simon Magus as the leader of the Gnostic assault on "truth" ("the devil who hates what is good") and traced all Gnostics to him: "Like brilliant lamps the churches were now shining throughout the world, and faith in our Savior and Lord Jesus Christ was flourishing among all mankind, when the devil who hates what is good, as the enemy of truth, ever most hostile to man's salvation, turned all his devices against the church."[1]

In Acts, Simon Magus is described as a magician who seduced people with his sorcery. He becomes impressed with Philip's preaching of the good news, believed, and was baptized. Simon Magus allegedly went to Rome in the early second century, joined other Gnostic schools (possibly the famous Valentinian), and was perceived as a threat to the early Church. Most of this is speculation.[2] Some say he was the founder of a sect, the Simonions who worshiped their founder as a manifestation of Zeus, but there is little evidence to support this conclusion.[3] Rudolph asserts that "Simonions themselves annexed Christian doctrines and thus threatened to subvert the Christian community as did most of the later Gnostics."[4] A number of his reported disciples are noted in the literature.[5]

BASILIDES

Alexandria is commonly known as the center of intellectualism of its time. It was in Alexandria Gnosticism reached its fruition with its first leader, Basilides. One of the most important representatives of Christian Gnosticism, Basilides had ambitions of becoming a Christian theologian. Origin attributes to him the composition of a gospel. According to some sources, Peter's interpreter was once his teacher. Basilides is said to have been in contact with East Indian scholars and is known to have been sympathetic to the Christian community. His teachings focused on a dualistic system, monistic theology and was strongly influenced by Greek philosophy. Among his writings are numerous commentaries and interpretations on early Jewish and Christian sacred writings.[6] He was succeeded by the most famous of all Gnostic teachers, Valentinus.

VALENTINUS

Valentinus (100–175 CE) claimed he had received a vision of working against heresies, but the early Church fathers viewed him as an arch-heretic second only to Marcion. He lived in the second century CE and, like Marcion, broke away from the Church. The most important surviving text prior to the Nag Hammadi find was the *Pistis Sophia*, allegedly written by Valentinus. However, scholars have assigned it to the fourth century or later. The document is in the British Museum; "a large part of the manuscript is concerned with esoteric instruction given to Mary Magdalene by Jesus."[7]

MARCION

Marcion lived in the second century and is believed to have been a wealthy ship owner of Sinope. He was converted from paganism, became an influential leader in the early Christian Church, and traveled extensively reaching Rome 140 CE. He is portrayed as an original thinker who wanted to institute reforms in Christian theology. He made generous contributions to the Church in Rome. When he drifted toward Syrian Gnosticism, his ideas were rejected and the money was returned to him.

Unlike other noted Gnostic thinkers of his time, Marcion did not found a school but rather a church. This church would last several centuries and become the first great dualist church and major carrier of Christian Gnosticism. Marcion never wavered in his determination to convert the Christian Church to what he considered to be the pure gospel. His own church, complete with creed, doctrine, organizational hierarchy, and sacraments, became a serious threat to the fledgling proto-orthodox Church of the early fathers. Ehrman writes compellingly: "The Marcionites . . . had a highly attractive religion to many pagan converts, as it was avowedly Christian with nothing Jewish about it. In fact, everything Jewish was taken out of it. . . . Not only were Jewish customs rejected, so, too, were the Jewish Scriptures and the Jewish God."[8]

Marcion's success was so significant the heresiologists unleashed volumes against him. Tertullian wrote five tomes attacking Marcion's views and theology.[9] Others followed suit. The successes of Marcionism have been validated by archeology. The earliest inscription found upon a Christian place of worship (320 CE) was over the doorway of a Marcionite meeting place.

Marcion was eventually excommunicated by Church elders in Rome who, as indicated, returned his money and bid him adieu. He returned to his home in

Asia Minor where he had a successful mission effort, establishing churches every-where he visited.

The "arch-heretic" passed on, but his churches and Marcionite brand of Chris-tianity continued. Bauer states that Ambrose, Bishop of Milan, was at one time in his early career a Marcionite.[10] In some parts of Asia Minor, Marcionism was the original form of Christianity and the only one people there knew. It was still around as late as the fifth century. Bishops are on record "warning members of their congregations to be wary when traveling, less they enter a strange town, attend the local church on Sunday morning, and find to their dismay that they are worshipping in the midst of Marcion heretics."[11]

Marcion was the first to recognize basic inconsistencies between the God of the Old Testament and the God of early Christian documents. (The New Testament at this point existed only as fragmentary, disconnected manuscripts.) There were two gods: A "Just God" and a "Good God." Paul was the only one who caught on to the mystery of these two Gods, and for this reason Marcion included his letters in the bible he fashioned.

More than any other individual or factor, Marcion was responsible for the for-mation of the New Testament and its canonization. He is credited with creating a canon of early Christian writings and awakening proto-orthodox proponents to the need for their own.[12] Marcion was impressed by Paul's writings, particularly his *Letter to the Galatians* in which the apostle clearly distinguishes between Jew-ish Law and the "good news," or Gospel of Christ,[13] a distinction that would become a guiding principle for him. The Law, based on justice and punishment, was given to the Jews by the God of the Old Testament. The Gospel, espousing love, mercy, and forgiveness, was proclaimed by Jesus Christ. For Marcion, they were two very different, mutually exclusive messages and messengers. In no way could the god of the Old Testament have anything to do with the God of the New Testament. Following this logic, Marcion created two Gods. The dualism was an affront to the early Church and would not be tolerated.

Once the dualistic premise was set, the remainder of Marcion's theology and subsequent writings fell into place. Jesus came into the world to save people, not condemn them. He had nothing to do with the material world created by the God of the Jews, that is, the Old Testament. Jesus was not part of the material world; he was not flesh, blood, and bones. He was complete and total spirit and only the *appearance* of physicality. Marcion's proof-text scripture was Romans 8:3—"For what the law was powerless to do in that it was weakened by the sinful nature, God did by sending his own Son *in the likeness* of sinful man to be a sin offering" (emphases added). In short, Marcion was a docetist. Jesus only seemed to be "in the flesh."

Marcion's "Bible" contained eleven books: a form of the Gospel of Luke and the ten Pauline letters found today in the New Testament. The Old Testa-ment was completely deleted. The three Pastoral epistles—1 and 2 Timothy and Titus—were not included.[14] The Gospel of Luke was truncated. Missing were those passages that did not fit the docetism of Marcion's dualistic theology.[15] Why

Luke and not Matthew, Mark, or John? Scholars speculate Marcion chose Luke because he was a companion of Paul. Another reason might be that Luke was on an intellectual level with Marcion.

With this cut-and-paste approach to the Bible, one might find it ironic that Marcion was a literalist.[16] He attacked Christian writers for their manner of textual interpretation, primarily their use of allegory.[17] "Controversy with Gnosticism also forced Origen to an extended examination of the right principles for interpreting the Bible. Against literalists, such as Marcion, he vindicated the claims of allegory to a place in Christian exegesis."[18]

CHRONOLOGY OF KEY DATES AND EVENTS

1500 BCE	Approximate time Zoroastrianism established
168 BCE	Antiochus IV Epiphanes began persecution of the Jews
167–165 BCE	The Maccabean Rebellion
160–ca. 150	Composition of the apocalyptic *Book of Enoch*
164 BCE	Composition of the *Book of Daniel*
27 BCE–14 CE	Reign of Caesar Augustus
ca. 30 CE	Crucifixion/Resurrection of Jesus
38–41	Composition of *Wisdom of Solomon*
55–70	Letters of St. Paul written
68	Death of Nero
70 CE	Jerusalem captured, the Temple destroyed by Titus; Dispersion of the Jews
70–90	Synoptic Gospels written
94	Clement of Rome's letter to the Corinthians written
100	Gospel of John written
96	Clement of Rome
130	Oldest NT fragment: Rylands Papyrus; John 18:31–33, 37
144	Shepherd of Hermas completed
160	Death of Marcion
165	Justin martyred
175	First recorded church council/against Montanism
180–225	Oldest papyrii of NT written: Chester Beatty and Bodmer Papyrus
130–200	Irenaeus of Lyons
190–203	Clement of Alexandria
210–276	Mani born; beginning of Manichaeism
220	Death of Tertullian
235	Hippolytus martyred
250	First general persecution of Christians
254	Death of Origin
303	Diocletion's persecution of Christians

306	Constantine proclaimed Emperor
313	Constantine's victory over Maxentius at the Milvian Bridge; Edict of Milan proclaiming universal religious toleration
319	Beginning of the Arian controversy
321	Constantine ordered law courts closed, Sunday established
324	Constantine became sole Emperor
325	Council of Nicea
326	Arius exiled
328	Athanasius became bishop of Alexandria
331	Constantine commissioned and financed new Bibles
325–450	Codex Vaticanus and Codex Sinaiticus compiled
336	Death of Arius in Constantinople; First exile of Athanasius
337	Death of Constantine
339	Death of Eusebius of Caesarea
340–350	Gnostic Gospels written and bound
361	Julian the Apostate succeeded Constantius
366	Final return of Athanasius from exile
367	Athanasius' thirty-seventh Festal Letter containing a list of twenty-seven New Testament books; Burial of Gnostic Gospels at the Chenoboskion Monastery
370	Basil became bishop of Caesarea in Cappadocia
373	Ambrose elected bishop of Milan
379	Accession of Theodosius the Great in the East
380	Theodosius outlaws Arianism
381	Council of Constantinople I
384–400	Jerome's (347–420) Latin Vulgate translation of the Bible
393	Synod of Hippo Regius ratifies Athanasius' New Testament list of twenty-seven books
397	Synod of Carthage confirms New Testament list of Hippo Regius Synod
410	Sack of Rome by Alaric and Visigoths
412–444	Cyril of Alexandria
419	Second Synod of Carthage makes final confirmation of New Testament canon
430	Death of Augustine
431	Cyril opens Council of Ephesus; Nestorius condemned and deposed; Nicene Creed approved to exclusion of all others
451	Council of Chalcedon; accepts creeds of Nicaea and Constantinople
481–511	Franks converted to Christianity
553	Council of Constantinople II
610–645	Reign of Heraclius
622	Muhammad's flight to Medina and the beginning of Islam; Muslim Invasion; Alexandria and Jerusalem lost to the empire

632	Death of Mohammed
680	Council of Constantinople III
711	Visigoth Spain overrun by Moors
738	Battle of Tours; Charles Martel
754	Pepin officially anointed, inaugurating the Carolingian dynasty: Donation of Constantine; the Pope supreme
787	Council of Nicaea II
800	Charlemagne crowned Holy Roman Emperor
950–1200	Bogomil heresy in Bosnia, Lombardy, and France
1095	Pope Urban II calls for the First Crusade
1099	Jerusalem captured by the First Crusaders
1150–1300	Albigensian/Cathar heresy in Southern France
1187	Battle of Hattin, Christians defeated by Saladin; Fall of Jerusalem
1446–50	Gutenberg's invention of the moveable type printing press
1453	Fall of Constantinople to Ottoman Turks
1455	printing of the Bible on Gutenberg's press
1514	First printed Greek New Testament (Cisnero's Polyglot Bible)
1516	First printed Greek New Testament to be published (Erasmus); Became the Textus Receptus from which King James was translated
1517	Martin Luther launched the Reformation
1611	King James Version of the Bible completed
1709–19	Publishing of First Greek New Testament based on ancient manuscripts and not the Textus Receptus
1730–70	First Great Awakening in America
1736	Beginning of Jonathan Edward's Northampton, Connecticut Revival
1738	Beginning of George Whitefield's revival tours in America
1741	Jonathan Edwards preached "Sinners in the Hands of an Angry God" in Enfield, Connecticut
1776	Beginning of the American Revolution
1782	First Bible printed in English in America (Robert Aitken in Philadelphia)
1800–82	John Nelson Darby, father of Dispensationalism
1800	Cane Ridge Revival in Kentucky and beginning of Second Great Awakening
1843–45	Millerite projected end of the world
1844	Von Tischendorf's discovery of the fourth-century Sinaiticus Codex at St. Catherine's Monastery on Mount Sinai
1845	Beginning of Southern Baptist Convention
1854	Catholic Infallible Doctrine of Immaculate Conception proclaimed

1870	Catholic Infallible Doctrine of Papal Infallibility proclaimed
1881	Publication of Hort & Westcott's Greek New Testament
1890	Gnostic Church reestablished in France
1910	General Assembly of Northern Presbyterian Church; the slogan "The Fundamentals" adopted
1910–15	Publication of The Fundamentals
1920	Curtis Lee Laws, editor of Northern Baptist newspaper adopts term "Fundamentalists"
1925	The Scopes "Monkey" Trial
1940–50	Beginning of Billy Graham Crusades
1945	Nag Hammadi discovery of the Gnostic Gospels
1947	Dead Sea Scrolls discovered
1979	Jerry Falwell founded the Moral Majority; beginning of the New Christian Right; Publication of Elaine Pagels' The Gnostic Gospels
1988	Pat Robertson founded the Christian Coalition

COMPOSITION CHRONOLOGY OF NEW TESTAMENT BOOKS

Scholars find it impossible to agree on the exact dates when the New Testament books were written. Table F.1 gives an idea of the variance of opinion among scholars. It is an amended version of one constructed by Dr. Albert E. Barnett, in *The New Testament: Its Making and Meaning* (Abingdon Cokesbury). An addition to Dr. Barnett's two columns is a third: Bart Ehrman's current version. The archeological scholar Albright expresses there is little basis for dating any New Testament book after 80 CE (*Harper's Bible Dictionary*, ed. Madeleine S. Miller and J. Lane Miller [New York: Harper & Brothers Publishers, 1961], 102).

Table F.1   Scholarly opinion on New Testament dates

Dr. A. E. Barnett	Others	Ehrman
Galatians 49 CE	53–58	1 Thessalonians 49
1/2 Thessalonians 50	52	
1/2 Corinthians 53–55	57	Remainder of Paul's
	Letters 49–62	
Romans 56	57–58	
Philippians (ca. 55) 60	63	
Colossians/Philemon (55) 61–62	58–60	
Mark 65–67	68–70	Gospel of Mark
	64–70	
Matthew 75–80	70–85	Gospels of Matthew and Luke 80–85
Luke, Acts 90–95	63–96	
Ephesians 95	58–60	
Hebrews 95	80	
Revelation 95	96	Deutero-Pauline Epistles; Pastoral Epistles, General Epistles 80–110
I Peter 95–100	61–63	

Table F.1   (*continued*)

Dr. A. E. Barnett	Others	Ehrman
Fourth Gospel 95–115	95–115	Gospel of John 90–95
Johannine Epistles 110–115	98	Book of Revelation 95–100
James 125–150	58–60	
Jude 125–150	81	
II Peter 150	98	
Timothy, Titus 160–175	64–67	

SUGGESTIONS FOR FURTHER READING

Ammerman, Nancy. *Bible Believers: Fundamentalists in the Modern World*. New Brunswick: Rutgers University Press. 1987.

Barclay, William. *The Making of the Bible*. Nashville, TN: Abingdon, 1963.

Barr, James. *Fundamentalism*. London: The Westminster, 1978.

———. *Voices from Cane Ridge*. Edited by Rhodes Thompson. St. Louis: Bethany, 1954.

Barrett, Charles. Kingsley. *The New Testament Background: Selected Documents*. 2nd ed. New York: Harper and Row, 1989.

Bauer, Walter. *Orthodoxy and Heresy in Earliest Christianity*. Translated by Robert Kraft. Philadelphia: Fortress Press, 1971.

Bettenson, Henry, trans. and ed. *The Early Christian Fathers*. 7th ed. New York: Oxford University Press, 1984.

Black, David Alan. *New Testament Textual Criticism*. Grand Rapids, MI: Eerdmans, 1992.

Boles, John B. *The Great Revival: Beginnings of the Bible Belt*. Lexington, Kentucky: University Press of Kentucky, 1996.

Bruce, F. F. *The New Testament Documents: Are They Reliable?* Grand Rapids, MI: Eerdmans, 1978.

Carpenter, Joel. *Revive Us Again: The Reawakening of American Fundamentalism*. New York: Oxford University Press. 1997.

Chesterton, G. K. *Orthodoxy*. San Francisco: Ignatius, 1995.

Conkin, Paul K. *Cane Ridge: America's Pentecost*. Madison, WI: University of Wisconsin Press, 1990.

Dibelius, Martin. *From Tradition to Gospel*. Translated by B. L. Woolf. New York: Scribner, 1934.

Dunn, James D. G. *Christology in the Making: A New Testament Inquiry into the Origins of the Doctrine of Incarnation*. 2nd ed. London: SCM, 1989.

Ehrman, Bart D. *After the New Testament: A Reader in Early Christianity*. New York: Oxford University Press, 1998.

———. *Lost Scriptures: Books That Did Not Make It Into the New Testament*. New York: Oxford University Press, 2004.

———. *The Text of the New Testament: Its Transmission, Corruption and Restoration*. New York: Oxford University Press, 2004.

Ehrman, Bart D., and Andrew S. Jacobs. *Christianity in late Antiquity 300–450 C.E.: A Reader*. New York: Oxford University Press, 2004.

Fitzmeyer, Joseph A. *Responses to 101 Questions on the Dead Sea Scrolls*. New York: Paulist, 1982.

Foerster, Werner. *Gnosis: A Selection of Gnostic Texts*. Translated by R. McL Wilson. Oxford: Clarendon, 1972.

Grant, R. M. *The Formation of the New Testament*. London: Hutchinson, 1965.

Greenlee, J. Harold. *Introduction to New Testament Textual Criticism*. Grand Rapids, MI: Eerdmans, 1964.

Harnack, Adolph von. *Marcion: The Gospel of the Alien God*. Translated by John E. Steely and Lyle D. Bierma. Durham, N.C.: Labyrinth, 1990.

Harris, William V. *Ancient Literacy*. Cambridge, MA: Harvard University Press, 1989.

Honegraaff, Hank. *Counterfeit Revival*. Nashville: Word Publishing, 2001.

Jenkins, Phillip. *Hidden Gospels: How the Search for Jesus Lost Its Way*. Oxford: Oxford University Press, 2001.

Johnson, Luke. *The Creed: What Christians Believe and Why It Matters* New York: Doubleday, 2003.

Jonas, Hans. *The Gnostic Religion: The Message of the Alien God and the Beginnings of Christianity*. 2nd ed. Boston: Beacon, 1963.

Keck, Leander. *Paul and His Letters*. Philadelphia: Fortress, 1979.

Kelly, Joseph. *Why Is There A New Testament?* Grand Rapids, MI: Eerdmans, 1967.

Kenyon, F. G. *Books and Readers in Ancient Greece and Rome*. 2nd ed. Oxford: Clarendon, 1952.

Knox, John. *Marcion and the New Testament*. Chicago: Chicago University Press, 1942.

Kurt, Rudolph. *Gnosis: The Nature and History of Gnosticism*. Translated by R. McL. Wilson. San Francisco: Harper and Row, 1987.

Layton, Bentley. *The Gnostic Scriptures: A New Translation with Annotations*. Garden City, NY: Doubleday, 1987.

Marsden, George. *Fundamentalism and American Culture. The Shaping of Twentieth Century Evangelism*. New York: Oxford University Press. 1980.

———. *The Shaping of Twentieth Century Evangelicanism, 1870–1925*. Oxford: Oxford University Press, 1980.

Marty, Martin, and Scott Appleby. *The Fundamentalism Project*. Chicago: The University of Chicago Press, 1991–95.

McDonald, Lee M. *The Formation of the Christian Biblical Canon*. Nashville, TN.: Abingdon, 1988.

Metzger, Bruce. *The Early Versions of the New Testament*. Oxford: Clarendon, 1977.

———. *Manuscripts of the Greek Bible*. Oxford: Oxford University Press, 1981.

Meyer, Marvin. ed. *The Ancient Mysteries: A Sourcebook*. San Francisco: Harper and Row, 1987

Nickle, Keith. *The Synoptic Gospels: Conflict and Consensus*. Atlanta: John Knox, 1980.

Nigosian, S. A. *From Ancient Writings to Sacred Texts: The Old Testament and Apocrypha*. Baltimore: Johns Hopkins University Press, 2004.

Pagels, Elaine. *Beyond Belief: The Secret Gospel of Thomas*. New York: Random House, 2003.

———. *The Gnostic Paul: Gnostic Exegesis of the Pauline Letters*. Philadelphia: Fortress, 1975.

Sandeen, Ernest R. *The Roots of Fundamentalism: British and American Millenarianism, 1800–1930*. Chicago: University of Chicago Press, 1970.

Sandmel, Samuel. *Judaism and Christian Beginnings*. New York: Oxford University Press, 1978.

Scholem, Gershom C. *On the Kaballa and Its Symbolism*. New York: Shocken Books, 1965.

Stowers, Stanley. *Letter Writing in Graeco-Roman Antiquity*. Philadelphia: Westminster, 1986.

Taylor, Isaac. *History of the Transmission of Ancient Books to Modern Times*. London: Jackson and Walford, 1859.

Torjesen, Karen Jo. *When Women Were Priests: Women's Leadership in the Early Church and the Scandal of Their Subordination in the Rise of Christianity*. San Francisco: HarperCollins, 1993.

Turcan, Robert. *The Cults of the Roman Empire*. Oxford: Blackwell, 1996.

Turner, Eric G. *Greek Manuscripts of the Ancient World*, 2nd ed. Oxford: Oxford University Press, 1987.

Underhill, Evelyn. *Mysticism*. Kessinger Publishing, 2003.

Vanderkam, James. *The Meaning of the Dead Sea Scrolls: Their Significance for Understanding the Bible, Judaism, Jesus and Christianity*. San Francisco: HarperSanFrancisco, 2002.

Vermes, Geza, ed. *The Dead Sea Scrolls in English*. 3rd ed. Baltimore: Penguin Books, 1987.

Warfield, Benjamin. B. *The Inspiration and Authority of the Bible*. Edited by Samuel Craig. Philadelphia: Presbyterian and Reformed, 1964.

Werner, Martin. *The Formation of Christian Dogma*. Boston: Beacon, 1963.

Williams, Michael. *Rethinking "Gnosticism": An Argument for Dismantling a Dubious Category*. Princeton, NJ: Princeton University Press, 1996.

Wright, N. T. Anglican Bishop, *Judas and the Gospel of Jesus: Have We Missed the Truth about Christianity?* York: Oxford University Press, 1984.

NOTES

PREFACE

1. Elsie E. Egermeier, *Egermeier's Bible Story Book: A Complete Narration from Genesis to Revelation for Young and Old* (Los Angeles: The Smithsonian Company, 1947).
2. Frederick L. Gwynn and Joseph L. Blotner, ed., *Faulkner in the University* (New York: Vintage Books, 1959), 167.
3. Philip Wise, *Against the Protestant Gnosticism* (New York: Oxford University Press, 1987), 282–83.

INTRODUCTION

1. In its original usage, the word "pagan" denoted someone who lived in the country, a "hillbilly" perhaps in our parlance. As Christianity became more and more urbanized, those living in the rural areas were considered non-Christian, thus pagan. Bart Ehrman, a well-known religious scholar, presents another etymological theory: "the term simply designates a person who subscribed to any of the polytheistic religions, that is, anyone who is neither a Jew nor a Christian. The term *paganism* then refers to the wide range of ancient polytheistic religions outside of Judaism and Christianity." *The New Testament: Its Background, Growth and Content* (Nashville: Abingdon, 2003), 20.
2. This geographical area would later become dominated by Manichaeism. Mani, who also called himself a disciple of Jesus Christ, is believed to have been a Mandaean, a sect that revered John the Baptist and rejected Jesus of Nazareth as a false prophet. He came from the region of Baghdad, had his first vision in 240 CE, and constructed a universal religion along Gnostic and dualistic lines, but also utilized elements from Zoroasticism, Christianity, and Buddhism. Mandaean is related to Marcionism in several ways. Mandaeanism and Marcionism are both characterized by dualism and belief in a Demiurge. Marcionism is extinct but Mandaeanism is not. However, some view Mandaeanism as a vestige of Marcionism. In that perspective, Marcionism lives on. In the eighth century there was a Manichean church in Peking. In the ninth century, Central Asia was Manichean. Until they were obliterated by the Mongols in the thirteenth century, the Manichees were strong throughout central and western Asia. From 373 to 382, Augustine was a Manichee and "though he bitterly attacked his former faith he never entirely rid himself of its doctrines." Michael Runciman, *The Medieval Manichee* (Cambridge: Cambridge University Press, 1984), 16.
3. Elaine Pagels, *The Gnostic Gospels* (New York: Random House, 1979).
4. Jay Tolson, *U. S. News and World Report* 141, no. 23 (2006): 75.
5. The man responsible for their translation to English was James Robinson, *Nag Hammadi Library*, 4th rev.ed. (Leiden: Brill, 1996).
6. Bruce Metzger, *The Text of the New Testament* (New York: Oxford University Press, 1992), 42.

7. Cf. Manly P. Hall, *Orders of the Quest*, 1996; *Orders of Universal Reformation*, 1999; and *Orders of the Great Work*, 1976, all published in Los Angeles by the Philosophical Research Society.

8. Included in this list are lesser known intellects, such as Adolph von Harnack, Richard Reitzenstein, and Walter Bauer, who contributed to creating a change in Gnostic studies. This renewed interest in Gnosticism was also joined by Madam Blavatsky and her student G. R. S. Mead. French esotericists led by Gerard Encausse and Jules Doinel reestablished the Gnostic Church, which, in various forms, continues today.

9. For more information on the Gnostic Socieity, go to their Web site: http://www.gnosis .org/gnostsoc/gnostsoc.htm.

10. Basilides (117–38 CE) was an early Christian teacher who may have studied under an alleged interpreter of St. Peter. His followers, Basilideans, formed a Gnostic sect. Very little is known about his teachings. He is alleged to have written twenty-four books on the Gospels, which, based upon the weight of criticism he received from Irenaeus of Lyon (ca. 130 CE), Clement of Alexandria (Bishop 190–203 CE), and Hippolytus (martyred 235 CE), this allegation could be true.

11. Cf. http://www.gnosis.org/gnostoc/gnostoc.htm.

12. Philip J. Lee, *Against the Protestant Gnostics* (New York: Oxford University Press, 1987).

13. Harold Bloom, *Omens of Millennium: The Gnosis of Angels, Dreams, and Resurrection* (New York: River Head Books, 1980), 27.

14. Bloom, *Omens of Millennium*, 31.

15. Fisher Humphreys and Philip Wise, *Fundamentalism* (Macon, GA: Smyth & Helwys, 2004).

16. Grand Rapids, MI: Zondervan, 1989.

17. *Webster's New World Dictionary*, College Edition (New York: World Publishing Company, 1960), 1035.

CHAPTER 1

1. Athanasius, *Epistolae Festales (XXXIX)*, in *Post and Post-Nicene Fathers*, series II, vol. IV (Baker Book House, 1983).

2. Athanasius' list of twenty-seven books were eventually accepted as canon by the Synods of Hippo Regius (393 CE) and Carthage (397 and 419 CE).

3. Athanasius, *Epistolae Festales (XXXIX)*, op. cit., emphasis added.

4. Historians and archaeologists place the Chenoboskian monastery near the small village of Tabinnisi. Its founder was a religious pioneer named Pachomius, who set up a code of solitary life, strict, militaristic discipline, and strenuous labor. The monks there were ascetics who believed bodily needs and sensations interfered with communion with God. Any form of pleasure was questioned. A contemporary of Pachomius was a famous and noted ascetic monk named Antony who never strayed from orthodoxy and later achieve sainthood.

5. Tobias Churton, *The Gnostics* (New York: Barnes & Noble, 1987).

6. *Codex* is Latin for block of wood or book. It contained separate pages bound together much in the way books of today are bound, only much less sophisticated. It is considered a Roman invention. The exact date is unknown, but during the first and second centuries CE, the writers of manuscripts that would later make their way into the New Testament canon shifted from using scrolls to using codices. Several reasons are conjectured. The codex was less cumbersome and more user friendly, especially for locating passages. Because both sides could be used, it was more economical. However, some scholars contend practicality and economics had nothing to do with the wholesale shift of Christian writers away from scrolls. They claim it was the intent of early Christians to distance

themselves in every way possible from the Jewish religion, which used only scrolls. Cf. E. Randolph Richards, *Paul and First Century Letter Writing* (Madison, WI: Inter Varsity, 2004).

7. Bart Ehrman reports that "the cache contained twelve leather-bound volumes, with pages of a thirteenth volume removed from its own, now lost, binding and tucked inside the cover of one of the others." Bart D. Ehrman, *Lost Christianities: The Battle for Scriptures and the Faiths We Never Knew* (New York: Oxford University Press, 2004), 53.

8. Ehrman, *Lost Christianities*, 53.

9. James R. Robinson, trans. *The Nag Hammadi Library* in English, 4th rev. ed. (Leiden: Brill, 1996).

10. Ehrman states this information came from the head of the archaeological team involved in the exploration of the site. Cf. Bart. D. Ehrman, *Truth and Fiction in The Da Vinci Code* (New York: Oxford University Press, 2004), 192. Stephen Hoeller, in his introduction to Manly P. Hall's classic *The Wisdom of the Knowing Ones*, points out that the exact place of the discovery is unknown.

11. Ehrman, *Truth and Fiction in The Da Vinci Code*, 37.

12. Manley P. Hall, *The Wisdom of the Knowing Ones* (Los Angeles: The Philosophical Research Society, 2000), 9.

13. Ehrman, *Lost Christianities*, 51. In order to console his companions who helped him find the vessel, Muhammad, the leader, tore the codices apart and doled out a fair share to each man. Suspecting some evil magic at work, his coworkers gave them back so Muhammad stuffed them in his turban and took them home. Sadly, his mother eventually confessed she used some of the papyrus sheaths to kindle their fire. Afterwards, the story becomes complicated and involves a blood feud with a neighboring tribe triggered by the murder of Mohammad's father, the mistaken revenge murder of a local sheriff's son. Fearing his house would be searched by authorities, Mohammad gave one of the books to the cleric of a local Coptic Church. The priest's brother-in-law, an itinerant teacher, realized the value of the books. There would be further intrigue before the books became the possession of James M. Robinson, the head of an international team of scholars and researchers.

14. It is also conjecture that the Essenes of Dead Sea Scroll notoriety hid manuscripts in similar urns in caves, possibly due to fear of their destruction by advancing Roman legions.

15. There were actually fifty-two treatises among the volumes, but six are duplicates.

16. For a complete list of the entire library, see Robinson, *The Nag Hammadi Library in English*.

17. The serpent appears throughout Gnostic literature as a voice of wisdom. Cf. also Joseph Campbell, *The Power of Myth* (New York: Doubleday, 1988).

18. *The Thunder, Perfect Mind* 13:16–14:18, in Nag Hammadi Library, 411–12.

19. Elaine Pagels, *The Gnostic Gospels* (New York: Random House, 1976).

20. "Gnosticism was the great heresy of the ante-Nicene period of church history. The fathers of primitive Christianity, having elected themselves the sole custodians of salvation, exercised their prerogative to stamp out all traces of Christianity as a philosophical code." Hall, *The Wisdom of the Knowing Ones*, 29.

21. Ehrman, *Lost Christianities*, 115.

22. Pagels and others correctly note that much of the terminology represents irrefutable Jewish heritage. However, other customs and culture also make up the multifaceted Gnostic collage.

23. Henry Chadwick, *The Early Church*, 3rd. ed. (London: Penguin Books, 1993), 34.

24. Bruce Metzger, *The New Testament: Its Background, Growth and Content*, 3rd. ed. (Nashville: Abingdon, 2003), 188.

25. Ehrman, *The New Testament*, 187.

CHAPTER 2

1. The word *hermeneutic* originally derived from Hermes, son of Zeus and the herald of the Greek Olympian gods. Among the many other hats he wore, Hermes was the god of shepherds, merchants, literature, athletics, thieves, and oratory. More importantly, he was the messenger of the gods, which makes his name important for us because that is one aspect of this study: understanding theological messages.

2. *Webster's New World Dictionary* (New York: The World Publishing Company, 1960), 680.

3. Bart D. Ehrman, *Misquoting Jesus* (San Francisco: Harper Collins, 2005), 217.

4. Kurt Rudolph, *Gnosis: The Nature & History of Gnosticism* (San Francisco: Harper, 1987), 307–8.

5. Bruce Metzger, *The New Testament* (New York: Oxford University Press, 2004), 190.

6. Elaine Pagels, *The Gnostic Gospels* (New York: Random House, 1976), xviii.

7. Pagels, *Gnostic Gospels*, xix.

8. From *The Apocryphon of James*, quoted by Tobias Churton, *Gnosticism and the New Testament* (Minneapolis: Fortress, 1993), 22.

9. From *The Book of Thomas the Contender*, quoted by Tobias Churton, Ibid.

10. *Gnosticism and the New Testament* (Minneapolis: Fortress, 1993), 58, 59.

11. Ibid., 67.

12. *Gospel of Thomas*, 3

13. *The New Testament*, 190 Some scholars, such as G. R. S. Meade ("Echoes from the Gnosis," Vol. 1, *The Gnosis of the Mind*, 1906), contest that the early Gnostics described themselves as *gnostikoi* but suggest they probably used the word *telestai*, "those who aimed," which would have aligned them with the mystery religions of the classical world. By their enemies, the likes of Tertullian and Origen, they would have been called *gnostikoi* or "know-it-all," which was an insult.

14. From *The Gospel of Thomas*, quoted in Churton, 23.

15. Stephen Hoeller, in his introduction to Manly P. Hall's *The Wisdom of the Knowers*, makes a distinction between Christian Gnostics and "pagan" Gnostics. This latter, he states, should be called Hermeticists because of their use of the Greco-Egyptian Hermes as their savior, which is very similar to the Christian Gnostics role for Jesus. This is a scholarly, and probably accurate, conclusion, but only marginally important for our purposes.

16. The Gnostic writer Basilides generated 365 gods.

17. Lee, 17

18. Ibid., 117.

19. An argument has been forwarded by some scholars, notably, Gershom Scholem, that the accurate name for "Jewish Gnosticism" was Essene (cf. Gershom Scholem, *Jewish Gnosticism, Merkaba Mysticism and Talmudic Tradition*, 1965).

20. This is an oversimplification but accurate in describing the "radical dualism" of many variations of Gnosticism resembling the "radical dualism" of such Eastern religions as Manichaeism and Zoroastrianism. Their ultimate source is probably Zoroastrianism which dates as far back possibly as 1500 BCE. Zoroaster (the Greek name is Zarathustra) is believed by many scholars to have invented the ideology of apocalypse and millennium, which reappeared in late apocalyptic Judaism, Gnosticism, and early Christianity. There were many variations on this theme. Some Gnostics favored what could be called a "mitigated" or watered-down dualism. In this form of dualism one of the two entities is inferior to the other. One classical Gnostic movement known as the Sethians believed the material world was created by a lesser divinity than the one true God who was the object of their worship and adoration. "Qualified Monism" would be another form of dualism, where the inferior deity might, or might not, be divine and might or might not be semi-divine.

21. The Apostle Paul referred to this phenomenon as evil powers and Elaine Pagels has even suggested Gnostic elements within his teachings and called him "The Gnostic Paul." Cf. *Gnostic Gospels*. Her reference is to Paul's comment that we struggle not against flesh and blood but against spiritual evil and wickedness in high places.

22. Ehrman, in *The Orthodox Corruption of Scripture* (New York: Oxford University Press, 1993) points out that this tripartite division was basically represented in only one form of Gnosticism: Separatist. The Separatists believed the spirit of the one God entered Jesus at his baptism and departed his physical body prior to his crucifixion. In this way Christ did not suffer. For a fuller discussion of the two basic forms of Gnosticism, Separatist, and Docetist, see the *Divine Redeemer* segment in this chapter.

23. Ehrman, *Orthodox Corruption of Scripture*, 123.

24. In the Gnostic Gospel of Thomas the story of the lost sheep sounds very similar to that told by the gospel writers but with a different, subtle, twist. In Thomas's version, the largest sheep went astray. The shepherd left the ninety-nine to find it. Upon finding it, he states, "I care for you more than the ninety-nine." Those who recall the parable, recognize immediately the shift. In the two Gospels where the story is found, the good shepherd looks for the sheep because the one sheep needs him. There is no concern for the flock, only the one sheep. This is just one more reflection of the elitism fostered by a dualistic, separatist theology. Lee, *Against the Protestant Gnosticism*, 34–35.

25. Ehrman, *Orthodox Corruption of Scripture*.

26. Hoeller, *The Wisdom of the Knowing Ones*, 16.

27. (Cambridge: Cambridge University Press, 1984), 5.

28. The Demiurge is mentioned in Plato's famous treatise *Timaeus*. Irenaeus, in his *Against Heresies*, credits Nicholas, founder of the Nicolaites, as the origin of the concept. Ibid.

29. This version is found in elements of the writings of Valentinian, a prominent Christian in the Roman Church who almost became elected Pope. Elaine Pagels points out that Valentinian Gnosticism is essentially different from dualism. *The Gnostic Gospels*)

30. For additional information Cf. William Schoedel, "Gnostic Monism and the Gospel of Truth," in *The Rediscovery of Gnosticism, Vol. 1: The School of Valentinus*, ed. Bentley Layton (Brill: Leiden, 1980).

31. Returning to the metaphor of the apple falling too far from the tree, one version of Sophia's fall portrays her breaking her boundaries by trying to understand and know all of the divine realm. By overstepping her authority, she separates herself from other divine spirits. The story creates images of Adam and Eve in the Garden and a tree that got them into trouble and exiled from Paradise. "The contribution of Genesis to Gnostic myth has long been recognized. The Gnostics, as well as other religious movements and systems of thought, were fascinated with the story of the Fall of Adam and Eve. Chadwick states: "The Fall of Eve was taken to symbolize a pre-cosmic catastrophe in which a female power, the Mother, went astray from the divinely intended path. Or the story might suggest exciting speculations about the role of the serpent" (37).

32. As Ehrman points out in his book *The New Testament* (New York: Oxford University Press, 2004) one of these beings is named Ialdabaoth in some Gnostic texts, which is closely related to the Hebrew name for God, which is Yahweh or Jehova.

33. A much more detailed and descriptive representation of this myth, along with its parallels in Judaeo-Christian mythology and relationship with Platonic philosophy, can be found in Manly P. Hall's *The Wisdom of the Knowing Ones*.

34. A number of texts in the Nag Hammadi library ridicule the concept of one good god who could create suffering and pain (cf. *On the Origin of the World, Secret Book of John, Hypostasis of the Archons*).

35. Op.cit., 18.

36. Some prominent names in Gnostic systems are Seth (third son of Adam), Jesus, and Mani, an Iranian prophet.
37. Lee, 9.
38. "The principle ingredient which Gnosticism derived from Christianity was the central idea of redemption. But not all second century sects included Jesus as redeemer." Chadwick, 37.
39. Jesus was not the only Redeemer around in those days. Second century sects could choose a Samaritan named Simon Magus, who was popular. In some systems, the Greek hero Heraclitus appears as a savior.
40. Both Basilides and the Platonist Valentinus, Gnostics who considered themselves Christian with belief systems very similar to orthodoxy, rejected any notion of incarnation.
41. There was a third interpretation of Jesus's sonship, namely, Adoptionism. In this theory, Jesus was adopted by God and was never divine, but always human. Proponents of this view were primarily a diversified group of Jewish Christians, most of whom were known as Ebionites, who based their understanding on elements of Paul's letters and on a text in Luke (3:22): "You are my Son, today I have begotten you." (Ehrman argues convincingly that this text is original with Luke.) They have little or no kinship with Gnosticism and are thus beyond the scope of this study.
42. Especially Bart Ehrman, *The New Testament: A Historical Introduction to the Early Christian Writings*; and Bruce Metzger, *The New Testament: Its Background, Growth and Content.*
43. The concept of the Trinity had not, at this point, been fully articulated, and would not become doctrine until the Council of Nicaea in 325 C.E. Even beyond Nicaea debates would continue to rage over the nature of Christ, how the paradox of his humanity and divinity could be explained. The Councils of Ephesus (431 C.E.) and Chalcedon (451 C.E.) both approved the Nicene Creed to the exclusion of all others.
44. Lee, 11.
45. A concept, we will see later, that resonates with some forms of Calvinistic doctrine.
46. This is attested in a number of Gnostic writings, particularly the works of Valentinus, who considered Christian sermons dull. Cf. Pagels, *The Johannine Gospel in Gnostic Exegesis* (Nashville: Abingdon, 1973).
47. *The New Testament*, 191–92.
48. Pagels, *Gnostic Gospels*, 25.
49. Ehrman, *The New Testament.*
50. *Strom.* III, 10.
51. *Against Heresies* I 6, 3 ff, quoted in Rudolph, 255–56.
52. Ibid., I 25, 4 quoted in Rudolph, ibid., 256.
53. *Panarion*, 26, 5, 7, quoted in Rudolph, ibid., 257.
54. Ibid.
55. *Omens of Millennium*, 184.
56. Ibid., 184.

CHAPTER 3

1. Pheme Perkins, *Gnosticism and the New Testament* (Minneapolis: Fortress, 1993), 91.
2. Kurt Rudolph, *Gnosis: The Nature & History of Gnosticism*, trans. Robert Wilson (San Francisco: HarperSanFrancisco, 1987), 275.
3. Perkins, *Gnosticism and the New Testament*, 9.
4. Bart Ehrman, *The New Testament* (New York: Oxford University Press, 2004), 187.
5. Greco-Roman is a term used by scholars to denote lands around the Mediterranean Sea within a time frame of roughly 300 BCE and 300 CE. The Hellenization process set in

motion by Alexander the Great (356–323 BCE) plus the political stability rendered by Roman government led to a complexly unified peaceful world (the *Pax Romana*).

6. Perkins, *Gnosticism and the New Testament*, 11.

7. A key Neo-Pythagorean teacher of the first century was one Appolonius of Tyana, whose biography reads like a duplicate of Jesus Christ's. Cf. Ehrman, *New Testament*, 19. Apollonius of Tyana.

8. T. R. Glover, *The Conflict of Religions in the Early Roman Empire* (Boston: Beacon, 1960), 18, but referencing Tertullian, *de Idol*. 9.

9. Hall, 124.

10. Ernst Troeltsch, *The Social Teaching of the Christian Churches*, vol. 1, trans. Olive Wyon (London: Allen & Unwin, 1931), quoted from Lee, 7.

11. Hall, 31.

12. Harold Bloom, prominent Gnostic scholar, agrees: "I myself believe that Gnosticism, like Christianity itself, began as a Jewish heresy, just as Islam rose as a kind of Jewish-Christian restoration movement." *The American Religion* (New York: Chu Hartley Publishers, 1992), 10. In addition to sharing similar traits of generic fundamentalism, Christian and Islamic Fundamentalism both stem from similar philosophic roots and are comparable psychologically. It is not surprising, therefore, that the loudest opposition to the mainstream Islam comes from both Islamic Fundamentalists and American conservative Fundamentalist camps.

13. Rudolph, 277. Cf. also Roman Catholic scholar, Father Daniélou: "It will have become clear by now that gnosis . . . cannot be regarded as it once was, as the result of Hellenistic influence, but must have been a characteristic of later Judaism." *The Theology of Jewish Christianity*, in of *A History of Early Christian Doctrine*, vol. 1, trans. John A. Baker (London: Darton, Longman and Todd, 1964), 34n. Cf. also R. M. Grant, *Gnosticism and Early Christianity* (New York: Harper & Row, 1966).

14. Perkins, *Gnosticism and the New Testament*, 81. She also notes how contemporary scholars are able to connect early Gnostic thinking with Jewish apocalypticism, a point also hammered by Rudolph. Others also believe Gnosticism was not a product of second century BCE Hellenism, as some have proposed but rather stems from Jewish Apocalypticism. Perkins presents a strong case: "The search for the origins of Gnostic mythology leads to Jewish sources that were taking shape in Palestine as well as Alexandria at the turn of the millennium." Perkins, 20. For a comprehensive study of the connection between Gnostic mythology and Jewish tradition, see Birger Pearson's study "Jewish sources in Gnostic literature," in *Jewish Writings of the Second Temple Period*, ed. Michael Edward Stone; vol. 2, print 2 (Philadelphia: Fortress, 1984).

15. Ehrman, *New Testament*, 117.

16. Ibid.

17. Paul J. Achtemeier, et al., eds. *The HarperCollins Bible Dictionary* (San Francisco: Harper-Collins, 1996), 930.

18. Perkins, *Gnosticism and the New Testament*, 24.

19. *HarperCollins Bible Dictionary*, 896.

20. For an in-depth study of Jesus as an apocalyptic figure, see Bart Ehrman's *Jesus: Apocalyptic Prophet of the New Millennium* (New York: Oxford University Press), 1999.

21. *The HarperCollins Bible Dictionary*, 223.

22. Ehrman, *New Testament*, 244 ff.

23. No other book in the Old Testament mentions a belief in resurrection and deals with the last day or eschaton.

24. Rudolph, 278.

25. Ehrman *New Testament*, 190. Harold Bloom reminds us that it was during this time, and in these writings, that angels and the concept of Satan entered Hebrew writings. He also notes that there are no fallen angels in the Hebrew Bible and that they are not a product of Judaic thinking. Satan in Job is an adversary and Lucifer in Isaiah (14:12–15) is clearly the King of Babylon. The closest the Hebrew Bible comes to a "bad" angel is in Daniel 10:13–21 and 12:1, where archangels Gabriel and Michael are opposed by angels of Persia and Greece. According to Bloom, all of this can be traced back to Babylonian and Sumerian mythology and the Gilgamesh Epic. What happens to Satan afterward, Bloom states, "is a leap from these to the New Testament, where Satan is truly an original invention." *Omens of Millennium*, 65.

26. 284.

27. Ibid., 285.

28. This world was a shadow of Plato's "real" world where all earthly and material things are found in perfect "Form" or "Idea." In this intelligible real world there is no corruption or change. This world also exists simultaneously with the ordinary world of perception, a world that is a shadow of the other, real world. According to the third-century neo-Platonist, Plotinus, Plato's intelligible world of ideas could be apprehended only by the *nous*, the higher intellect or reason, a perfect vehicle for the Gnostics and one that they used prolifically. It has even been noted by one scholar that "Plotinus castigated certain gnostics in Alexandria and Rome precisely for not employing this faculty" (Churton, 103)

29. Of less importance was Pythagorean symbolism, which was adopted by various Gnostic systems (Cf. Metzger, *New Testament*). Gnostics may have been influenced by Yogic and Yogic disciplines, which were around as early as Pythagoras and part of Neo-Platonic mysticism (Cf. Hall, 130). Secret discipline was important to Gnosticism. "The Gnostics believed that salvation must be earned." Hall, 130.

30. Alexandria was also the headquarters of Philo, the most vocal and able spokesperson of Jewish mysticism. It was while visiting in Alexandria that Vespasian had the imperial purple conferred upon him. During that time he met and became an admirer of Apollonius of Tyana, a foremost Pythagorean, and ordered Gnostic emblems on Alexandrian coins (cf. Hall).

31. The names of some may be familiar: Demeter, Persephone, Eleusis, Mithra, Isis, Dionysus, and Cybele, or Magna Mater as it was often called. Almost all were introduced into the Greco-Roman world from The East and had initiation rites with vows of secrecy comparable to Masonic rites and vows of our own time. In Orphism, an ancient Greek theosophic school connected with the cult of Dionysus, only the initiated who led a righteous life and observed a diet free from meat (vegetarianism) could find salvation. The un-pious are condemned to eternal hell and damnation. A similar phenomenon would surface later in the Middle Ages with the Cathars of Southern France and be viciously prosecuted by the State and Church. For more information on the mystery religions of the Greco-Roman world, please see the following: Harold R.Willoughby, *Pagan Regeneration: A Study of Mystery Institutions in the Graeco-Roman World* (Chicago: University of Chicago Press, 1929); Joscelyn Godwin, *Mystery Religions in the Ancient World* (San Francisco: Harper & Row, 1981); Robert Turcan, *Cults of the Roman Empire* (Oxford: Blackwells, 1996).

32. A central idea of Gnosticism was the ascent of the soul through consecutive stages of life form. Hall opines that "this doctrine probably originated in the astrolatry of Babylon with its doctrine of a series of heavens, each under the sovereignty of a planetary god. The soul must ascend through these heavens and their gates by means of magical passwords delivered to the guardians of the doors" (Hall, 31–32). The ladder concept, by which souls ascend and descend, is well known in eastern mythological lore. The symbolism is

reflected in Jacob's ladder (Genesis 28:10–15) and in the royal arches of Enoch and the seven heavens of St. John of Revelation. The ladder motif also served as a symbol of hope for both Gnostics and Christians. "The ladder in Egypt was tipped so that the top of it pointed toward the constellation of the seven stars. The Great Bear was the symbol of initiation into the mysteries and of the heavenly ascent of the soul. This was the ladder in the vision of Jacob in which the angels ascended and descended" (ibid., 139).

33. Perkins, *Gnosticism and the New Testament*, 40
34. Ehrman *New Testament*, 187ff.
35. Chadwick, 33ff.
36. 282–83. 11.
37. Cf. Eric Robertson Dodds, *The Greeks and the Irrational* (Los Angeles: University of California Press, 1951); and Gilles Quispel, *Gnostic Studies*, 2 vols. (Istanbul, 1974); also *The Rediscovery of Gnosticism: Proceedings of the International Conference on Gnosticism*, "Gnosis and Psychology," ed. Benton Layton (Numen Book Series, 1997).
38. Edward Conze, "Buddhism and Gnosis," in *Le Origini dello Gnosticismo: Colloquio di Messina 13-18, April 1966* (Leiden, 1967).
39. Michael Runciman, *The Medieval Manichee* (Cambridge: Cambridge University Press, 1984), 172. Bardesanes, a Christian teacher of the second century and the last of the great Gnostics (though he would probably disagree he was Gnostic), may have been influenced by Buddhist metaphysics. The soul's ascension of consciousness into the ultimate state of nonconsciousness or nonbeing, a goal of Gnosticism, is reminiscent of the state of Nirvana in Buddhism
40. 15.
41. *The Gnostic Religion* (Boston: Beacon, 1963), 25.
42. Chadwick, 35. Cf. Also Metzger, *The New Testament*, 78.
43. 36.
44. The development of Christianity into something resembling organized religion did not occur until it became evident to the early believers that the eschaton, the last day, was much further away than predicted and adjustments had to be made to accommodate the delay of the *Parousia*.
45. Perkins, *Gnosticism and the New Testament*, 3.

CHAPTER 4

1. Gnosis is a modern term, invented by modern scholars. For almost a century, Christianity also had no name and was viewed as an apocalyptic reform movement within the Jewish religion.
2. Cf. also Walter Bauer, *Orthodoxy and Heresy in Earliest Christianity*, trans. Robert Kraft, et al, ed. Robert Kraft (Philadelphia: Fortress, 1971).
3. Kurt Rudolpf, *Gnosis: The Nature & History of Gnosticism*, trans. Robert Wilson (San Francisco: HarperSanFrancisco, 1987), 300; cf. also Acts 20:29ff.
4. Arthur Darby Nock, posthumously published article, quoted by Lee in *Against the Protestant Gnostics*, 4.
5. Nock, in *Against the Protestant Gnostics*, 4. It was difficult for early Christians to know a Gnostic when they saw one. In Rome Justin Martyr worshiped with Gnostic Valentinus who could recite the same confession, which included "resurrection of the flesh." For Valentinus, people in the flesh represented entrapped divine sparks who can ascend to the *Pleroma* through gnosis. Walter Bauer points out that St. Ambrose and Augustine had both, at one time, been members of heretical sects; Ambrose with the Marcionites and Augustine, the Manichees. Cf. *Orthodoxy and Heresy in Earliest Christianity*. Also, see Runciman, *The Medieval Manichee*.

6. Manley P. Hall, *The Wisdom of the Knowing Ones* (Los Angeles: The Philosophical Research Society, 2000), 54. This process spawned several schools, including Marcionites, Sethians, Valentinians, and Thomas Christians. All became influential and drew the fire of those Christians who would later be called heresiologists. Brief bios of some of these are in Appendix D.

7. Pheme Perkins, *Gnosticism and the New Testament* (Minneapolis: Fortress, 1993).

8. Christians were not guiltless of this tactic and used additional means (baptism, creeds, etc.) of separating true from untrue believers.

9. "Jewish Scriptures" and "Hebrew Bible" refer to what would later be called "The Old Testament." The term "Old Testament" would not be used until the end of the second century AD. Some scholars believe the Old Testament canon was decided upon at the Council of Jamnia, sometime around 90 CE. Others argue that it was later. Cf. Arthur G. Patzia, *The Making of the New Testament* (Downers Grove, IL: InterVarsity), 1995.

10. *Apocrypha* is a term applied to books that were "hidden," from which we get our word "cryptic." *HarperCollins Bible Dictionary*, 39–40.

11. Bart D. Ehrman, *Lost Christianities: The Battle for Scripture and the Faiths We Never Knew* (New York: Oxford University Press, 2003), 10.

12. Ehrman, *Lost Christianities*, 10.

13. The word *synoptic* meant, literally, "seen together." Because they had so much in common, these three gospels could be either placed side by side or viewed together. Cf. Ehrman, *The New Testament*, 84.

14. Patzia, Arthur G. *The Making of the New Testament* (Downers Grove, IL: InterVarsity, 1995).

15. Downers Grove, IL: InterVarsity, 2004.

16. Patzia, *The Making of the New Testament*.

17. Richards, *Paul and First Century Letter Writing*.

18. Ehrman, *Lost Christianities*, cf. 154–55.

19. With this abundance of literature one would deem a high literacy rate for that world in those times. Yet, the literacy rate was quite low, about 10 percent. More often than not, letters were read to congregations. Cf. Ehrman, *The New Testament*; and E. Randolph Richards and Patzia.

20. For a more expansive list, see Ehrman's *Lost Christianities*, xi–xv.

21. Ehrman, *Lost Christianities*.

22. Ibid.

23. Ibid.

24. Ibid.

25. "Although Gnostic speculation may not have caused any particular writing in the NT, Gnostic mythologizing does form part of the horizon within which the NT should be interpreted." Perkins, *Gnosticism and the New Testament*, 4.

26. Metzger, *The New Testament*, 311.

27. For further reading: *The New Testament in the Apostolic Fathers*, Oxford Society of Historical Theology (Oxford: Clarendon, 1905).

28. For a more thorough examination of the Synoptic Gospels please see the following: Rudolph Bultmann, *The History of the Synoptic Tradition* (Oxford: Blackwell, 1963); Arthur G. Patzia, *The Making of the New Testament*; Bruce Metzger, *The Early Versions of the New Testament* (Oxford: Clarendon, 1981); Bernard Orchard and Harold Riley, *The Order of the Synoptics: Why Three Synoptic Gospels?* (Macon, GA: Mercer University Press, 1987); William Farmer, *The Synoptic Problem: A Critical Analysis* (New York: McMillian, 1964); Keith Nickle, *The Synoptic Gospels: Conflict and Consensus* (Atlanta: John Knox,

1980); and Robert Stein, *The Synoptic Problem: An Introduction* (Grand Rapids, MI: Baker Book House, 1987).

29. *The Making of the New Testament*, 52.
30. For further inquiry, please see Dale Allison, *The Jesus Tradition in Q* (Harrisburg, PA: Trinity Press International, 1997); J. Kloppenborg, *The Formation of Q: Trajectories in Ancient Wisdom Collections* (Philadelphia: Fortress, 1987); Christopher M. Tuckett, *Q and the History of Early Christianity* (Edinburgh: T & T Clark, 1996).
31. Ehrman, *Lost Christianities*, 57–64.
32. For comparison, cf. *The Gospel of Truth* and the *Trimorphic Protennoia*.
33. Cf. for a discussion on the sources of John see Ehrman, *New Testament*.
34. This gospel, like the Synoptics, was written anonymously. The writer never mentions his name. Ehrman and others are of the opinion the gospel was the product of several writers. Cf. Ehrman, *The New Testament*.
35. This introductory passage is different from the rest of the narrative. Its poetic quality has led some scholars to theorize that it may be a hymn, meditation, or poem. If that is the case, the material about John is creatively spliced into the larger narrative.
36. *The New Testament*.
37. Perkins, *Gnosticism and the New Testament*, 139.
38. Ehrman, *New Testament*.
39. Ibid.
40. According to Perkins, this position can be found in second- and third-century Gnostic writings.
41. Kurt Rudolph, *Gnosis: The Nature & History of Gnosticism*, trans. Robert Wilson (San Francisco: HarperSanFrancisco, 1987), 302.
42. Ibid.
43. Perkins, *Gnosticism and the New Testament*, 80.
44. *The Gnostic Gospels*. It is her opinion that Gnostics of that era also drew the same conclusion. She evokes the name of one important Gnostic, Valentinus, who claimed he learned some of Paul's secret teachings from one Theudas, alleged to have been one of Paul's disciples.

CHAPTER 5

1. Henry Chadwick, *The Early Church*. Rev. ed. (New York: Penguin Books, 1993), 286.
2. Irenaeus. *Against Heresies (or Refutation and Overthrow of False Gnosis or of Knowledge Falsely So-Called)*. I.18.1. I Harvey; 1.27.1-2 A.-N.C.L. In Stevenson's *A New Eusebius* (London: S.P.C.K., 1963).
3. *Against the Heresies*, 1. 21. 5, quoted in Bart Ehrman, *The New Testament* (New York: Oxford University Press, 2004), 188.
4. *Against the Heresies*, quoted in Ehrman, *The New Testament*, 3. 16.8.
5. Interestingly, Gnostics considered Christians as difficult to know. Celsus complained of their slippery interpretations in their use of allegory and their manipulation of texts. From day to day their beliefs changed.
6. Ehrman, *The New Testament*, 317.
7. Gnosticism was more philosophy than religion, another major reason it attracted the fury of the Church fathers: "It sought to interpret Christian mysticism in terms of the metaphysical systems of the Greeks, Egyptians and Chaldeans." Hall, 30.
8. Elaine Pagels, *The Gnostic Gospels* (New York: Random House, 1976), 30.
9. "Tertullian declares that anyone who denies the resurrection of the flesh is a heretic, not a Christian." Pagels, *Gnostic Gospels*, 5.

10. Ibid., 7.
11. Ibid., 30.
12. Pagels notes that German scholar and theologian Hans van Campenhausen presents a compelling theory that Peter was the first, primarily because he was the first leader of the Christian community in Jerusalem. *The Gnostic Gospels*. Harold Bloom in *Omens of Millennium* presents a compelling argument that James the Just, or Jesus's brother, was probably the leader of the early Jerusalem community.
13. Pagels, *Gnostic Gospels*, 45.
14. Chadwick, *The Early Church*.
15. Official lists of popes give the early succession of Peter, Linus, Cletus (or Anacletus), Clement. . . . The dates usually given to his papacy (though that term was not in vogue until centuries later) were 90–100 CE. Cf. P. G. Maxwell-Stewart, *Chronicle of the Popes* (New York: Thames and Hudson, 2006).
16. Jaroslav Pelikan, *The Emergence of the Catholic Tradition (100–600)* (Chicago: University of Chicago Press, 1971).
17. *The Epistle of Clement to the Corinthians*, also referred to as *1 Clement*, can be found in collections of writings of the Apostolic Fathers. Penguin Paperbacks *Early Christian Writings* by Maxwell Staniforth is one source. Excerpts from the work are also available in Henry Bettenson, trans. and ed., *The Early Christian Fathers* (New York: Oxford University Press, 1956).
18. *Trallians* 3.1.
19. Cf. Chadwick, *The Early Church*, chap. 2.
20. Pagels, *Gnostic Gospels*, 126, 128.
21. Ibid., 139.
22. Ibid.
23. Rudolph Bultmann, *Theology of the New Testament*, I, trans. Kendrick Groebel (New York: Scribner's, 1954), 170–71. Walter Schmitals advances the same argument: *Gnosticism in Corinth* (Nashville: Abingdon, 1971); and *Paul and the Gnostics* (Nashville: Abingdon, 1972).
24. Others place it within different time frames. For example, Rudolph places them closer to their composition (49–50). Metzger . . . Rudolph also states, in agreement with Metzger, Trobisch, et al. that both letters are "more precisely a collection of letters," ibid., 301.
25. Kurt Rudolph, among others, advances this theory, and draws support from German theological heavyweights W. Schmithals and G. Theissen.
26. Metzger, *The New Testament*.
27. Ibid., 267.
28. Ibid., 303.
29. Rudolph, *Theology*, 306. Also cf. Metzger, *The New Testament*.
30. Recent scholarship questions Paul's authorship and suggests one of his disciples composed this letter.
31. For brief biographies on each, please see Appendix C.
32. Ehrman, *The New Testament*.
33. *Against Heresies*, 1:29:1.
34. Pelikan, *Emergence of the Catholic Tradition*.
35. 64 [d] k syr Dial Tim and Aqu'. These notations are the manuscript sources Ehrman is referencing.
36. Ehrman, *The Orthodox Corruption of Scripture*, 137.
37. Ibid., 188.
38. *Encountering the Manuscripts* (Nashville: Broadman & Holman Publishers, 2005), 287–88.
39. Ehrman, *Orthodox Corruption of Scripture*.

40. Philip Comfort, *Encountering the Manuscripts: An Introduction to New Testament Paleography & Textual Criticism* (Nashville: Broadman & Holman, 2005), 288.
41. Comfort, *Encountering the Manuscripts.*
42. Origin, *Commentary on Matthew*, 15.14, quoted by Ehrman, *Misquoting Jesus*, 52. The great Latin scholar Jerome would make a similar comment when asked by Pope Damasus to create a Latin bible.
43. Origin, *Against Celsus*, 2.27, quoted in Ehrman, Ibid.
44. *Adv. Haer.* E.11. Cf. also Perkins, 190.
45. Pagels, *The Gnostic Gospels*, 68.
46. Ehrman, *Misquoting Jesus*, 183–86. The verses in question create a seam and do not fit into the flow of the passage. Ehrman further notes that this passage is also found in different contexts in other textual witnesses. Also, previously in the same letter, at 11:2–16, Paul uplifts women and has no problem with their speaking in church.
47. "In Egypt women had attained by the first century A.D., a relatively advanced state of emancipation, socially, politically, and legally." Pagels, *The Gnostic Gospels*, 74. Pagels also cites this passage from the Gospel of Mary: "Under the empire: women were everywhere involved in business, social life, such as theaters, sports events, concerts, parties, traveling—with or without their husbands. They took part in a whole range of athletics, even bore arms, and went to battle." Ibid., 75.
48. *Apocryphon of James*, 1.31–2.9, in *Nag Hammadi Library in English 99*, trans. James M. Robinson. 3rd ed. (New York: Harper and Row, 1988).
49. *Gospel to the Hebrews*, cited in Origen, *COMM. JO* 2.12, taken from Pagels, *The Gnostic Gospels*, 62.
50. *Gospel of Philip*, 71.3–5, in *Nag Hammadi Library*, 143, quoted from Pagels, *The Gnostic Gospels*, 63.
51. Pagels, *The Gnostic Gospels*, 72.
52. *Apostolic Tradition*, 18.3, quoted in Pagels, *The Gnostic Gospels*, 78–79.
53. Ibid., 79.
54. Tertullian, *De Praescr*, 41.
55. *De Baptismo* 1, quoted from Pagels, *The Gnostic Gospels*, 72.
56. *De Virginibus Velandis 9* quoted from Ibid., 72.
57. 1 Clement 1.3 quoted in Ibid., 76.
58. Ibid.
59. Rudolph, *Theology*, 367.
60. Philip J. Lee, *Against the Protestant Gnostics* (New York: Oxford University Press, 1987), 7.
61. A priest called Bogomil (i.e., loved of God) is responsible for the heresy that was well under way by 950 CE. It lasted for several centuries and influenced most of Europe. They were dualists who believed the devil created the world, which meant rejection of the Old Testament. Their renunciation of the world, the reason they denounced the Sacraments and the cross, was complete and thorough. By the twelfth century, their highest level of activity and influence was in Bosnia, Lombardy, and France. Cf. Runciman, *The Medieval Manichee.*
62. Rudolph, *Theology*, 368.
63. *Omens of Millennium*, 229
64. Martin Buber, *The Eclipse of God*, trans. Stanley Goodman (New York: Harper & Brothers, 1952).
65. Lee, *Against the Protestant Gnostics*, 14
66. *The Plague* (New York: Vintage Books, 1972), 287.
67. Pagels, *The Gnostic Gospels*, 56.

CHAPTER 6

1. *Webster's New World Dictionary*, 4th ed., ed. Michael Agnes (New York: Simon & Schuster, 2003), 264.

2. Karen Armstrong, *The Battle for God* (New York: Alfred A. Knopf, 2001), ix.

3. Fisher Humphreys and Philip Wise, *Fundamentalism* (Macon, GA: Smyth & Helwys, 2004). 2.

4. James Innell Packer, *Fundamentalism and the Word of God* (Grand Rapids, MI: Wm. B. Eerdmans Publishing Co., 1977), 19.

5. Packer, *Fundamentalism and the Word*, 264.

6. Martin Marty and Scott Appleby, *The Fundamental Project*, chap. 15 (Chicago: The University of Chicago Press: 1991–95).

7. Ibid., 835. Also quoted in Humphreys and Wise, *Fundamentalism*, 15.

8. "Pseudo-Fundamentalists: The New Breed in Sheep's Clothing," online at http://www.bju.edu/resources/faith/1978/issue1/pseudo.html.

9. Bruce Bawer, *Stealing Jesus: How Fundamentalism Betrays Christianity* (New York: Three Rivers, 1997), 6–7.

10. Generic fundamentalism will be discussed more fully in Chapter 9 on "The Differences between Gnosticism and Fundamentalism."

11. The concept of dispensationalism is associated with John Nelson Darby. Dispensationalism is a form of premillennialism that teaches that biblical history was a number of successive economies or administrations called dispensations, each of which constitutes continuity with the Old Testament covenants God made with his chosen people through Abraham, Moses, and King David. Dispensationalism gained adherents among fundamentalists.

12. Humphreys and Wise, *Fundamentalism*, 18–20.

13. Ibid., 19.

14. Some consider another conference to be the beginning of Fundamentalism: The Niagara Bible Conference of 1883. This was a group of conservatives who met annually at Niagra-on-the-Lake, Ontario, to hear the founding fathers of Fundamentalism, names familiar to most Fundmentalists: W. E. Blackstone, James Brookes, Cyrus Ingerson Scofield, Charles Erdman.

15. Humphreys and Wise, *Fundamentalism*, 24.

16. Curtis Lee Laws, "Convention Side Lights," *The Watchman-Examiner* 8, no. 27 (July 1, 1920): 834.

17. Packer, *Fundamentalism and the Word*, 28–29.

18. Bawer, *Stealing Jesus*, 9.

19. Philip J. Lee, *Against the Protestant Gnostics* (New York: Oxford University Press, 1987), 103.

20. Lee, *Against the Protestant Gnostics*, 78. Cf. also chapters 3–5, where Lee tracks the Gnostic influence from colonial days to the present.

21. Ibid., 104

22. Robert Middlekauff, *The Glorious Cause* (New York: Oxford University Press, 1982), 102.

23. Middlekauff, *The Glorious Cause*.

24. Edwin S. Faustad, *The Great Awakening in New England* (New York: Harper, 1957). Schools among those founded by Great Awakening revivalists include Brown (Baptist), Harvard, Yale and Dartmouth (Congregational), and Princeton (Presbyterian).

25. Greven, *The Protestant Temperament*, 67–68.

26. Lee, *Against the Protestant Gnostics*, 87.

27. Ibid.

28. Ibid.

29. Ibid., 87.
30. Cf. also Gilles Quispel, *Gnostic Studies* (Istanbul: Nederlands-Historisch-Archaeologisch Instituut in het Nabije Oosten, 1974). The alternative school of thought states that Basilides, Valentinus, and Marcion found St. Paul's doctrine of election much to their liking and extrapolated it for their own theological purpose.
31. "Delimitation of the Gnostic Phemnomenon—Typological and Historical," in *Le origini dello gnosticismo*, ed. Ugo Bianchi, Proceedings of the Colloquio di Messina, April 1966 (Leiden: E. J. Brill, 19670, 98–99. Quoted in Lee, *Against the Protestant Gnostics*, 104; emphasis added.
32. Lee, *Against the Protestant Gnostics*, 102.
33. Ibid. "It is clear that an economic scheme based on individualistic achievement benefits from a religion based on the divine calling of the individual," 104.
34. Middlekauff, *The Glorious Cause*, 48.
35. "It should be noted that religious revivals are not confined merely to the years designated *the revival phase*. Revivals have been more or less continuous since the eighteenth century, although some periods have a higher incidence of conversions than others." Robert William Fogel, *The Fourth Great Awakening: The Future of Egalitarianism* (Chicago: University of Chicago Press, 2000), 18.
36. *The American Religion*, 47.
37. Ibid. The word *enthusiasm* stems from a Greek word, *entheos*, which means possessed by a god. Originally associated with supernatural inspiration and prophetic ecstasy, it morphed into meaning eager interest, zeal, and fervor. The first example of this theological orientation in the early days of Christianity was probably Montanism, a form of revivalism that lasted several centuries. Montanists, whom the noted Church father and heresiologist Tertullian joined, distrusted the intellect and relied solely on inspiration. A Syrian sect of the fourth century was known as The Enthusiasts. Their beliefs were basically Gnostic: prayer, ascetic practices (the world is evil), contemplation, and inspiration by the Holy Spirit a ruling evil spirit. Some Protestant sects of the sixteenth and seventeenth centuries were called enthusiasts. In the eighteenth century, John Wesley and George Whitefield were accused of blind enthusiasm or fanaticism.
38. Ian Frederick Finseth, "Liquid Fire Within Me": Language, Self and Society in Transcendentalism and Early Evangelicalism, 1820–1860. MA Thesis in English, University of Virginia, 1995.
39. For additional information on the Cane Ridge Revival, see the following: *Voices from Cane Ridge*, ed. Rhodes Thompson (St. Louis: Bethany, 1954); Hank Honegraaff, *Counterfeit Revival* (Nashville: Word Publishing, 2001); John B. Boles, *The Great Revival: Beginnings of the Bible Belt* (Lexington, KY: University Press of Kentucky, 1960; Paul K. Conkin, *Cane Ridge: America's Pentecost* (Madison, WI: University of Wisconsin Press, 1990).
40. *American Religion*, 208.
41. Ibid., 206.
42. Ibid., 252.
43. Humphreys and Wise, *Fundamentalism*.
44. Ibid., 30.
45. *The American Religion*, 302.

CHAPTER 7

1. R. A. Torrey, ed. *Fundamentals, The* (Grand Rapids, MI: Baker Books, 2003).
2. Humphreys and Wise, *Fundamentalism* (Macon, GA: Smyth & Helwys, 2004), 37.
3. Humphreys and Wise, *Fundamentalism*, 42.
4. Ibid., 43

5. For a comprehensive review, see Ernst R. Sandeen, *The Roots of Fundamentalism: British and American Millenarianism 1800–1930* (Chicago: The University of Chicago Press, 1970), xiv–xv, 251–53; and George Marsden, *The Shaping of Twentieth-century Evangelicanism, 1870–1925* (Oxford: Oxford University Press, 1980), 262n30.

6. For a full discussion of these, see Chapter 10, "The Case against Inerrancy."

7. J. I. Packer, *"Fundamentalism" and the Word of God* (Grand Rapids, MI: Wm. B. Eerdmans, 1977), 21.

8. Packer, *"Fundamentalism" and the Word of God*, 47.

9. *Webster's New World Dictionary*, ed. Michael Agnes, 4th ed. (New York: Simon & Schuster, 2003), 855.

10. Packer, *"Fundamentalism" and the Word of God*, 91

11. Ibid., 77. For a thorough presentation of this viewpoint, see Benjamin Breckinridge Warfield, *The Inspiration and Authority of the Bible*, ed. Samuel Craig (Philadelphia: Presbyterian and Reformed, 1964).

12. Packer, *"Fundamentalism" and the Word of God*, 79.

13. Ibid., 90.

14. Ibid., 96

15. Fisher Humphreys, "The Baptist Faith and Message and the Church Statement on Biblical Inerrancy," in *Proceedings of the Conference on Biblical Inerrancy1987* (Nashville: Broadman, 1987), 329.

16. The Roman Catholic Church continues to refer to Mary as "The Mother of God," the title approved at the Council of Ephesus in 431 CE. In the Ave Maria, the Virgin is addressed not only as "Holy Mary" but also as "Mother of God." She is, therefore, referred to as both "mother of Christ" and "mother of God." In 1854 Pope Pius IX declared the concept a dogma of the Church that Mary "at the first instant of her conception was preserved immaculate from all stain of original sin, by the singular grace and privilege granted her by Almighty God, through the merits of Jesus Christ, savior of mankind." Cf. *In Ineffabilis*, in Henry Denzinger, *The Source of Catholic Dogma* (St. Louis: B. Herder Book Company, 1957), 1950. For further research on the development of this dogma, see Edward Dennis O'Connor et al., *The Dogma of the Immaculate Conception* (Notre Dame, IN: University of Notre Dame Press, 1958).

17. Yom Kippur, the tenth day of the Hebrew month *Tishrei*, is a ritual derived from the sixteenth chapter of Leviticus. It is a solemn fast of twenty-five hours marked by intense prayer.

18. Two more, lesser known, are the Acceptance Theory (introduced by John Scotus, circa 1300 CE), in which atonement is solely by the arbitrary choice of God, and the Moral or nonviolent theory propounded by Liberal Christians and currently being developed.

19. Humphreys and Wise, *Fundamentalism*.

20. Ibid., 52.

21. Bruce Bawer, *Stealing Jesus: How Fundamentalism Betrays Christianity* (New York: Three Rivers, 1970), 7.

22. William Loader, *Jesus and the Fundamentalism of His Day* (Grand Rapids, MI: Wm. B. Eerdmans, 2001).

23. Loader, *Jesus and the Fundamentalism*, 8.

24. Ibid.

25. One need only to search online for "Primitive Christian Churches" to obtain a lengthy catalogue of the variations along this religious theme. Wikipedia.com has a "List of Christian Churches" along with a flow chart tracking the development and evolution of the major branches of Christianity from the early Church until the present.

CHAPTER 8

1. Tobias Churton, *The Gnostics* (New York: Barnes & Noble Books, 1987), 36–38.
2. Churton, *The Gnostics*, 38.
3. Elaine Pagels, *The Gnostic Gospels* (New York: Random House, 1976), xxiii.
4. Ehrman, *Lost Christianities* (New York: Oxford University Press, 2003), 1.
5. Quoted from Jay Tolson, "U.S. News & World Report," December 18, 2006, vol. 141. no. 23.78.
6. Harold Bloom, *The American Religion* (New York: Chu Hartley Publishers, 1992), 4.
7. *American Religion*, 219. Bloom goes on to say that Mormons and Southern Baptists are competing Gnosticisms.
8. Philip J. Lee, *Against the Protestant Agnostics* (New York: Oxford University Press, 1987), 84.
9. Lee, *Against the Protestant Agnostics*.
10. Lee, *Against the Protestant Agnostics*, 239.
11. The term "dualism" did not appear in religious language until 1700 when Thomas Hyde introduced it in his attempt to describe Manichaeism and other religious systems that postulate God and the devil, or Satan, as two separate, coeternal entities. The term was later introduced into philosophical discourse to describe Descartes' distinction between mind and matter as separate substances. Yuri Stoyanov, *The Other God* (New Haven: Yale University Press, 2000). Harold Bloom also points out that Gnosticism "as a term did not exist before the seventeenth century." *Omens of Millennium* (New York: Riverhead Books, 1980), 185.
12. Pheme Perkins, *Gnosticism and the New Testament* (Minneapolis, MI: Fortress, 1993), 80.
13. For a thorough presentation of the early church councils see Leo Davis, *The First Seven Ecumenical Councils, 325-787* (Collegeville, MN: The Liturgical, 1983).
14. Conjured up are images of Gnostic ascetics, where flesh is vilified and sex denigrated, often to the point of rejecting marriage. Perkins describes Gnosticism as having "a radical asceticism that opposed sexuality, procreation and any other ties that might bind an individual to the dominant social powers. . . . Paul's own example may have been responsible for those who insisted that Christian couples should renounce sexual intercourse," 9, 146–47. She goes on to point out that "Paul's account of the struggle between good that one knows and the 'other law' of sin found in one's members (Rom. 7:14–25) is closely related to the 'two spirits' tradition found in *Apocryphon of John*." Davis, *The First Seven Ecumenical Councils*.
15. *Webster's New World Dictionary*, ed. Michael Agnes, 4th ed. (New York: Simon & Schuster, 2003), 447.
16. *Webster's*.
17. Ibid.
18. Bloom points out that "American Baptists descend from two rival sects of Inner Light English Puritans of the early seventeenth century: General Baptists, who believed that everyone in general could be redeemed and Particular Baptists, who held onto the Calvinist convictions that only those elected in particular would be saved." Bloom, *American Religion*, 208. In 1801 at Cane Ridge two groups merged and compromised, but the distinction between General and Particular redemption was blurred and the Particular form is still prevalent among some Baptist circles.
19. The most radical form of this predestinarian view of humanity, which has its origins in second-century Sethian Gnosticism, is the "Two-Seed-In-The-Spirit" ideology. From the beginning God implanted a good seed in Eve and a bad seed in Satan. (Ancient Gnostics

believed Seth was the offspring of the good seed and Cain of the bad seed.) All humanity proceeded from one or the other, therefore, those descendants from Seth (the "good" seed) are elect and descendants of Cain are damned.

20. Perkins, *Gnosticism and the New Testament*, 32–33. This is also true of the far right in the political process . . . the more spiritually endowed, the closer to the truth, the more believable, the more God-chosen.

21. Bloom, *American Religion*, 211. In 1908 Southern Baptist leader Edgar Young Mullins proposed *The Axioms of Religion*. Among these tenets was "soul competency" stating religion was a personal matter between God and individual. The individual soul is competent to deal with God without third parties, that is, the organized church. An unmediated fellowship exits between God and the believer and God. The faith relationship is one-on-one with the Almighty. Soul competency sounds very similar to the Southern Baptists reliance on an inner light and the Gnostic "inner light." Lee makes the following supportive comment: "Salvation, for present-day Gnostics as for ancient Gnostics, can be found only through discovering the spark within" (197). The end result of this approach is the reduction of corporate worship to a private psychological event. In the words of the old hymn, Fundamentalists and Gnostic Christians do indeed "come to the garden alone."

22. *American Religion*, 238.

23. Lee, *Against the Protestant Agnostics*, 10.

24. Manly P. Hall, *The Wisdom of the Knowing Ones* (Los Angeles: The Philosophical Research Society, 200), 19.

25. Some popular hymns that carry this theme are "I Know The Lord," "I Know Whom I Have Believed," "Sweet, Sweet Spirit," and "Come My Way, My Truth, My Life."

26. Hall, *The Wisdom*, 130.

27. John Atack, *A Piece of Blue Sky: Scientology, Dianetics and Ron Hubbard Exposed* (New York: Carol, 1990).

28. The word Christ (Greek *Christos*) stems from the Hebrew for Messiah, or *mashiah*. Both mean "anointed one." Cf. *HarperCollins Bible Dictionary*, 677.

29. For a fuller discussion of these two very different portrayals of Jesus in Mark and Luke see Bart Ehrman, *The New Testament* and *Misquoting Jesus*.

30. *The American Religion*, 222.

31. Elaine Pagels, *The Gnostic Gospels* (New York: Vintage, 1981), 23.

32. Irenaeus, *Against Heresies*, 1.13.3–4.

33. George Fox, founder of the Quakers told of his encounter with the "inner light." He would go on to condemn Puritan authority.

34. In the understanding of a clear distinction between body and spirit, and ascendancy of the spirit from the body, shades of Platonism surface. In Platonic theory the physical body imprisoned the spiritual soul, which, at death escaped its material bondage. It has been pointed out how both early Gnostic and Christian thought borrowed from Platonism.

35. *Webster's*, 972.

36. Ibid., emphasis added.

37. "In the widest sense, mysticism is every guidance to the immediate awareness of that which is not reached by either perception or conception, or generally by any knowledge. The mystic is opposed to the philosopher by the fact that he begins from within, whereas the philosopher begins from without. The mystic starts from his inner, positive, individual experience, in which he finds himself as the eternal and only being, and so on. But nothing of this is communicable except the assertions that we have to accept on his word; consequently he is unable to convince." *Schopenhauer, The World as Will and Representation*, vol. 2, chap. 48.

38. Orhan Pamuk, *Istanbul* (New York: First Vintage International, 2006), 91. These words were recently encountered while reading this work by the famed Nobel author. His comment was made in reference to the *hüzün* (melancholy) of Istanbul, how its mood "evokes a way of looking at life that implicates us all, not only a spiritual state, but a state of mind that is ultimately as life-affirming as it is negating." Ibid. And it is very attractive, almost seductive. His careful words seemed to fall right into place with the mystic experience.

39. There are some who differ with this assessment, notably M. Scott Peck who, in his book, *The Different Drum* (New York: Touchstone, 1998), asserts that mysticism is the equivalent of nonduality while human life exists in duality.

40. Perkins, *Gnosticism and the New Testament*, 142

41. Quoted in Bloom, *Omens of Millennium*, 17.

42. (Harper Collins: San Francisco, 2005), 217.

43. Hall, *The Wisdom*.

44. Bloom, *American Religion*, 225.

45. For a thorough review of the word "orthodoxy" and Orthodox Christianity, see G. K. Chesterton, *Orthodoxy* (San Francisco: Ignatius, 1995).

46. Pagels, *The Gnostic Gospels*, 31.

47. The word "mystic" derives from the Greek *mustikos*, which means "initiate" and is associated with esoteric cults.

48. Bloom, *American Religion*, 244.

49. An anecdote told by United Methodist Bishop Earl Gladstone Hunt, Jr., has relevance. While traveling with a colleague to hear him preach, the colleague remarked about his sermon preparation, how it were as though a funnel was inserted in his brain and the Holy Spirit was pouring all he would need. Following the sermon the colleague asked the bishop if he liked his sermon. Bishop Hunt responded: "Well, it was okay, but I had the impression the funnel was pointing in the other direction."

50. *Webster's New World Dictionary*, 377.

51. Ehrman, *The Orthodox Corruption of Scripture and Misquoting Jesus*.

52. Jaroslav Pelikan, *The Riddle of Roman Catholicism* (New York: Abingdon, 1959), 82–83.

53. Pelikan, *The Riddle*, 82.

54. Bruce Bauer, *Stealing Jesus: How Fundamentalism Betrays Christianity* (New York: Three Rivers, 1997), 5.

55. Perkins, *Gnosticism and the New Testament*, 149.

56. Ibid., 19.

57. Lee, *Against the Protestant Agnostics*, 163. Cotton Mather took offense that Christ could die for *all* people. Jonathan Edwards sounded a similar theme: "Only visible saints can be accepted as member of visible churches."

58. Tolson, "U.S. News & World Report," 78.

59. Hall, *The Wisdom*, 52.

60. Patrick Henry honed his oratory skills listening to revivalist preachers, memorizing their sermons and practicing in his family's buckboard wagon on return trips home from camp meetings. Cf. Henry Mayer, *A Son of Thunder* (New York; Grove, 1991).

61. Pagels, *The Gnostic Gospels*, 50.

62. Lee, *Against the Protestant Agnostics*, 183.

63. Hall, *The Wisdom* 131.

64. Lee, *Against the Protestant Agnostics*, 122.

65. Millerites were disciples of William Miller, a New York farmer who proclaimed that Jesus's return, according to the Bible, would occur in April of 1843 and the elect, or worthy, would all ascend to heaven on October 23, 1844. Through mostly tent revivals, an estimated one million people became followers. Many sold all their worldly possessions and

climbed high mountains to be closer to heaven on the day of expectation. The Great Millerite Disappointment, as it has become known, led to spin-off religions, such as the Seventh-day Adventists and Jehovah Witness. Cf. George R. Knight, *Millennial Fever and the End of the World* (Boise, ID: Pacific, 1993).

66. Bloom, *American Religion*, 169.

67. John Nelson Darby was an Anglo-Irish evangelist who is considered by many to be the founder of modern-day dispensationalism.

68. Bloom, *Omens Millennium*, 30. It is equally ironic that for centuries, Persia (Iran) and Israel were friends and supportive of each other. There is no harsh word in the Old Testament toward the Persians, who treated them kindly.

69. Henry Chadwick, *The Early Church* (London: Penguin Books, 1993), 36.

70. Philip Greven, *The Protestant Temperaiment: Patterns of Child-Rearing, Religious Experience and the Self in Early America* (New York: Knopf, 1977), 66.

71. Recently, the senior Muslim cleric in Australia publicly blamed immodestly dressed women who do not wear their headdress for being raped and likened them to meat that attracts wild animals. *The Australian*, October 26, 2006.

72. Pagels, *The Gnostic Gospels*, 31.

73. Lee, *Against the Protestant Agnostics*, 18.

74. Perkins, *Gnosticism and the New Testament*, 139.

75. Ibid.

76. Ibid., 142

77. Ibid.

78. Ibid., 162–63.

79. Kurt Rudolph, *Gnosis: The Nature & History of Gnosticism*, trans. Robert Wilson (San Francisco: HarperSanFrancisco, 1987).

80. Lee, *Against the Protestant Agnostics*, 21.

81. Ibid., 205.

82. Ibid., 116.

83. A. D. Nock, *Early Gentile Christianity and Its Hellenistic Background* (New York: Harper & Row, 1964), 16.

CHAPTER 9

1. Henry Chadwick, *The Early Church* (London: Penguin Books, 1993), 55–56. More recently some Fundamentalists in a number of states, principally Montana, have become proactive in supporting the Green Party based on biblical reasons. They take Genesis literally, that is, we are custodians and stewards of the earth. There may be others of which I am not aware as this book goes to print. But there does appear to be some movement in that area of concern.

2. Chadwick, *The Early Church*, 56.

3. Tobias Churton, *The Gnostics* (New York: Barnes & Noble Books, 1987), 61.

4. Bart Ehrman, *The New Testament* (New York: Oxford University Press), 129.

5. Ehrman. *The New Testament*.

6. Harold Bloom, *American Religion* (New York: Chu Hartley, 1992), 470.

7. *American Religion*, 52.

8. Based upon this understanding, it would seem those finding meaning in these liturgical expressions would gravitate more to the Gospel of Mark, where an anguished and distressed Christ is more clearly portrayed as the suffering Son of God. The scripture in Luke regarding his sweating blood has been demonstrated to be an interpolation.

9. Elaine Pagels, *The Gnostic Gospels* (New York: Vintage Books, 1981), xx.

10. Act I, Scene 3. The reference to the devil is intended only symbolically as a part of the quote and not intentionally associated with Fundamentalists.
11. Tertullian, *De Carne Christi*, letters for his canon best support his theological positions.
12. Luke's social message aside, Marcion's choice of that Gospel and Paul's letters for his canon best support his theological positions.
13. Ehrman, *The New Testament*, 400.
14. Ibid.
15. Ibid., 401. Cf. also Karen Jo Torjesen, *When Women Were Priests: Women's Leadership in the Early Church and the Scandal of Their Subordination in the Rise of Christianity* (San Francisco: HarperCollins, 1993).
16. Most scholars agree these two epistles, along with others (Ephesians, Colossans, and probably 2 Thessalonians) were probably not composed by Paul.
17. "Gnostic mythology takes shape in a cognitive environment accustomed to philosophical discourse about origins. Consequently, it has an abstract character that differentiates it from more primitive mythologies." Pheme Perkins, *Gnosticism and the New Testament* (Minneapolis, MN, 1993), 12.
18. Max Weber, *The Sociology of Religion* (London: Methuen, 1965), 131.
19. Perkins, *Gnosticism and the New Testament*, 177.
20. Manly P. Hall, *The Wisdom of the Knowing Ones* (Los Angeles: The Philosophical Research Society, 2000), 53.
21. "It is known that Gnosticism affirmed the Oriental belief in reincarnation, and probably found some support among the followers of the old Platonic and Pythagorean systems. Unfortunately, however, Gnosticism was bitterly assailed by Neo-Platonism, probably because of its emphasis upon transcendentalism and esoteric practices." Hall, 78.

CHAPTER 10

1. O. C. Edwards, *How Holy Writ Was Written* (Nashville: Abingdon, 1989), 13.
2. Arthur G. Patzia, *The Making of the New Testament* (Downers Grove, IL: InterVarsity Press, 1995), 136.
3. Bart Ehrman, *Misquoting Jesus* (San Francisco: HarperSanFrancisco, 2005), 210–11.
4. Patzia, *The Making of the New Testament*, 136.
5. Ibid.
6. For an in-depth study of ancient writing, see Patzia, *The Making of the New Testament*; Frederick G. Kenyon, *Books and Readers in Ancient Greece and Rome*, 2 ed. (Oxford: Clarendon, 1952); Philip Comfort, *Early Manuscripts and Modern Translations of the New Testament* (Wheaton: Tyndale, 1990); Stanley Stowers, *Letter Writing in Graeco-Roman Antiquity* (Philadelphia: Westminster, 1986); Isaac Taylor, *History of the Transmission of Ancient Books to Modern Times* (London: Jackson and Walford, 1859); Eric G. Turner, *Greek Manuscripts of the Ancient World*, 2nd ed. (Oxford: Oxford University Press, 1987); and Solomon A. Nigosian, *From Ancient Writings to Sacred Texts: The Old Testament and Apocrapha* (Baltimore: Johns Hopkins University Press, 2004).
7. Ehrman, *Misquoting Jesus*.
8. Ibid., 45.
9. Ibid.
10. William Loader, *Jesus and the Fundamentalism of His Day* (Grand Rapids, MI: William B. Eerdmans Publishing Company, 2001), 138.
11. Bart Ehrman, *New Testament* (New York: Oxford University Press, 2004), 180.
12. For an detailed history of the texts of the New Testament, see Bart Ehrman, *Misquoting Jesus*, chap. 3; and Bruce Metzger and Bart Ehrman, *The Text of the New Testament: Its*

Transmission, Corruption and Restitution, 4th ed. (New York: Oxford University Press, 2005).

13. This was the Vulgate translation originally commissioned near the end of the fourth century by Pope Damasus and produced by the great Latin scholar of that time, Jerome. Cf. Chadwick, *The Early Church.*

14. Ibid.

15. Ehrman, *Misquoting Jesus*, 79.

16. F. H. A. Scrivner, *A Plain Introduction to the Criticism of the New Testament*, 4th ed., ii (London, 1894), 185. Quoted from Bruce Metzger, *The Text of the New Testament* (New York: Oxford University Press, 1992), 99.

17. Metzger, *The Text of the New Testament.*

18. Ibid. For a comprehensive review of the *Textus Receptus*, see Metzger, *The Text of the New Testament*, chap. 3.

19. Ehrman, *Misquoting Jesus.*

20. Quoted from Ehrman, *Misquoting Jesus*, 81.

21. Ibid., 82.

22. Metzger, *The Text of the New Testament.*

23. Quoted in Patzia, *The Making of the New Testament*, 141.

24. Latin was the language spoken in the Western part of the empire and Greek in the eastern. But the New Testament was available in non-Greek and non-Latin speaking regions so Christians in those indigenous tongues could have access. For example, Syriac was spoken in Syria and Coptic in Egypt. Probably in the mid- to late second-century texts were translated in these languages, then in turn translated by other scribes and copyists. Ehrman, *Misquoting Jesus.* For a list of current available texts (witnesses) in these various languages, see Metzger, *The Text of the New Testament*, chap. 2. A more comprehensive list of Greek manuscripts is in Philip Comfort's *Encountering the Manuscripts*, chap. 1.

25. *The Making of the New Testament*, 125. Patzia also points out that the literacy rate in the Western world at that time was only about 10 percent. This is also confirmed by Ehrman in *The New Testament* and Richards in *Paul and First-Century Letter Writing.*

26. Patzia, *The Making of the New Testament.*

27. Ibid., 13.

28. Ibid.

29. *The Making of the New Testament*, 126–27. Lectionaries, from the Latin *lector*, or reader, were biblical texts and accompanying lessons arranged according to the Church year.

30. So-called because of the legend that seventy-two Jewish translators gathered in Alexandria for its production. More accurate research indicates it was a process that began in the third century BCE in Alexandria (*HarperCollins Bible Dictionary*).

31. Kurt Aland and Barbara Aland, *The Text of the New Testament: An Introduction to the Critical Editions and to the Theory and Practice of Modern Textual Criticism*, trans. E. F. Rhodes, 2nd ed. (Grand Rapids, MI: Eerdmans, 1989), 70.

32. 2nd ed. (Oxford: Hammond and Scullard, 1970), 1048.

33. Patzia, *The Making of the New Testament*, 136.

34. Ibid., 136. For more information on the survival of ancient manuscripts, see Joseph Kelly, *Why Is There A New Testament?* (Grand Rapids, MI: Eerdmans, 1967); and F. F. Bruce, *The New Testament Documents: Are They Reliable?* (Grand Rapids, MI: Eerdmans, 1978).

35. Philip Comfort, *Encountering the Manuscripts* (Nashville: Broadman & Holman, 2005), 289.

36. *Text of the New Testament*, 156.

37. Ibid.

38. Ehrman, *Misquoting Jesus.*

39. Ehrman credits Johann Albrecht Bengel (1687–1752), a Lutheran professor, for this guideline as well as Bengel's work in grouping "textual families."
40. *Text of the New Testament*, 209.
41. Ehrman, *Misquoting Jesus*.
42. If one letter attesting to have been written by Paul—2 Timothy—is very different in terms of all of the other, one would deduce the manuscript was probably not written by Paul and that it was written at a later time. Transcriptional probability has little to do with authorship but focuses instead on the copyist. A guiding maxim here is: the more difficult the reading, the more likely it is original. Also, in general, there is higher preference for a shorter reading as opposed to the longer. Metzger, *Text of the New Testament*.
43. Ibid., 132. In his book *Misquoting Jesus* (chap. 5, 133–49), Ehrman provides concrete, eye-opening, New Testament examples of textual decisions based upon three textual variants.
44. See also Mark 3:14, 9:29, 16:8; John 3:13, 7:53–8:11; Ephesians 1:1; Colossians 1:14.
45. Patzia, *The Making of the New Testament*.
46. Metzger, *The Text of the New Testament*, 186–206; Patzia, *The Making of the New Testament*, 138–40.
47. Metzger breaks these down into "substitution of synonyms . . . variation in sequence of word . . . transposition of letters within a word . . . the assimilation of the wording of one passage to the slightly different wording in a parallel passage" and "errors of judgment." Ibid., 193–94.
48. Patzia, *The Making of the New Testament*.
49. Patzia points out a classical error of this type in Luke 6:42: "How can you say to your brother, 'Brother, let me take the speck out of your eye,' when you yourself fail to see the plank in your own eye?'" The Greek word for "plank," or "log" as it is translated in the King James Version, is *karphos*. One transcribed the word *karpos*, which, in Greek, means "fruit." Ibid.
50. *The Text of the New Testament*.
51. "Not only does the text tend to grow, it becomes more stylistically polished, conformed to the rules of Greek grammar." Aland and Aland, *The Text of the New Testament*, 285.
52. Metzger, *Text of the New Testament*. Patzia also points to "an attempt to harmonize the accounts of Paul's conversion in Acts 9:5–6 and 26:14–15" (141). Other illustrations abound and are noted in other authorities.
53. Patzia, *The Making of the New Testament*.
54. Metzger, *Text of New Testament*.
55. *Text of the New Testament*.
56. Ibid.
57. Ehrman offers a good encapsulation in *Misquoting Jesus*, chap. 6.
58. An example of antiadoptionist alteration of text is 1 Timothy 3:16. Early manuscripts speak of Christ "who was made manifest in the flesh," whereas with later texts this becomes "God who was made manifest in the flesh." The difference, of course, insists that Christ was God all along and not merely adopted by God as some of the Ebionite Jews contended. An illustration of antidocetic alteration is found in Luke 22:43–44 where Jesus is portrayed as sweating drops of blood. As mentioned earlier, this passage, not in earlier manuscripts, was added later to emphasize Jesus's humanity against the docetic view that he was not flesh and blood. An antiseparationist example of alteration is Hebrews 2:9 in which the original text read Jesus died "apart from God." The later altered text read "by the grace of God." Because it was intolerable to them that the deity suffer, the Separatists, as already mentioned, believed God entered Jesus at baptism and departed his body at the crucifixion. The earlier translation would be fuel for their theological fire. Therefore, it

had to be changed. Cf. Ehrman's, *Misquoting Jesus*, 151–73; *The Orthodox Corruption of Scripture*; and Metzger, *Text of the New Testament*.

59. Metzger, *Text of the New Testament*, 206.
60. Ehrman, *The New Testament*, 487.
61. For a thorough review on New Testament texts the following are recommended: Philip Comfort, *Encountering the Manuscripts* (Nashville: Broadman and Holman Publishers, 2005); Bruce Metzger, *The Text of the New Testament*; Patzia, *The Making of the New Testament*; Bart Ehrman, *Misquoting Jesus*; *Studies in the Theory and Method of New Testament Textual Criticism* (Grand Rapids, Michigan: Eerdmans, 1992); David Alan Black, *New Testament Textual Criticism* (Grand Rapids, Michigan: Baker Publishing, 1994).

CHAPTER 11

1. *Webster's New World Dictionary*, ed. Michael Agnes, 4th ed. (New York: Simon & Schuster, 2003), 544.
2. Cf. Joe Edward Morris, "Humanistic Psychology and Religion: Steps Toward Reconciliation," *Journal of Psychology and Religion* 19, no. 12 (Summer 1980); Gordon Allport, *The Individual and His Religion* (New York: MacMillan, 1950); William H. Clark, *The Psychology of Religion* (New York: MacMillan, 1958); Abraham Maslow, *Motivation and Personality* (New York: Harper, 1954); J. Havens, *Psychology and Religion* (Princeton, NJ: D. Van Nostrand Company, 1968).
3. Descartes is a philosophical descendant of Plato who, in his work *Phaedo*, describes how true substances are not physical bodies. They are eternal Forms of which the bodies are imperfect copies. Body and soul are two distinct entities. The soul resides, is imprisoned, in the body. Aristotle, Plato's pupil believed "forms" (lowercase "f") are the substances themselves, the union of body and soul. The soul is the form of the body; a person's soul is no more than his nature as a human being. Most Western thought stems from, and is a representation of, these two interpretations of reality. One can detect in Aristotle's hermeneutical key the philosophical framework that could be applied to the incarnation of Christ, whereas Plato provides the basis for the Gnostic spiritual Christ. Cf. Frank Thilly, *A History of Philosophy*, rev. by Ledger Wood (New York: Holt, Rinehart and Winston, 1964); Will Durant, *The Story of Philosophy* (New York: Washington Square, 1969).
4. "The notion that our souls are flesh is profoundly troubling to many, as it clashes with religion. Dualism and religion are not the same: you can be dualist without holding any other religious beliefs, and you can hold religious beliefs without being dualist. But they almost always go together. And some very popular religious views rest on a dualist foundation, such as the belief that people survive the destruction of the bodies. If you give up on dualism, this is what you lose." Michael LaTorra, "Trans-Spirit: Religion, Spirituality and Trans-humanism," *Journal of Evolution and Technology* 15 (August 2005): 43.
5. *Webster's New World Dictionary* (New York: World Book, 1960), 234.
6. From *In Memoriam*, quoted from *The College Survey of English Literature*, ed. by B. J. Whiting, et al., 2nd ed. (New York: Harcourt, Brace & World, Inc., 1942).
7. "For whose sake is it that proof is sought. Faith does not need it; aye, it must even regard the proof as its enemy." Kierkegaard, Søren, *Concluding Unscientific Postscript*, trans. David F. Swenson and Lowrie Walter (Princeton: University of Princeton Press, 1941), 31. In that same work he stated: "without risk there is no faith" (182); and "if Christianity is the highest good, it is better for me to know definitely that I do not possess it, so that I may put forth every effort to acquire it, rather than that I should imagine that I have it, deluding myself so that it does not even occur to me to seek it" (340). All of these statements reflect incarnational theology.

8. Scholars produce convincing arguments that St. Paul, in 1 Corinthians, was striking at the very heart of Gnosticism when he proclaimed "If I have the gift of prophecy and can fathom all mysteries (*mysteria*) and all knowledge (*gnosis*) (2a) . . . but have not love, I am nothing . . . where there are tongues (*glossai*), they will be stilled; where there is knowledge (*gnosis*), it will pass away. For we know in part." (13:2–9).

9. Fisher Humphreys and Philip Wise, *Fundamentalism* (Macon, GA: Smyth & Helwys, 1989) chap. 4.

10. Humphreys and Wise, *Fundamentalism*, 59.

11. (Lynchburg, VA: Liberty House Publishers, 1997), 385.

12. (New York: Oxford University Press, 1987), 115.

13. Herbert Benson, M.D., *The Relaxation Response* (New York: Avon Books, 1975), 24.

14. Philip J. Lee, *Against the Protestant Gnostics* (New York: Oxford University Press, 1987), 26.

15. Lee, *Against the Protestant Gnostics*, 29.

16. Ibid., 117.

17. In his book, *The Protestant Temperament: Patterns of Child-Rearing, Religious Experience and the Self in Early America* (New York: Knopf, 1977), Philip Greven points out how even children were considered part of the natural landscape and not blessings sent from heaven. He notes how John Wesley, founder of Methodism, even admonished parents to "break their will that you may save their souls" (44). Jonathan Edwards referred to them as "young vipers . . . infinitely more hateful than vipers." Ibid., 31.

18. Lee, *Against the Protestant Gnostics*, 31.

19. This attitude seemed to reverse over the years as the Roman Catholic Church preferred intellectuals who could read Latin and viewed, with great alarm, the education of the masses, who were deemed to be ignorant. The Church's position was to keep them ignorant and the language of the Church, Latin, in the hands of the intellectual clerics. Martin Luther thought otherwise and printed the Bible in German for the masses. The rest, as the saying goes, is history.

CHAPTER 12

1. Steven Runciman, *The Medieval Manichee* (Cambridge: Cambridge University Press, 1984) 171.

2. This may be one of the reasons for the success of Islam, that is, its simplicity. As Runciman notes, "In Islam the tendency to heresy is smaller; for the revelation of Islam is a simpler thing, contained in the word of Mahomet. . . . The Christian revelation is far harder to fit into simple language; the room for error is infinitely great." *The Medieval Manichee*, 2.

3. Ibid., 174.

4. *Webster's New World Dictionary* (New York: The World, 1960), 326.

5. *Fear and Trembling*, trans. Walter Lowerie (Garden City, NY: Doubleday, 1954), 47.

6. Trans. John W. Harvey (New York: Oxford University Press, 1958).

7. Philip Lee, *Against the Protestant Gnostics* (New York: Oxford University Press, 1987), 45.

8. Lee, *Against the Protestant Gnostics*, 205.

9. Ibid., 27.

10. Quoted in Lee, *Against the Protestant Gnostics*, 58.

11. Ibid, 32.

12. Ibid., 69.

13. Elaine Pagels, *Gnostic Gospels* (New York: Vintage Books, 1981).

14. Joachim Jeremias, *The Origins of Infant Baptism*, trans. D. M. Barton (London: SCM, 1963), 85.

15. Quoted from Pagels, *Gnostic Gospels*, 146.

16. Paul L. Lehmann, *Ethics in a Christian Context* (New York: Harper & Row, 1963), 67–68.

17. Lee, *Against the Protestant Gnostics*, 220.

18. Bart Ehrman, *Misquoting Jesus* (San Francisco: HarperSanFrancisco, 2005), 217.

19. Emil Brunner, *The Mediator* (Philadelphia: The Westminster, 1947).

CHAPTER 13

1. Harold Bloom, *The American Religion* (New York: Chu Hartley, 1992), 4.

2. Yuri Stoyanov, *The Other God* (New Haven, CT: Yale University Press, 2000), xi.

3. Weber, Max. *The Sociology of Religion*. London: Methuen, 1965.

4. Ernst Troeltsch, *The Social Teaching of the Christian Churches, I*, trans. Olive Wyon (London: Allen & Unwin, 1931), vol. 1.

5. Philip Lee, *Against the Protestant Gnostics* (New York: Oxford University Press, 1987)

6. Lee, *Against the Protestant Gnostics*, 12.

7. The famous existentialist writer Albert Camus spent two years in a French monastery. A monk there asked him what the Church could do to survive. Camus is reported to have said: "Speak up clearly and pay up personally."

8. The following statistics are from *The World Almanac* and *Yearbook of American Churches* on Christian Church Membership in the United States: 1960–2002. These declines in mainstream Protestant churches are Registered: American Baptist Association, -57.6 percent; American Baptist Church in the United States of America, -5.7 percent; Christian Church (Disciples of Christ), -56.4 percent; Churches of Christ, -30.7 percent; Episcopal, -32.6 percent; Evangelican Lutheran Church of America, -5.9 percent; Presbyterian Church U.S., -21.1 percent; United Methodist Church, -23.6 percent. In sharp contrast, the following Fundamentalist churches show significant percentage gains: Church of God in Christ, +1,299 percent; Church of God (Cleveland, TN), +425 percent; Church of Jesus Christ of Latter-day Saints (Mormons), +277 percent; Evangelical Free Church of America, +684 percent; International Church of Foursquare Gospel, +269 percent; Jehovah's Witness, +274 percent; Pentecostal Assemblies of the World, +3233 percent; Seventh-day Adventists, +190 percent. This represents only a sampling of a much larger assessment, but the trends are significant.

9. The Gnostic Institute, http://www.gnosticshop.com.

10. An example of this blending is seen in Manichaeism. Stoyanov records, "The violent reaction of official Zoroastrianism to Mani's Religion of Light was provoked partly by the use of Zoroastrian concepts in his new and essentially Gnostic religion, where Iranian, Jewish, Christian, Buddhist and Egyptian traditions were synthesized in what is usually described as the supreme syncretistic system of late antiquity." Stoyanov, *The Other God*, 1070. In the Middle Ages, the priest Bogomil "synthesized elements of earlier heretical traditions, usually identified as Paulician and Massalian, but sometimes direct Manichaean, Marcionite, or separate Gnostic influences." Ibid., 162.

11. Hans Jonas, *The Gnostic Religion* (Boston: Beacon, 1963), 26.

12. Jonas, *The Gnostic Religion*, 26.

13. Stoyanov, *The Other God*, 294.

14. Peter Baker, *Washington Post*, September 13, p. A05.

15. During this time the social gospel gained momentum simultaneously with a global missionary effort. It was also during this period that new religious groups emerged—Holiness (Assembly of God and Pentecostal), Salvation Army, Nazarenes, Christian Science.
16. Bush apologized for his use of the word "crusade" in 2001. Baker, *Washington Post*.
17. *The Fourth Great Awakening: The Future of Egalitarianism* (Chicago: University of Chicago Press, 2000), 18.
18. *Mauve Gloves and Madmen, Clutter and Vine* (New York: Bantam Books, 1977).
19. Quoted in Lee, *Against the Protestant Gnostics*, 197.
20. Ibid, 197–98.
21. Robert William Fogel, *The Fourth Great Awakening: The Future of Egalitarianism* (Chicago: University of Chicago Press, 2000).
22. Lee, *Against the Protestant Gnostics*, 262.
23. Fisher Humphreys and Philip Wise, *Fundamentalism* (Macon, GA: Smyth & Helwys, 2004), 32.
24. *American Religion*, 192.
25. Maxentius tolerated Christians but remained a pagan and reminded Romans of their glorious past.
26. Quoted in Bloom, *American Religion*, 226.
27. Ibid., 240.
28. Ibid.
29. Ibid., 242.
30. Ibid.
31. Bruce Metzger, *The Text of the New Testament* (New York: Oxford Univeristy Press, 1992), 34.
32. Metzger, *Text of the New Testament*.
33. Lee, *Against the Protestant Gnostics*, 183.
34. Humphreys and Wise, *Fundamentalism*, 61.
35. Ibid.
36. (London: STM, 1964), 8–9.
37. Lee, *Against the Protestant Gnostics*, 219.
38. Ibid., 229.
39. Ibid., 13.
40. Elaine Pagels, *The Gnostic Gospels* (New York: Random House, 1976), 174–75.
41. Pagels, *Gnostic Gospels*, 181.

APPENDIX C

1. Henry Bettenson, *The Early Christian Fathers* (New York: Oxford University Press, 1956), 10.
2. Bettenson, *The Early Christian Fathers*, 13.

APPENDIX D

1. Eusebius of Caesarea. *Ecclesiastical History*, trans. with introduction and notes by Lawlor, H. J. and Oulton, J. E. L., 2 vols., London, 1927–28, *Ecclesiastical History*, IV 7, 198.
2. Gnosticism may have originated in the Syrian teachings of Simon Magus; George Robert Stow Meade discusses this point at some length in his book *Simon Magus*.
3. Pheme Perkins, *Gnosticism and the New Testament* (Minneapolis, MN: Fortress Press, 1993).

4. Kurt Rudolph, *Gnosis* (San Francisco: HarperSanFrancisco, 1984), 297.

5. One named Meander allegedly came from Samaria but worked in Antioch and lived until about 80 CE Another, Satornilos, had views dependent on Meander. The world was created by inferior angels and Christ is portrayed as a gnostic redeemer. Satornilos was a contemporary of Basilides.

6. Rudolph.

7. Manly P. Hall, *The Wisdom of the Knowing Ones* (Los Angeles: The Philosophical Research Society, 2000), 58.

8. Bart Ehrman, *Lost Christianities* (New York: Oxford University Press, 2003), 103.

9. Tertullian. *Against Marcion*. I.19. In J. Stevenson's *A New Eusebius* (London: S.P.C.K., 1963).

10. Walter Bauer, *Orthodoxy and Heresy in Earliest Christianity*, Trans. Robert Kraft, et. al., Ed. Robert Kraft and Gerhard Krodel. Philadelphia: Fortress Press, 1971.

11. Ehrman, *Lost Christianities*, 109. Stanley Hall records that "Traces of the sect are to be found as late as the tenth century CE and the questions which Marcion pondered were revived in the years of the Protestant Reformation" 58.

12. One school of thought considers St. Paul to have been the first to consolidate a group of writings as a canon. David Trobisch, in his book *Paul's Letter Collection* (Bolivar, Missouri: Augsburg Fortress, 2001) presents a strong and convincing argument that Paul made copies of every letter, which was the custom of the time, kept copies and before his death, edited, and consolidated several in a single edition for friends in Ephesus. The edition included Romans, 1 and 2 Corinthians, and Galatians. Trobisch also presents an equally compelling argument of similarity of themes linking the four letters.

13. The Greek word for "gospel" is *euangelion* and later became *evangelion*. The word meant literally "good news." In ancient times runners bearing news from a battle, if their side had won, would approach a city shouting "*Euangelion, euangelion.*"

14. "We may never know why these three were not included as well. It may be that they were not as widely circulated by Marcion's time and that he himself did not know of them." Ehrman, *Lost Christianities*, 106.

15. Henry Chadwick, *The Early Church* (London: Penguin Books, 1990).

16. Ehrman explains how Marcion, in his book *Antithesis*, "was not willing to explain away . . . passages by providing them with a figurative or symbolic interpretation; for him, they were to be taken literally." *Lost Christianities*, 107. In his work *Gnosis*, Rudolph also points out that Marcion was "the first in the history of Christianity to draw up a 'canon' of the New Testament . . . rigorously selected and arranged according to his basic principles" (315). He further notes Marcion's "lack of mythological speculation . . . and his limitation to the Bible. In this respect, he is a 'biblical theologian' through and through" (316).

17. Ibid.

18. Some Gnostics rejected literalism. Cf. Elaine Pagels, *Gnostic Gospels* (New York: Vintage Books, 1981),160. Based upon some of the poems discovered at Nag Hammadi, some were more interested in the nonliteral, symbolic meaning of language. The author of the *Gospel of Philip*, a follower of Valentinus, "criticizes those who mistake religious language for a literal language." Pagels, *Gnostic Gospels*, 160–61.

BIBLIOGRAPHY

Aland, Kurt, and Barbara Aland. *The Text of the New Testament: An Introduction to the Critical Editions and to the Theory and Practice of Modern Textual Criticism.* Translated by E. F. Rhodes. 2nd ed. Grand Rapids, MI: Eerdmans, 1989.

Allport, Gordon. *The Individual and His Religion.* New York: MacMillan, 1950.

Apocryphon of James. Nag Hammadi Library in English. Translated by James M. Robinson. 3rd ed. New York: Harper and Row, 1988.

Apocryphon of John. Nag Hammadi Library in English. Translated by James M. Robinson. 3rd ed. New York: Harper and Row, 1988.

Armstrong, Karen. *The Battle for God.* New York: Alford A. Knopf, 2001.

Atack, Jon. *A Piece of Blue Sky: Scientology, Dianetics and Ron Hubbard Exposed.* New York: Carol, 1990.

Athanasius. *Epistolae Festales.* XXXIX. In *Post and Post-Nicene Fathers,* series 2I, vol. 4. Baker Book House, 1983.

Baker, Peter. *Washington Post.* September 13, 2006, p. A05.

Basilides, *Exegitca, XXIII* in Clement of Alexandria. *Stromateis,* IV.12.81.2–82.2. In *A New Eusebius,* edited by J. Stevenson.

Bauer, Walter. *Orthodoxy and Heresy in Earliest Christianity.* Translated by Robert Kraft, et al. Edited by Robert Kraft and Gerhard Krodel. Philadelphia: Fortress, 1971.

Bawer, Bruce. *Stealing Jesus: How Fundamentalism Betrays Christianity.* New York: Three Rivers, 1970.

Benson, Herbert, M.D. *The Relaxation Response.* New York: Avon Books, 1975.

Berkouwer, Gerrit C. *The Conflict with Rome.* Philadelphia: The Presbyterian and Reform Publishing Company, 1958.

Bettenson, Henry, trans. and ed. *The Early Christian Fathers.* New York: Oxford University Press, 1956.

Bloom, Harold. *Omens of Millennium: The Gnosis of Angels, Dreams, and Resurrection.* New York: Riverhead Books, 1996.

———. *The American Religion.* 2nd ed. New York: Chu Hartley Publishers, 2006.

Browning, Robert. *The Poems and Plays of Robert Browning.* New York: Modern Library, 1934.

Brunner, Emil. *The Mediator.* Philadelphia: The Westminster, 1947.

Buber, Martin. *The Eclipse of God.* Translated by Stanley Goodman. New York: Harper & Brothers, 1952.

———. *The Writings of Martin Buber.* Edited by Will Herberg. Cleveland: World, 1968.

Bultmann, Rudolph. *Theology of the New Testament, I,* New York: Scribner's, 1954.

Campbell, Joseph. *The Power of Myth* New York: Doubleday, 1988.

Chadwick, Henry. *The Early Church.* Rev. ed. New York: Penguin Books, 1993.

Chesterton, Gilbert Keith. *Orthodoxy.* San Francisco: Ignatius, 1995.

Churton, Tobias. *The Gnostics.* New York: Barnes & Noble, 1987.

Clark, W. H. *The Psychology of Religion.* New York: MacMillan, 1958.

College Survey of English Literature, The. 2nd ed. Edited by B. J. Whiting, et al. New York: Harcourt, Brace & World, Inc. 1942.

Comfort, Philip. *Encountering the Manuscripts: An Introduction to New Testament Paleography & Textual Criticism.* Nashville: Broadman & Holman Publishers, 2005.

Couglan, Robert. *The World of Michalangelo.* New York: Time-Life Library of Arts, 1970.

Daniélou, Jean. *The Theology of Jewish Christianity.* In *A History of Early Christian Doctrine*, vol. 1. Translated by John A. Baker. London: Dartman, Longman and Todd, 1964.

Davis, Leo. *The First Seven Ecumenical Councils (325–787).* Collegeville, MN: The Liturgical Press, 1983.

Denzinger, Henry. *The Sources of Catholic Dogma.* St. Louis: B. Herder Book Company, 1957.

Durant, Will. *The Story of Philosophy.* New York: Washington Square, 1969.

Edwards, O. C. *How Holy Writ was Written.* Nashville: Abingdon, 1989.

Egermeier, Elsie E. *Egermeier's Bible Story Book.* Los Angeles: The Smithsonian Company, 1947.

Ehrman, Bart D. *The Orthodox Corruption of Scripture: The Effect of Early Christological Controveries on the Text of the New Testament.* New York: Oxford University Press, 1993

———. *Jesus: Apocalyptic Prophet of the New Millennium.* New York: Oxford University Press, 1999.

———. *Lost Christianities: The Battle for Scripture and the Faiths We Never Knew.* New York: Oxford University Press, 2003.

———. *Misquoting Jesus.* San Francisco: HarperSanFrancisco, 2005.

Eliade, Mircea. *Myth and Reality.* New York: Harper and Row, 1963.

Eusebius of Caesarea. *Ecclesiastical History.* Translated and with introduction and notes by H. J. Lawlor and J. E. L. Oulton. 2 vols. London, 1927–28.

Fadiman, James and Robert Krager. *Essential Sufism.* New York: HarperCollins, 1999.

Falwell, Jerry. *Falwell: An Autobiography.* Lynchburg, VA: Liberty House, 1997.

Faustad, Edwin, S. *The Great Awakening in New England.* New York: Harper, 1957.

Finseth, Ian Frederick. *"Liquid Fire Within Me": Language, Self and Society in Transcendentalism and Early Evangelicalism, 1820–1860.* M.A. Thesis in English, University of Virginia, August, 1995.

Fisher, Humphreys. "The Baptist Faith and Message and the Chicago Statement on Biblical Inerrancy." In *The Proceedings on the Conference of Biblical Inerrancy 1987.* Nashville: Broadman, 1987.

Fisher, Humphreys, and Philip Wise. *Fundamentalism.* Macon, GA: Smyth & Helwys, 2004

Fogel, Robert William. *The Fourth Great Awakening: The Future of Egalitarianism.* Chicago: University of Chicago Press, 2000.

Fundamentals, The. Edited by R. A. Torrey. Grand Rapids, MI: Baker Books, 2003.

Glover, T. R. *The Conflict of Religions in the Early Roman Empire.* Boston: Beacon, 1960.

Gospel of Philip, Nag Hammadi Library in English. Translated by James M. Robinson. 3rd ed. New York: Harper and Row, 1988.

Gospel of Thomas. Nag Hammadi Library in English. Translated by James M. Robinson. 3rd ed. New York: Harper and Row, 1988.

Gospel of Truth. Nag Hammadi Library in English. Translated by James M. Robinson. 3rd ed. New York: Harper and Row, 1988.

Grant, R. M. *Gnosticism and Early Christianity.* New York: Harper & Row, 1966.

Greven, Philip. *The Protestant Temperaiment: Patterns of Child-Rearing, Religious Experience and the Self in Early America.* New York: Knopf, 1977.

———. *Orders of the Great Work.* Los Angeles: The Philosophical Research Society, 1976.

Hall, Manly P. *Orders of the Quest.* Los Angeles: The Philosophical Research Society, 1996.

————. *Orders of Universal Reformation.* Los Angeles: The Philosophical Research Society, 1999.

————. *The Wisdom of the Knowing Ones.* Los Angeles: The Philosophical Research Society, 2000.

HarperCollins Bible Dictionary, The. Edited by Paul J. Achtemeier, et al. San Francisco: Harper-Collins Publishers, 1996.

Harris, William V. *Ancient Literacy.* Cambridge, MA: Harvard University Press, 1989.

Havens. *Psychology and Religion.* Princeton, NJ: D. Van Nostrand, 1968.

Hippolytus. *Refutation of All Heresies.* VII.20.1 (A.-N. C.L. VII.8). In *A New Eusebius.* Edited by J. Stevenson.

Hoffman, Mark S. The World Almanac. Ann Arbor, MI: Pharos Books, 1992.

Holy Bible, The: New International Version. Grand Rapids, MI: Zondervan, 1989.

Holy Bible, The. New Revised Standard Version. The American Bible Society, New York: Harper Collins1989.

Hopewell, David. W. *Christian Fundamentalism: A Journey into the Heart of Darkness.* Austin, TX: American Atheist, 1998.

Ignatius. *Trallians.* In *A New Eusebius.* Edited by J. Stevenson. London: S.P.C.K., 1963

Irenaeus. *Against Heresies (or Refutation and Overthrow of False Gnosis or of Knowledge Falsely So-Called.* I.24.25. I Harvey; 1.27.1-2 A.-N.C.L. In *A New Eusebius.* Edited by J. Stevenson. London: S.P.C.K., 1963.

Irenaeus. Irenaeus. III. 40.2. Harvey III.25.3 A.-N.C.L. In *A New Eusebius.* Edited by J. Stevenson. London: S.P.C.K., 1963.

Jeremias, Joachim. *The Origins of Infant Baptism.* Translated by D. M. Barton. London: SCM, 1963.

Jonas, Hans. *The Gnostic Religion.* Boston: Beacon, 1963.

————. "Delimitation of the Gnostic Phenomenon—Typological and Historical." In *Le origini della gnosticismo.* Edited by Ugo Bianchi. Proceedings of the Colloquio di Messina, April 1966. Leiden: E. J. Brill, 1967.

Jones III, Bob. *"Pseudo-Fundamentalists: The New Breed in Sheep's Clothing."* http://www.bju .edu/resource/faith/1978/issue1/pseudo.html.

Knight, George R. *Millennial Fever and the End of the World: A Study of Millerite Adventism.* Boise, ID: Pacific, 1993.

Laws, Curtis Lee. "Conventional Side Lights." *The Watchman-Examiner* 8/27, July 1, 1920.

Lee, Philip J. *Against the Protestant Gnostics.* New York: Oxford University Press, 1987.

Loader, William. *Jesus and the Fundamentalists of His Day.* Grand Rapids, MI: William B. Eerdmans, 2001.

Marty, Martin, and Scott Appleby. *The Fundamentalism Project.* Chicago: University of Chicago Press, 1991–95.

Maslow, Abraham. *Motivation and Personality.* New York: Harper, 1954.

Mayer, Henry. *A Son of Thunder.* New York: Grove, 1991.

Maxwell-Stewart, P. G. *Chronicle of the Popes: The Reign-by-Reign Record of the Papacy from Peter to the Present.* New York: Thames and Hudson, 2006.

Meade, G. R. S. *Simon Magus: An Essay on the Founder of Simonianism Based on the Ancient Sources with a Re-evaluation of His Philosophy and Teachings.* R. A. Kassinger, 1940.

Metzger, Bruce. *The Canon of the New Testament: Its Origin, Development and Significance.* Oxford: Clarendon, 1987.

Metzger, Bruce and Bart Ehrman. *The Text of the New Testament: Its Transmission, Corruption, and Restoration.* 4th ed. New York: Oxford University Press, 2005.

Morris, J. E. "Humanistic Psychology and Religion: Steps Toward Reconciliation." *Journal of Psychology and Religion* 19, no. 12 (Summer 1980): 67–79.

Nock, Arthur Darby. "Gnosticism." *Harvard Theological Review* 57 (1964).
————. *Early Gentile Christianity and Its Hellenistic Background.* New York: Harper & Row, 1964.
Otto, Rudolph. *The Idea of the Holy.* Translated by John W. Harvey. New York: Oxford University Press, 1958.
Oxford Classical Dictionary, The. 2nd ed. Oxford: Hammond and Scullard, 1970.
Packer, J. I. *"Fundamentalism" and the Word of God.* Grand Rapids, MI: 1977.
Pagels, Elaine. *The Johannine Gospel in Gnostic Exegesis.* Nashville: Abingdon, 1973.
————. *The Gnostic Gospels.* New York: Random House, 1976.
Patzia, Arthur G. *The Making of the New Testament.* Downers Grove, IL: InterVarsity, 1995.
Pearson, Birger. "Jewish Sources in Gnostic Literature." In *Jewish Writings of the Second Temple Period.* Edited by M. Stone. CRINT II/2. Assen: Van Gorcum; Philadelphia: Fortress, 1984.
Peck, Scott. *The Different Drum.* New York: Touchstone, 1998.
————. *The Riddle of Roman Catholicism.* New York: Abingdon, 1959.
Pelikan, Jaroslav. *The Christian Tradition: A History of the Development of Doctrine, The Emergence of the Catholic Tradition (100–600).* Chicago: University of Chicago Press, 1971.
Perkins, Pheme. *Gnosticism and the New Testament.* Minneapolis: Fortress, 1993.
Plato. *Timaeus.* Translated by Peter Kalkavage. Focus Philosophical Library. Newburyport, ME: Focus, 2001.
Richards, E. Randolph. *Paul and First Century Letter Writing.* Downers Grove, IL: InterVarsity, 2004.
Robinson, James, ed. *The Nag Hammadi Library in English.* 3rd ed. New York: Harper and Row, 1988.
Rudolph, Kurt. *Gnosis: The Nature & History of Gnosticism.* Translated by Robert Wilson. San Francisco: HarperSanFrancisco, 1987.
Runciman, Michael. *The Medieval Manichee.* Cambridge: Cambridge University Press, 1984.
Schmitals, Walter. *Gnosticism in Corinth.* Nashville: Abingdon, 1971.
————. *Paul and the Gnostics.* Nashville: Abingdon, 1972.
Schoedel, William. "Gnostic Monism and the Gospel of Truth." In *The Rediscovery of Gnosticism, Vol. I: The School of Valentinus.* Edited by Bentley Layton. Brill: Leiden, 1980.
Spence, Lewis. *The Encyclopedia of the Occult.* London: Bracken Books. 1994.
Stevenson, J., ed. *A New Eusebius: Documents Illustrative of the History of the Church to A.D. 337.* London: S.P.C.K., 1963.
Stoyanov, Yuri. *The Other God.* New Haven, CT: Yale University Press, 2000.
Tertullian. *De Praescriptione haereticorum (On the Prescription of Heretics).* Translated by Rev. Peter Holmes. Edited by Alexander Roberts and James Donaldson. Edinburgh: T & T Clark, 1868.
————. *Against Marcion.* I.19. In *A New Eusebius.* Edited by J. Stevenson. London: S.P.C.K., 1963.
Thilly, Frank. *A History of Philosophy.* Rev. by Wood, Ledge. New York: Holt Rinehart, and Winston, 1964.
Tolson, Jay. "The Gospel Truth." *U.S. News & World Report.* December 18, 2006.
Torjesen, Karen Jo. *When Women Were Priests: Women's Leadership in the Early Church and the Scandal of Their Subordination in the Rise of Christianity.* San Francisco: HarperCollins, 1993.
Trobisch, David. *Paul's Letter Collection.* Bolivar, MO: Augsburg Fortress, 2001.
Troeltsch, Ernst. *The Social Teaching of the Christian Churches,* I. Translated by Olive Wyon. London: Allen & Unwin, 1931.
Weber, Max. *The Sociology of Religion.* London: Methuen, 1965.

Webster's New World Dictionary. New York: The World, 1960.

Webster's New World Dictionary. 4th ed. Edited by Michael Agnes. New York: Simon & Schuster, 2003.

Wisse, F. "Prolegomena to the Study of the new Testament and Gnosis." In *The New Testament and Gnosis: Essays in honour of Robert McL. Wilson.* Edited by A. H. B. Logan and A. J. M. Wedderburn. Edingurgh: T. & T. Clark. 1983.

Wolfe, Tom. "The Me Decade and the Third Great Awakening." In *Mauve Gloves and Madmen, Clutter and Vine.* New York: Bantam Books, 1977.

Yamauchi, Edwin M. *Pre-Christian Gnosticism.* 2nd ed. Grand Rapids: Baker Book House, 1983.

Yearbook of American Churches. National Councils of Churches of Christ in the United States of America, Nashville: Abingdon, 1972.

INDEX